The Keys to the Kingdom

by
Michael E. Morgan

Keys to the Kingdom

Copyright © 2024 by Michael E. Morgan

All rights reserved. No part of this book may be reproduced or transmitted in any form or by any means now known or to be invented, electronic or mechanical, including photocopying, recording, or by any information storage and retrieval system without written permission from the author or publisher, except for the inclusion of brief quotations in a review.

For information write to:
Dawntrader Books, LLC
P.O. Box D120-413
Scottsdale, Arizona
85266

If you are unable to order this book from your local bookseller, or Amazon.com, you may order directly from the publisher.
Quantity discounts for organizations are available.

Many Thanks to Alexa Lombardi for her Illustrations

Cover and book design by
Michael E. Morgan

Publisher's Cataloging-in-Publication Data
ISBN 978-1-7322981-9-4

10 9 8 7 6 5 4 3 2 1

Table of Contents

Introduction: Returning Home..4
Chapter 1. The Creator-Source..20
Chapter 2. Tiamat..71
Chapter 3. Earth: Salvation's Child..83
Chapter 4. Androgyny To Polarity..97
Chapter 5. Anunnaki History on Earth..110
Chapter 6. Jahwey, Elohim, Storm God of Israel..119
Chapter 7. The Robot, Shell of the Fallen..130
Chapter 8. Trans-Humanism, Living Forever..157
Chapter 9. The Soul, Ghost in the Shell..163
Chapter 10. Physical Alachemy and the Atom Bomb..179
Chapter 11. Spiritual Alchemy and the Philosoper's Stone..188
Chapter 12. Reincarnation: The Wheel of Birth and Death..196
Chapter 13. Time Loop..204
Chapter 14. Law of Cause and Effect..212
Chapter 15. The Law of Octaves..218
Chapter 16. The Right Use of Will..228
Chapter 17. Yoga..236
Chapter 18. Right Use of Breath..247
Chapter 19. Digestion of Light..259
Chapter 20. Mitochondria Avalanche and Singularity..265
Chapter 21. The CSF, The Pineal and Pituitary Glands..278
Chapter 22. What is Ascension..291
Chapter 23. Quest for Power..294
Chapter 24. Djinns and Daemons..302
Chapter 25. Beelzebub and the Antichrist..305
Chapter 26. Rapture, Myth of the Chosen..311
Chapter 27. Dreams: Portents of Consciousness..336
Chapter 28. Astrology, The Lunar Return..348
Chapter 29. Hemispheric Synchronization..353
Chapter 30. Jeshua, Mary and The Holy Grail..376
Chapter 31. The Second War in Heaven..379
Chapter 32. Reality Simulation..414
Chapter 33. The Secret Decoded..427
Epilogue: Warnings on the Path..437
Bibliography..442

When terms such as "kingdom" are mentioned in religious sources such as biblical scripture, there can be many assumptions drawn from its meaning. Usually, the term is further described as the 'kingdom of heaven', the dwelling place of God. This is assumed to refer to God's realm. This would be a gross misrepresentation in the viewpoint of the author. In the case of the Hebrew translation into the King James English version of the bible from Genesis, 'Elohim', being a plural form is interpreted in the English translation as a singular term for meaning God, but in truth, the literal translation is 'those on high'.

This literal translation places a completely different perspective on the Genesis story. Otherwise, the translation offered as God-singular inferring to Yahwey or Jehovah, who is mentioned in Sumerian texts dating 6000 years prior to the Hebrew accounts is an Anunnaki (extraterrestrial) demi-god.

In terms of esoteric knowledge, there are three heavens: lower heaven which would describe the lower atmosphere of earth and or the lower Astral Realm. Midheaven which would describe the high

Introduction

Astral Realm as well as the physical multiverse and finally Upper Heaven which describes the Quantum, the true definition of the kingdom of the Highest God or the Source, a non-anthropomorphic representation of the prime mover and creator of all existence.

The evolution of the human being refers religiously to the so called 'redemption' in religious terms of the soul, sin from the original fall from grace. Ascension, therefore, must refer to the return to grace and the realm of the Highest God by the spirit. Then ascension is to talk about the evolution of spirit or soul from a mortal component of the body anima to an immortal being who would then be resurrected in a perfect divine immortal body and reside in the kingdom of the Highest God.

This brings into question many conditions which stand in the way of such an evolution. On the earth, the first problem is, there is and has always been a sharp division between the masses and the priestly class or overseers who are in charge and responsible for the 'care' of the masses through their dissemination of the 'word' and doctrines of correct behavior.

Down through the ages, through many civilizations, this hierarchy is abusive, where the masses are kept ignorant of many truths regarding their redemption and return. Knowledge of the secrets of evolution are kept and retained by the priesthood. This comes from the influence of the demi-god race that created man 450,000 years ago for their own purposes. (Note: This information will be expanded into greater detail later in this treatise).

From the beginning, mankind has been a slave race in service to the extraterrestrial influences and kept under control by the overlords. The subsequent rulership over the slaves was engendered to continue by the priesthood after the overlords left the planet.

If one reads the bible from the Old Testament to and through the New Testament it is a compilation of more than 100 books of stories relating the accounts of and between the experiences of man and the 'Gods' from the beginning to and including prophecy of the end of the world or the Apocalypse.

Introduction

Both Testament accounts have experienced several translations: from Arabic, Greek, Hebrew and finally into English. The New Testament has been challenged to its authenticity, since the dating of the writings often shown they have been written at a time some 150 - 250 years after their alleged occurrences and therefore suspect as to the 'true' writers who did not live to see what happened. So that leaves the authenticity of the writings as nothing more than mere here say by others.

Arguments have recently emerged as to the scriptural authenticity from all the translations that are supposedly perfect renditions of the word of God, yet curiously, there is a warning within the writings that if one word is taken away or added to these scriptures, a curse is pronounced to those who would defy this commandment indicating the possibility of corruption.

It is historically accurate to show that the New Testament was altered in major ways by the council of Mycenae in the 4th century, by the direction of Alexander the Great.

Many books originally included were removed and only four books remained as part of the new cannon gospels while the others were declared heretical. The reason for this was due to Alexander wanting an accurate means by which he could rally and control those under his rule without confusion and chaos.

Many scholars have determined that Alexander was not Christian but merely used this system of belief as the moral foundation of his empire. Even so, during that council investigation it was found that the four gospels; Mathew, Mark, Luke, and John did not agree in their accounts. So, Alexander ordered the scribes to adjust each of the writings to essentially agree on all important points, which is what we have today.

Some tribes of Israel were exiled when Babylon attacked Jerusalem in 587 BCE and captured the Israelites bringing them back to Babylon as slaves. The Israelites remained as slaves in captivity for 500 years. The author believes it was during that time they studied the Sumerian accounts of history and comprised their own historical narratives in the Torah, changing the names and dates and places to fit their own needs of Jewish historical reference to formulate the Old Testament.

Introduction

The origins of man in the Sumerian tablets were called the Enuma Elish (the Sumerian Genesis). In Hebrew, it was just called Genesis. The Sumerian account of the Flood was the account of Gilgamesh. In Hebrew, it was called the Flood of Noah and the survival of his family replacing the story of Gilgamesh. Since the time reference of the Sumerian account was 6000 years or more before the Jewish accounts, some plagiarizing seems obvious.

Prior to the present time, church and state were always joined. Ultimate authority of the regents and their rule was bolstered by the priesthood. The path of spiritual life was a twin path, one for the priesthood and one for the masses.

In Egypt, the pharaohs were considered Gods incarnate and thus shared the knowledge of the temple secrets. In Greece, it was the Mantis, or Oracles providing knowledge of the future and guidance for the leaders in their battles with other nations.

During the empire of Rome, The Roman gods ruled the empire and later the Christian church in Rome continued to rule down through the Middle

Ages even until the British empire ruled the known world.

The knowledge of the history and the true path to evolution has always taken a twin path, one diluted for the sake of the masses and the other secret path relegated to members of the elite and priesthood. The priesthood has always condemned the pursuit of the secret knowledge as heretical and or diabolical and forbidden under penalty of death (ex., persecution of Joan of Arc by the holy church and the Spanish Inquisition). Also, the dogma prescribed to the masses is the concept of being born into sin leaving the masses unable to claim their right to divine inheritance through the enforcement of guilt and inherent shame from the fall, (original sin).

The importance of authority was demonstrated even in the opening of the New Testament where the entire lineage of Jeshua was established by who begat who from the line of David down to Jesus (Jeshua or Joshua), thus making Jeshua the true Messiah and the words he spoke reliable and authentic. Jeshua began his ministry around AD 27-29 and ended around AD 30 -36. There were as

Introduction

many as 25 prophets at the time of Jeshua in Jerusalem, all claiming to be the Messiah. It was important to prove only one was truly the reflection of the original source, the direct line of King David which was purported to have spoken directly with the demigod (Yahwey) or Jehovah during his reign.

2000 plus years before the present day, the secret knowledge was alluded to by Jeshua, more popularly known as Jesus of Nazareth. Jeshua left Jerusalem at the age of 12 and traveled to India, Egypt, and Tibet. He was given the keys of the kingdom by the monks, a knowledge that extended from Atlantis, through Thoth, an Atlantean priest of the temple of knowledge. He returned to Jerusalem at the age of 30 to begin his ministry.

His mission was to confront the Sanhedrin, the pharisees, their corruption and overbearing rulership of the masses while they politically aligned with Rome who sought to keep the Jews under their thumb and never wanted to share the truth or their power with the masses.

Jeshua often spoke in riddles to the masses

daring them to pursue the knowledge on their own. For this he was condemned as a blasphemer to the laws of Moses and declared a seditionist to Rome. But before he departed the earth, he bestowed the secret knowledge to his closest followers, Mary the Magdalene, his wife, and the disciples, in the form of the Keys to the Kingdom.

After Jeshua was nailed to the tree by order of Pontius Pilate, he told the disciples that they should be wise as to whom they would impart the keys. So, later in their gospels, they told the story of how Jeshua was born in Bethlehem, of an immaculate birth, his crucifixion, and resurrection (all secret coded language).

They described many miracles performed by him including raising Lazarus from the dead, casting out demons and placing them in swine. He turned water into wine once at a wedding and fed multitudes of believers with only two loaves of bread and a couple of fish. This magic he accomplished was by virtue of his training in foreign lands. At the end, they describe how he was crucified on the cross (a tree in life, not a cross-but described in coded language) was dead

Introduction

to the world in the tomb of Joseph of Arimathea, then after 3 days he rose in his astral body and was seen by Mary. Then again, he appeared to the disciples and continued to appear to them in the astral until his physical death. The disciples believed he had been resurrected and finally ascended into heaven.

The disciples continued to teach his way to many believers throughout the known world until all the disciples were hunted down by Rome and killed. Their stories were retold by those they taught, without knowing the real secrets of evolution thus expanding the growth of Christianity until the modern era.

This story has been passed down for many generations in the celebration of Christmas and extended to include the celebration of Easter and the resurrection.

First, these holidays are pagan in origin. Christmas is the Druid candlemas. The Easter holiday is based on the rites of spring, another Druid ceremony. Jeshua's story is an allegory only, not real. For Jeshua was born a normal birth in the month of October in a hovel alongside the road, not in a manger. He was secretly spared his death by Pontius Pilate, a friend and believer, while upon the tree as a man, because he only carried the Christ force for only three and a half years (also coded language) He lived out his life in Egypt secretly until the age of 70 years.

This was his secret, even unto his wife Mary and the children who had escaped to France. They never saw him again. According to the gospel of Thomas, Jeshua said, "I am the way, the light, follow me and you will have everlasting life." Again, these are coded words referring to the 'Keys to the Kingdom,' the real secret of evolution.

Caligula Feared that the children and Mary would be a continued threat to Rome, were sought out and killed by Roman assassins. The assassins found the children in France with Martha, killing all, thinking also they had killed Mary, the Magdalene, the last threatening seditionist. But Mary escaped their treachery by chance. They were betrayed by Simon Peter in his deal with Caligula to preserve the lives of the disciples, but even Peter was later betrayed by Caligula.

Mary continued Jeshua's ministry to teach the

Introduction

'keys' to the knights of Christ who later Meta-morphed into the Knights Templar. In 1307, Pope Clement the fifth and King Phillip the fourth conspired to have all the Knights Templar executed on Friday the 13th, now a lingering supernatural fear of this ominous date by God fearing people. The 'Keys' again went underground, stored in the 'false' crypt of King Herod in the Cistern below the temple in Jerusalem and reemerged through the investigations of Hermes Trismegistus, Paracelsus and Sir Isaac Newton under the guise and secret practice of spiritual alchemy.

To understand evolution, one must consider the realms of existence. The first three are mineral, vegetable and animal. Though the idea that the mineral kingdom has consciousness is a reach for most persons, but the level of the consciousness is only on the elemental level. The next is the vegetable kingdom and again the average person would not consider the world of plants and trees to have consciousness. The Druids of Gaul (early France) also carried this belief and understanding. The trees do communicate with each other. Plants also have a rudimentary form of consciousness akin to and like the mineral kingdom. The animal kingdom has a higher form of intelligence and is enjoying greater awareness of their environment, as well as each other. That form of consciousness is not very different from a hive type consciousness like the insect world. Since man is also an animal, we must therefore define the differences. The lower animals are conscious but not self-conscious. They can dream yet they cannot imagine anything beyond their own beingness. Whereas, man is aware of himself, can imagine himself separate from his environment. The differences cannot be settled merely because of thinking, as the expression goes, 'I think therefore I am'.

   The gorilla in captivity named Koko for example, who was taught to sign and communicate with humans. In many instances Koko proved that the animal was self-consciousness and the animal's awareness demonstrated a command well beyond the mimicking of human language. And intelligence cannot separate man from other animals just because he can make tools. That myth was debunked when they discovered that apes also make tools. Remarkably, while a secret camera was set up as an experiment to observe the social behavior of apes approaching a predator as a dummy tiger, the apes used clubs in defense while planning to assault a fake tiger. More importantly, the head of the tiger was torn away. Then, after the successful assault, the apes carried the head of the tiger away in triumph as a trophy! Obviously, a surprisingly human trait.

The knowledge of the history and the true path to evolution has taken a winding and circuitous path, one diluted for the sake of the masses and the secret path relegated to members of the elite and priesthoods. The Jewish have their secret Talmud and Zohar texts within the Torah. The Taoists monks have secret meditations and formulas to affect a spiritual evolution within the physical body. The Yogis of India and Tibet have their secret meditations given only through initiation by their masters. Even the Druids of France have their secret elemental knowledge and secret ceremonial practices not shared unless you speak their language. Once while in France, the author excitedly had a chance private meeting with an

Arch Druid and he told the author he would share all his knowledge, but sadly only if the author could speak Gaelic. That was disappointing!

Even today, the church's priesthood has a separate bible (the codex 1209) different from the bible of the masses. The only way a lay person would be allowed to see or read the Codex1209 is to enter the priesthood and become a priest. The author spoke with a catholic seminary teacher in Warsaw, Poland about the Codex and the seminary priest told the author the rules regarding access to the Codex. He would not reveal any of the content despite several efforts on the author's part. The priesthood has always condemned the pursuit of the secret knowledge as heretical and or diabolical and forbidden under penalty of death.

Keys to the Kingdom come from Jeshua's own hidden words of wisdom cloaked for only those who have eyes to see and ears to hear. Decoded from his riddles and allegories retold from the heretical gospels of his disciples. This work tells the history of man's beginnings, obstacles and the aspirations for the resurrection from ignorance and slavery toward a possible ascension into a life of

Introduction

freedom through the Keys to the Kingdom.

The following are excerpts and adaptations taken from a previous work by Michael Morgan, called The Untold History of Planet Earth.

In the time before time began, a realm exists that is described by some as the void, but it's true name is the quantum. There would be those who would call it a dark and empty place but that is because their understanding falls short of the true meaning of emptiness. What would seem to be empty is just the opposite. What fills the quantum cannot be seen. It is the highest realm where physical matter does not exist, but this reality is filled with something that is not yet manifest, but exists as an infinite potential, literally a field of all possibilities, a standing wave. In terms of the science of quantum mechanics, another expression by man's limited consciousness, a purely mathematical perception of the highest form of consciousness.

In religious terms, it would be that third part of the trinity that is the Holy Ghost. In the midheaven, the realm of the multiverse, where there are countless stars bound by the forces of gravity and electromagnetism. They coalesce to form a multitude of galaxies, where countless worlds whirl about those stars in measured orbits that form the many solar systems. Upon many of those worlds, life has arisen through the divine program called evolution.

Looking upon this vast firmament of teaming life-filled expanse, all manner of life emerges within these spaces and proceed to unfold their realities within these currents of relative time, growing and expanding continuously while in the same moment, contracting and decreasing in the awareness of the standing waves of chaos that collapse into nothing only to reemerge into higher forms of order. Like a giant egg that has no shell, vibrating with a myriad of frequencies folding upon itself with a tumultuous writhing and heaving like a breathing infant that is at once a newborn and yet beyond ancient.

Such is the realm of the Highest God, the creator of all existence that is omnipresent expressing her power without so much as whimper or a shout. One would ask who is this being, where did she come from and how did she come to be? The answers to these simple but profound questions must rest within the cocoon of divine mystery waiting to unfold before the humble seeker of truth.

The finite mind, separated and disconnected from this revelation of realization, must demand with a terrible agony and the need to know, a beginning and an end to this spectacle. All the while, feeling speechless with certain awe and even dusted with some disbelief that all this is real.

Deep in the vast regions of this primordial space existed several immortal races, god-like creatures that were quite comfortable in their existence without knowing either time or space and totally quiescent in their nature. They would simply emerge as it were, from the obvious pregnant condition of that space as a sudden regurgitation. Each with its quality defined as a unique signature, a semi-permanent wrinkle out of the vibratory pattern from that space, much like the fingerprints left as a final mark upon the digits of the hand while it grows into maturity.

This race is known as the Djinn, bound with a self-imposed construct of laws and structure that provided a foundation for their existence. They were beings of energy and intelligence. Usually, intelligence is relegated to a quality of action and behavior coming from something having more substance such as, the brain of a human.

Their world existed by virtue of their undivided view of a rigid control of their reality. They were normally emotionally neutral in human terms but did not lack the possibility of an emotional response. They continued to exist in a group known as the Collective. Their way of being was defined by their control of their reality which was known by them as the way of dominion. Though expressing often with a certain unique individualism, they functioned as a hive mind.

The immortal energy of the Collective had always reached its breadth just before an explosive manifestation. This was a sign that the will of the collective would bring forth another of its kind, and it was again near the point of emergence. This always brought about a surge of pride and excitement raging through most of the fabric of the Collective. A flood of telepathic exchange rippled around the zone. Not all were so inclined to be exuberant about the event. They considered this turbulent region the backwater zone of the void, known by the Djinn as the Archway of Praxxis.

The energy at the Archway was unpredictable and chaotic. Their conflict and consternation about the emergence came from the assurance that a Djinn would arise. Some even dared to suggest that the emergence was spontaneous. The Collective considered the idea to be blasphemous. Still, when an emergence was about to occur, despite any misgivings, the Collective readjusted itself and yielded to the outcome of its own nature.

The area of Praxxis became more turbulent with an energetic froth rising out of the splashing of energy against energy upon the greater densities of the void, much like a series of ocean waves crashing against a rocky cove. The maelstrom of light emerging in that place was an awesome fountain of wonder. To be present was quite disturbing and disruptive for the Djinn. They usually avoided that place.

The experience was considered both seductive and terrifying toward their way of control. It always seemed mystifying that there was such a place in the realm of the Djinn. After all, their way was strong, traditional, and represented a conservative framework and the exact nature of the Collective had not changed for many eons.

The area of Praxxis was fertile, brimming with the promise of something new and remarkable.

The Djinn tried to ignore their instincts and rallied with hope and measured caution that something refreshing could come out of this region, but above all, they would not allow anything non-traditional amongst their ranks. Anything unexpected or construed as disruptive was unimaginable. Yet many of the High Council held a strong belief that festered, something special could arise in this most chaotic of places in the realm. Some quietly believed in the idea of fresh blood, if added to the Collective, would be the most desirable event imaginable.

This new emergence suggested the Collective had reached an involuntary breach. They could not embrace the disturbing aspect in an already well-established quadrant of the Dominion. Speculation about the true nature of the emergence and how it was to be channeled was the subject of several recent High Council meetings.

The moment had come when members of the High Council, along with delegates of other quadrants, formed a ring to surround the event horizon. The void heaved repeatedly under the influence of the standing wave streaming forth from the One. All was unfolding as expected. With each wavelet, the potential rose to capture and gather the space nearby, compressing and moving it toward the center. The stress on the space in the surrounding area forced a spontaneous leaning inward toward the event center by those present, adding to the remarkable focus of immortal energy.

Each wave recurring past those in the surrounding ring caused a murmuring arising in unison, pressing forth like a rhymical chant. The prayer continued within each Djinn that said: "stronger be the force of power, ring pass not this exalted tower, majestic sage to rule oblivion, by divine decree we grant dominion."

The energy pressed on. Folding back upon itself while increasing, gathering to itself a greater sense of everything, and with itself an increased knowledge of the boundary growing denser while at the same time shrinking. Blinding light from the crushing force of space folded on itself and rushed toward the center, gobbling the space surrounding its core. The space collapsed like a giant avalanche of vortexes in cavitation, rotating the void in and out of matter and anti-matter at a frightening pace.

    Light emitting from the spectacle suspended itself as if frozen in an endless moment. Form from formlessness shimmered in the night, as a great crystal with many colored facets standing clear for all to see. All the facets reflected the light within and without. The One was complete. All was well with the quadrant of turmoil and chaos. The One had come into its midst to establish a new calm, a renewed structure, and a renewed way of dominion ruling over the realm. The dominion held secure in its framework of stability and assured constitution, a permanent solution to the chaos.

    There was a sigh of relief as the ring of Djinn broke up, greeting each other with pleasure and confidence, knowing all was well in their reality. When they retreated into their own spheres and zones of reality, a wave of intense pressure burst from the crystalline form of the One in their midst. A sudden thunderclap exploded from the form, followed by an outcry, as if a thousand trumpets blasted a mournful note at the same time. The utterance shocked the Djinn nearby. Never in the eons of the dominion had they experienced this kind of vibration.

From the One came an outburst that spread like a brush fire driven by high wind.
Radiant light filled the dark space surrounding the One, casting sharp shadows beyond those in its midst. The facets turned in unison. Cracks formed along certain facets, letting out brilliant blue and golden energy, spewing forth more foreign vibrations, and sending out ripples of fear. The Djinn were repulsed by its magnificence. Horrible tremors of the force moved with greater power and radiance until the penetration reached members of the High Council. The tremors moved like shafts of broken glass blasting through their inner most being.

Members of the High Council rushed to the Archway of Praxis to grasp the situation at first hand. To their horror, they saw something had gone terribly wrong. The One continued with another metamorphosis. No one in the Collective could do anything except observe the unfolding phenomenon. The wondrous event rumbled through the vast structure of the Djinn as an earthquake of monumental proportions, rattling the foundations of their stability. Many began to mutter to themselves and to others what it could mean. The members of the High Council approached cautiously, aghast over what they saw. Those of the other quadrants looked to the elders of the Collective with certain desperation, longing for a settlement of this disturbance and restoration of calmness and stability known for an eternity.

The danger was clear to the younger Djinn. They looked upon the elders and saw in their gaze the unsettled appearance revealing the obvious fact there was no distinct solution to the debacle. Not unlike their younger brethren, the elders stood by helpless to effect anything meaningful. They too awaited the eventual outcome of this disturbing and unpredictable event unfolding. As every change unfolded, gasps of horror and dread followed from the onlookers. Blinding light streamed from the One, seeping from the fracturing crystal, too strong and painful to embrace. These searing rays were too bright against the dark velvet realms of the Djinn. Each ray split the darkness with violent passion.

The changes kept coming, speeding up the metamorphosis before the elders could grasp the situation. There was no chance to offer any kind of cogent response. Each change presented by the One brought more serious considerations, implying greater consequences for their influence on the Collective.

Meanwhile, within the core of the One, conscious awareness multiplied and amplified with greater intensity. Her passion focused on an irresistible urge growing within her being. A certain intolerance emerged in her awareness, pressing against her form, clearly defining the outline of her boundaries. This aspect was unusual. It was a sharp departure from the traditions found in the normal emergence of a Djinn in the Collective. This singular difference pressed outward from her core, causing a blast of heat and light like hot plasma, building with eruptive pressure against her boundary. There was only one burning thought in her passion, to be free of the boundary and the form that bred her.

With one more final outcry she erupted with frustration, caring no longer for her existence, she surrendered with trust toward the purest evolution of her divine will,
to be greater than she was, or nothing. Her passion for freedom rushed through the dark void, past the elders of the High Council. A spherical envelope of spiritual substance and energy spewed forth, containing many bright star clusters of concentrated intentionality, surrounded by divine energies swirling about the centers of the clusters of pure consciousness, each embedded with the finite aspects of her essence of divine freedom.

The Djinn retreated from the magnificent display of insurrection to their traditional divine structure, and the One expanded further her envelope of evolving expression of freedom. Thinking the final explosion would be like a candle burning twice as bright and lasting half as long, the elders went to their own realms to deliberate on this ominous debacle.

At once they lodged charges against the abomination of the One, claiming nothing calm or stable could ever come out of the forsaken zone of chaos, the Archway of Praxxis. Some wanted the Archway declared inviolate, where no Djinn should ever venture. They gave little consideration about the fate of the One since they believed she had exploded out of existence.

The High Council could not comprehend what had happened. The true mystery unfolding in their midst was inconceivable to them. They had given birth to what some would call a biological sport, an evolutionary mistake. Hidden within their essence was the possibility their nature could degenerate into something that represented their compliment as well as their opposite. The High Council had to learn more of her evolutionary essence that was growing. The full implications of the far-reaching confluence to their foundation, beyond structure and without structure, the embodiment of the purest energy free of form, the first formless Djinn.

The speed of the One's sphere of influence slowed, while the surface of Her volume grew larger. The size of the volume could not be determined without the reference of time. Space was indiscernible. To offer spatial reference,

Creator - Source

humanity measures space by the speed at which light travels within one year. Hundreds-of-thousands of light years measured in parsecs could not define the ever-expanding boundary.

Countless starry clusters represented psychic nuclear points of her consciousness. Each of these clusters, like cells of the whole, combined as the One's divine mind. Each point represented one Stellar Mind, an individual spiritual aspect of Her energetic form. There were a finite number of Stellar Minds, but the exact number was not known. Like the One's original energetic form, the components possessed the same quality of the One's intent, expressing free will, but through their individual aspects and perspective.

Unlike the attributes of the Collective rising beyond Her, the witness aspect of the One's awareness existed as part but beyond the individual cluster cells. Her will and purpose acted as an invisible binding force. Her witness functioned as the highest overseeing influence. This influence was a positive propulsive energy, not dissimilar to the male positive propulsive energy of the Djinn but appearing distinctly as the

Divine Feminine. This prime mover, the Mother Goddess, instilled with passion of joy and happiness while creating and recreating Herself, multiplied with each wave of intention.

The expression to be everything without limit frightened the Djinn. Rumors spread while outspoken complaints continued among the Collective. They grew intolerant of Her existence.

Each component of Her crystallized being since Her explosion spawned numerous facets and each facet of consciousness were the Stellar Minds. They expressed Her will and intention, reflecting the One's unique light and love like beacons projecting throughout Her volume to the outermost fringe. The immense patterns of conscious energy in Her system were like neural networks found inside the brain of a human being. They connected in a unified family of neuronal-like synapses. Energy exchange occurred constantly with each as they evolved into more complicated networks in the expansion of Her increasing omniscient potential.

From the start, the Djinn did not describe the form of the One as wrong. It was more about their fear of something so different. Her strangeness made them uncomfortable. They were not accustomed to Her spontaneous and unpredictable energy disrupting the static balance through their realms. The Collective turned to the elders for a definition of the phenomenon. They wanted answers and solutions to resolve this disturbance. They wanted to return to the peace and calm of the expected, the structure of controlled reality restored.

The most disturbing aspect of the event from the point of view of the elders was the clear dissolution of the One's form and core. They could not grasp the meaning and continued dispersal of Her essence into countless secondary centers of influence called Stellar Minds. To them, the One functioned like a hive of spores, spreading among their kind. The general lack of Her focused presence appeared to the elders like an absentee host, or as humans might put it, a ghost in Her own shell.

The dominant opinion among the elders was to stop the expansion of the foreign expression. Factions in the Council represented various points of view, and not all the Djinn were against the phenomenon. Some were hopeful of the outcome and waited to see the result. Despite forming a loose alliance to the One's expression, elders of the High Council continued to push for a resolution.

They insisted the young Djinn had shown in Her rogue expansion a cavalier disregard for traditional values instilled in the Collective. They further stated Her presence might threaten the foundation of the Collective, the Way of the Dominion. During the furor, a new wrinkle appeared.

In the world of the Djinn, energy and expression of their light is always male propulsive. The constant Djinn light streamed from each of their cores. It was a quality not as vibrant or white hot as the One. Each was powerful on their own, unique in their realms. A separate vibration defined each realm. Each had its own sphere of influence and existed in each other like dimensional spheres within spheres.

Near the fringe of the One's expression, the positive propulsive blue and golden light shifted in color. The harmony and unity of consciousness from some Stellar Mind altered. The value of their light became almost monochromatic, possessing an unusual singularity in their value.

A lackluster quality eroded the dazzling appearance of Her light, which first was so positive and alive. A significant change occurred in some individual Stellar Clusters. Hesitation appeared in their movement, retarding their individual will toExpand.

The One, aware of the emerging in Herself, did not react negatively to their shift.
In the framework of Her passionate paradigm, freedom to express was good and righteous. The One took no interest to consider this alteration. To Her, it was a variation, a continued differentiation of Her ever-expanding and evolving pattern of consciousness.

True darkness emerged for the first time in the realm of the immortal Djinn. It may sound strange to say, since their realm comprised the continuum of the dark void. This made different by the polarity in the light that emerged. Shifts of reality became harsh and disruptive. The freedom that expanded throughout their existence took on a shadowy and foreboding quality.

This shift of light into dark did not arise due to doubt about the One's intentions. Among the Stellar Minds, curiosity led them to explore this direction of contraction. They were innocent to the implications of the movement, and pursued the direction with the same dedication, fervor, and steadfastness that defined the will of the One.

As most of the Stellar Minds continued to expand the gold-blue light of love and freedom of expression modeled by the One, the others explored something most peculiar in their experience of themselves. They explored the opposite of expansion…the act of contraction. This movement had never been witnessed by the Djinn, which included other immortal beings in the vast dark void alongside them.

The nature of the contraction was simple. The Stellar Minds wanted to implode.

Her expression in the opposite direction and reduce their ever-increasing consciousness in the harmony of the one's realm. They eliminated their sensitivity to everything of the One, step by step. They wanted to observe and experience the effects of the process.

To the One, this seemed plausible. The One considered the idea to be consistent with free expression, so long as there is joy and passion in the movement their way of expressing Her will was sanctioned.

The elders of the High Council approached the One.

"Have you given your word for these individual parts to undertake this most unusual way to express?"

"No, we have not given the word, but do We need to? Is it not true that in the freedom to express, there is no need of the word to approve or disapprove?"

The elders balked at her response.

"How dare you reject the Way of Dominion. This is the way of kindred immortals, the foundation of the Collective, the only way possible and allowed. If you do not give your word, there will be disorder and chaos."

"What you say may be true in a bound structure. As you can witness, our movement is free of any binding structure. A preordained structure requires order to maintain itself. Our lack of structure

allows the freedom to alter the form at will.
In Our way, if a need arises, let the one drawn to fulfill the need respond of their own volition. Then there is no need to give Our word."

The elders back away, aghast of the One's views. They turned to assimilate Her thought-forms. Then Bael, leader of the elders and Supreme Chancellor of the High Council, stood and addressed Her.

"What you say is blasphemy. Only disorder can come from spontaneity. We can see no reason to this lack of responsibility in your manifestation. You must cease and desist movement at once."

The primordial law, known beyond and recognized by the first of our kind, states That which is undertaken cannot be undone, for the primary cause set in motion, you are bound to the effects."

The One smiled after this statement, knowing it would be an inescapable argument of their own decree, and a dilemma for the High Council.

"Be careful, young one, said Bael. In your cleverness to use the law, you have sealed your fate. For it is also true, that the absolute doctrine of the law governs all reality. This defiant action on your part is lawless and could warrant the Council's recommendation for the elimination of your expression. You have not been confirmed yet, young one. You would do well to yield to an elder's wisdom in this case. The wisdom to follow an elder's guidance is a fundamental requirement set down in the Djinn doctrine."

"Dear brothers, said the One. Don't be upset with my movement. We are here to fulfill the law, not break it. Let the cause we have set in motion be evaluated by results. The effects express the law, and we must experience it. If there be the need to judge our expression, let the witness of the law unfold, what will be, as well as the seal of our fate."

Bael turned his back on the One with scorn. He motioned for the others to leave. Then he turned his attention once more to her.

"This is not over yet, young one. The time of your reckoning grows nigh. Your ways will not pass without judgement. Let us see then how clever you will be."

Later

In the central portion of the great regions of the

One's expansion, a vast stellar mist swirled with brilliant hues of emerald, green. Those colors succumbed to soft reddish tones followed by purple swaths pulsating in a dance of light.

The One could not help being pleased. This pleasure exuded from everywhere and invited a smile while she observed the shimmering surfaces ripple and unfurl from the wake of Her invisible breath. Her vision of beauty and passion raced across the depths of the dark void like great interstellar sails. Deep in the mists of the triune stream of two Stellar Minds, Pollux and Childra, exhibiting qualities distinct from the original crystalline One. They were the first to emerge from the expansion. They explored their unique essence and expression with innocence in. their movement.

As Pollux and Childra merged during their continuous expansion, an epiphany rose between them. They discovered another way to be realized. Instead of exploring expansion in their expression, they could explore what it would be like to be less. Why not exchange their passion for outward movement to an inner movement? In that moment, what could happen?

This changed the quality of their light and the outpouring from them became less. The unusual effect fascinated the pair. They had accomplished the unimaginable with the creation of a new quality of light. This quality differed from the dark void around them. It seemed present and discernable in their space, yet they observed the quality as though it were independent of their existence.

The darkness was alluring and mysterious, and the reduction caused the creation of something beyond them. It appeared separate, but still coming from their inseparable quality of united expression.

"How could this be?" asked Childra.

Pollux was troubled and bewildered, without an immediate answer, as was always the case before. They had found an end to the unlimited realm of the all-knowing and discovered a boundary they did not know existed. Had they created the boundary, they wondered. Now came an insatiable curiosity. They discerned this amazing perception with a slight individual perspective.

Darkness moved away like a shadowy wave, dimming the efflorescence of the One's light.

Other Djinn witnesses to the phenomenon were displeased by is presence. By now, the Collective was aware of the disturbing quality called darkness.

The One's presence was enough to manage, but the new substance could not be categorized, analyzed, or processed within normal Djinn thought, the dark beyond dark void, the beginning of something dense and repulsive to the Collective, as a quality reflected in everything they were not. The experience represented a lack, like nothingness or deadness, with a final touch of numbness. Consideration of it caused their spiritual hackles to rise.

Polarity was unknown to the Djinn. They knew only an expression of their consciousness as a singularity of light. They described the darkness as the absence of consciousness. The horror brought a whole new fear experience to the Collective, an immortal sense of xenophobia. The substance approached them, posing a real threat to conscious existence in the Collective.

In the Meantime

Creator - Source

The Stellar Minds in the vicinity of Pollux and Childra looked on with bewilderment. Several drew near to comprehend this experience of darkness along with the causes of the phenomenon coming from their brothers.

In the human experience, when siblings of the family group become distant with each other, a psychic separation is generated in the energy fabric of the family, a knowledge that something has gone awry. The family instinct declares the family structure is in trouble. When the family feels a separation or a loss of the connection in the group, the individuals draw together to resolve, if possible, the issues causing the rift.

Here too, other Stellar Minds approached their brothers to offer help and compassion for their separation. They expected stress or anguish in the situation, but there was none. This stimulated curiosity from the others, forcing a deeper telepathic empathy with Pollux and Childra.

As much as the incident caused anguish for the Djinn, there was also a strong reaction from other Stellar Minds. In an act of love and compassion, they too wanted to understand their brother's discovery of contraction. This act was a desire to help and support Pollux and Childra. However, the incident as noted in fragmented human records of bygone spiritual events describes a conspiracy against the One. In their attempts to comprehend the darkness, others added to the darkness and thus multiplied the phenomenon. The situation grew worse with every moment of their experience.

An inescapable cause set in motion through the combined mental and emotional components of divine imaging, these Stellar Minds, together with their combined consciousness, brought into existence the first Cause, a lower vibratory state of being consciousness. This became known as the Causal Plane.

This emergence of lesser out of greater consciousness was classified as evil in human terms. In the realm of the One, it was only a different manner to express Her life essence., an experiment of reduced life. The expression was necessary and allowed in the realm of the One.

In the same manner, within a democracy where freedom of speech exists, this idea argues that this creed must also allow for talk of revolt or sedition against a democratic nation's foundation, which conceived such freedom. (This might reflect on some of the scripture in Genesis 1:4, And God saw the light, that it was good, and God divided the light from the darkness.)

   Andrais and Ardenax, Stellar Minds representing courage and steadfastness in the origins of the One, examined the Causal plane of consciousness. They declared it was a perfect example of absolute freedom. This movement of decline, they argued, should carry on, and suggested this variation on the theme of the One warranted further experimentation and exploration. They explained that the experience of Causal existence with presence, was just as an extension of another state of being. This possibility existed because there was no prior sense of three-dimensional space.

   As an example, if a person were in a room with a friend, enjoying an exchange of conversation by mutual contact, and then leaves the room to enter an adjacent room, there could still be limited communication with the friend in the original room. Even without close contact paranoia or alarm would not arise. The distancing would not represent a deliberate attempt on the second person's part to separate from the other.

So, it was with those who discovered the reduction of consciousness. It seemed harmless and non-threatening. From an observer's point of view, it seems sad those Stellar Minds did not anticipate the ramifications of their combined movement.

The identification with their experimentation was the source of their separation from unity consciousness. They were helpless but to continue blinded by their curiosity, pushed further and deeper into separation and polarity, intrigued by the effect of reducing their being into something realizably felt.

Before the development of the Causal plane of existence, nothing of the physical multiverse existed. The light of Stellar Minds from the One and the light of the Djinn are not from stars, nebula, or other celestial objects of the night sky. After the physical multi-verse emerged containing those objects, the Djinn Collective coexisted and cohabited in and about these starry apparitions within their own regions, defined by their unique vibrations of existence and being.

Casiel, Meluziel, and Saganagriel brought the process down to the next level of Midheaven existence. They were intoxicated with this spiritual sort of narcotic and absorbed and shared the perceptions of degradation with ease and anticipation. They moved downward with a rush of discovery. The dramatic effects of each level of reduction remained mesmerizing. In each discovery brought excitement, but a slight twinge of regret loomed over the adventurous spirits. Unexplainable feelings were experienced and a sense of distance of. space and time emerged. Longing, sadness, and a subtle sense of loss of orientation was felt. What they took for granted, with their poise and sense of spiritual direction of the One, now seemed beyond their reach.

The One was still present. They remembered her, her essence, but no longer had any direct or even indirect contact with Her, or with any of the other Stellar Minds in the ascension and expansion of Her realm.

They continued despite their growing isolation, assured that the effects were only temporary, believing they could be reversed at any time should they decide to do so. They were divine immortal beings with free will. They believed in the freedom to explore in both directions.

The situation of this downward direction grew more deleterious. These bold spiritual explorers stretched their will, reducing their consciousness stage by stage, with each exhalation of their vital force. They expanded downward and continued to contract deeper than before. From their first separation, an unwitting letting go of the divine Mother binding them to the energetic fabric of the One caused the fabric to heave and swell, giving birth to their departure. With each stage from the whole of the One, descending to the first Cause, the be-Cause or Causal level, re-emerged into a denser state. The One's essence of energy, form, and witness collapsed into regions of the fallen Stellar Minds, lowering to the essence of imagination, awareness, and will.

With the next in-breath, the fallen broke into greater density and created several polarized aspects defining the next lower level of existence called the Etheric plane. The awareness of the fallen then fractured again and dissolved into three separate parts. The parts divided into male and female bipolar opposites representing active and passive principles. In the first part, the passive form of awareness presented its shadow active side of understanding. In the second part, the passive component of wisdom revealed its shadow active side of insight and imagination. The third part, the lower will is expressed passively as concentration with its active shadow of expansion.

The expression of the Etheric plane led the fallen further from the whole of the One. Increasingly, other Stellar Minds joined the original group mesmerized by the dark light of the debacle they created. The experience was exotic and yet tranquil. They found solace in the clear sensations of separate feeling that the whole of vibrant consciousness didn't seem to satisfy somehow. This consciousness was sanguine, without responsibility, and narcotic. While at the same time promising pleasures apart from anything else the One could offer with Her loving cocoon of wholistic mindfulness.

Though it was not yet clear, the fallen leaned

from the desirable support of the whole, and moved toward independent thought and expression, an unheard-of concept shared by those in the inner circle of the fallen.

Beleth stood before them, whirling his being in a column of vapor shining with the deepest red and burgundy. His prideful glare penetrated the others with disdain. He had a hideous laugh that was both mocking and impish. Beleth paced before them like a stocky peacock and yet like an impatient father waiting for his first-born offspring.

Then he finally spoke.

"You don't get it, do you? You search, experiment, and explore, yet it's plain to see. We set the course, the way is clear, yet you hesitate. Why?"

"What do you mean, Beleth? asked Childra. We have labored to understand this manifestation with our combined will and divination. Troubled that the reduction doesn't lead us anywhere. Many of us feel we have failed the One, trying to express Her complete free will, but this movement doesn't seem to lead us to any worthwhile conclusion."

"My dear Childra. You are intelligent. Your

powers of divination are better than most, yet you are blinded by your foolish devotion to the misguided prophet of freedom. The One is making this up as She goes. The One stumbled on the profound truth you have uncovered by accident."

The rest laughed loud at the inference of something accidental in the realm of the Djinn. Pollux raised his vision from a bow of disappointment.

"Beleth, its over. We have gone as far as we can. WE must return to inform the One, this line of decline leads to nothing. Worse, it leads us into shame."

"I cannot believe my senses. You stand on the brink of the monumental and you want to turn away, cowering before what you have done like slithering things. On the contrary, my friends, you cannot stop now. You must follow through with what you have started. You owe the One that much, don't you?"

His vision bore down on them like daggers to a target. Beleth refused to let up his goading. In what Beleth believed to be their greatest hour, the only recourse was to finish the work of absolute defiance. He focused his will on his essence of fortitude. Like a great spear, he plunged it into their core to cauterize their wounds of shame and harden their cores. They pushed on to the ultimate sacrifice.

With one final thrust, another level of being manifested. From the Etheric plane the lighter and delicate qualities of imagination, higher awareness and softer will exuded a darker level with a hellish blast of exhalation. They were fused together, developing a combination of even denser energy forming in the crucible of defiance. With a focused and determined lower will to exist beyond that of the One, negative intellect seethed, pure independent reason reckoned with the One. The Mental Plane now looming into existence allowed them to act on their own terms. The One's realm, challenged by the combined downward movement, took on heavier substance. The name of that substance was rebellion.

Meanwhile at the High Council

The Djinn elders Bael, the Arch Chancellor,

Beliel, second to the Chancellor, and Arjaxx, adjutant to Beliel, returned to the Hall of Justice for a meeting with the rest of the High Council. The chambers appeared like a classic Greek amphitheater.

The moment came to deliberate on the One. High Council members gathered when considering important matters in the crescent-shaped bowl with the eldest at the bottom and the youngest near the top tier creating a parabolic focus of energy. Their focus was toward the arena, or as the Djinn referred to it, the Platform of the Just.

When decisions were handed down, the form changed to a twelve-member panel with a three-tier cluster of crystalline forms called Tiers of Judgement. Three elders sat in the row at the top. They descended in order of position to the second tier of four and at the bottom tier of five where the youngest sat. Discussion around the issue was already underway. Groups huddled and argued the points with many heated exchanges.

They lingered on the singular point that one of their own could emerge amidst such chaos as the Archway of Praxxis. The shock of this incident continued to ripple through the Collective, which represented widespread catharsis. A centrifuge of anger fueled most of the complaints. It became the center stage for many outbursts at the meeting.

Tago the lesser addressed the members.

"I speak for many who want to know why we have an abomination rising in our midst. Why are you, our leaders, not doing something about the One?"

Beliel spoke next.

"With due respect to brother Tago, we recognize his enthusiasm on this issue. We must consider these matters carefully. Being young, impatient, and following brashly made conclusions will only add to the disruptive pattern and chaos already present in our realms."

Saixx jumped in.

"We share the concern and urgency voiced by Tago. How long before we shall see action on this matter? Every lingering moment has some occurrence caused by this thing growing like a tumor among us. Do you not see this kind of change is dangerous?"

Bael stood beside Beliel to support the wisdom

put forth by his brother.

"This is not the moment to divide in our purpose. We agree this is of the utmost urgency and yet we must weigh all the evidence."

Three representing the Ursa Major quadrant; Anodon, Arinaxx the Bold, and Deloi the Just waited for the noise and clamor to subside.

"We of the Council of Nine bid for a moment to offer a different point of view. Said Deloi. Brothers of the High Council of the Collective, we are strong in our presence and need not fear the One."

Haboro interrupted the Deloi's answer, with grumbling and dispute.

"What say you, Deloi? Your quadrant is in the outreach, what have you to offer? Your voice is heard, but it is small and has no meaning!"

"Haboro, we must exhibit patience and allow every brother to make his point,
Answered Beliel. The issue and conclusions dawn must never be questioned later. We must be sure this meeting is not construed as ill conceived or an illegitimate suppression of our own intention, please continue, brother Deloi from the Ursa quadrant."

"Thank you, brother Beliel, for your support. This represents an important transition for the Collective. Do not misunderstand our meaning: we recognize the overwhelming importance of tradition. Many have had questions about the survival of the Collective for eons, whether they want to admit it or not. The disturbance is meaningful because the One reflects our underlying consideration of paths to ensure our continuation, that we remain strong, or to become stronger."

"Yes, brothers, and hail to the wise elders who will lead us through these treacherous waters." Said Anadon.

"What say you then, Anadon?" Asked Beliel.

"We are not here to sow seeds of discontent but to reveal something in each of us. Like it or not, the One is showing us a new way."

More grumbling rose in response to Anadon's strong words. Malachais then reached forward from his position with a grimace of disapproval.

"And you, Anadon, also have the audacity to proclaim yourself aged with enough wisdom to cast judgement on the Way of Dominion?"

"Her coming into our midst has stirred us to such malfeasance and shows weakness about our structure. The Dominion needs support from a new perspective, if not a readjustment." Proclaimed Anadon.

Argument between the Djinn increased the noise to a deafening roar. Bael raised his staff and brought it down on the floor of the Hall of Justice, causing a thunderclap. Only the Eldest of Djinn carried the Jaram scepter, a symbol and artifact of great power and authority. Waves of compelling force rippled out among the Djinn until the Hall became silent.

"Brothers. Said Bael. Let us be an example of calm and order."

"Brothers of the Hall of Justice, our strength flows from Maoi, the primordial energy of vibration." Said Arinaxx. Then a sigh of acknowledgement came from the audience.

"We must prevail by not allowing the Maoi to become too stiff and rigid to move. Remember the words set down in our venerable records by the first Djinn: 'That which moves all, is Maoi, and that which preserves Maoi shall also move all with it, or all shall perish in the remnants of its passing.' Let our youngest deliver us from rigidity and restore the nimbleness of Maoi."

This brought many whisperings from the audience. A pause kept lingering, indicating no reply to Arinax's words. The elders did not want to leave the Hall on a somber note.

Anadon spoke.

"On this point, the new One's vitality is without question. We must observe the quickness with which the new One can expand, like no other before us. We can learn from the One, even though she is the youngest among us."

Demiel, a Djinn of the Anasa quadrant, reiterated the issues.

"We have listened to the Ursa quadrant and hold these views self-evident with respect. But many aspects of the new One warrant closer scrutiny. What of the dark substance she manifests? Can it be hiding her true intention? Isn't this breaking the rule of the first directive: 'Thou shalt not hold separate thyself from the whole'?

"Thus, she does not blend with us, not even at her emergence. Beliel admitted her defiance of the elders and manipulation of the law to defend her actions. Further, why does she segregate into many while hiding her own boundary? This suggests a sinister agenda. What if she multiplies herself through these altered cores to launch a siege on us?"

A voice cried out from the audience.

"Is this true, Beliel? What say you to these claims?"

Beliel turned to Bael and dropped his gaze to the floor.

"I am cautious to lay accusations when she is new among us. Her lack of experience calls for patience. It pains me to say, I have observed the young One is provocative in her actions. And I declare that the law should judge her."

Bael stood before the body of immortals and brought down the Jaram septer twice to the Hall floor.

"We cannot assimilate these deliberations without information from the young One. Summon her at once. We shall discern her provocative nature for ourselves, and have her fate determined by the evidence of her machinations." Bael declared,

The One responded to the summons without delay. She appeared in the Hall of Justice in a flash of blue light. She smiled on the august body seated before her. The Hall became silent while the Djinn gazed at her with wonder and bewilderment. Bael turned to the youngest of the Collective with surprising patience.

"Young One from the Archway of Praxxis, it is not without grave concern we have summoned you to our presence. We have heard from many in the Council about your actions. There are many allegations. We elder among the High Council want you to respond and defend these actions."

The One said.

"Dear brothers of this most auspicious gathering of the Collective, we are honored and pleased to stand before you. We look forward to answering your inquiries."

Malachais jeered.

"There, you, see? Why do you not honor us with only the One, your core? What are these 'we' you refer to?"

"We are One, but we express as many, each with

their perspective, all equal in their place in the whole, without hierarchy. But allegiant to the purpose of our will." The One said.

The audience gasped in astonishment.

Haboro then raised another question.

"How can there be existence without hierarchy in your core? This is a pure example of your defiance to the Way of Dominion. For it is known the Way of Dominion is always from the order and structure of hierarchy, since the dawn of the first Djinn."

The words of the One reflected an absolute assurance in her way of existence.

"We share mutual responsibility in matters of interest with equal status. As a need arises, those most aligned to the matter at hand respond with love and compassion. There is no need for a decree to say which of the whole will do this or that."

The audience reared back with surprise at her remarks.

Then Beliel stared at the One with intense focus, seeking the opportunity to trap her with his questions.

"So, you admit to delegating your authority to these separate parts, without regard to their direction? You do this in secret behind your wall of darkness. With this wall of darkness, do you have another agenda? You have expressed a desire to change everything. Perhaps you seek to undermine or overthrow the Collective? What say you to this, defiant One?"

The One turned serious with this charge. She looked at Beliel as well as, the rest.

"Brothers, you mistrust our way. You ask these questions with suspicion. Yet, be assured we mean no harm to you or the Collective. We only seek to reflect a new way of expressing the law, which invites trust, unconditional love, and greater mobility with the great Maoi. We seek to strengthen the Collective through relaxing the structure, suggesting a looser approach with greater freedom of expression.

"Our separation from the whole of the Collective is only that our way isn't confirmed. We need continued development before merging with the whole.

"As to the 'darkness' that emerged in our form, it is a byproduct of freedom of expression. When something new begins, it can be expected."

Bael reached forward and stopped Beliel from another round of questions. He raised his scepter, letting it fall to the floor with a thunderous noise.

"We of the elders have heard enough. We declare these proceedings closed. We shall retire to deliberate on the evidence presented.

Bael turned to the One.

"You are free to return to your realm for now, until there is judgement."

The One smiled and nodded her acknowledgement.

Later, the Judgement

Beliel turned to Bael for his reaction.

"What are your conclusions regarding the young One?"

"The matter is difficult and requires careful consideration because there is not the unity I hoped for. There are many dissenters. That makes the situation more complicated." Bael said solemnly.

"I thought the platform for her dissolution was clear. We have more than a quorum for this decision, Bael. You need not worry." Assured

Beliel.

"You are impatient on this and assume it is well to proceed, but I am less sure. Her dissolution may not be the best solution. What you suggest will satisfy the needs for the moment, but what if another of her kind appears? I want a permanent assessment of the effects of the One, and a long-term resolution to establish a benchmark for any of her kind that may arise later."

Beliel retorted.

"You are far too concerned with the One. She is a freak of nature, one of a kind, and must be reckoned with to bring order back to the Collective and reaffirm your leadership as Grand Elder of the High Council. This will give assurance of your continuation."

Bael challenged.

"Beliel, I would say you have just informed me that my leadership is in question. Do you seek my position, brother?"

Beliel bowed his head and dropped to a kneeling position in a posture of obedience.

"Forgive me for being presumptive and insolent."

"Get up brother! Bael demanded. You look

ridiculous prostrating before me."

"There has been talk… Beliel went on. I do not wish to speak out of turn here, but yes…of your delay in handling this matter, but you must know it is not my perspective. I have the highest regard for your ability to lead the High Council."

"I tell you, brother, we must move with care here. The solution must serve us all. It must be broader in its application to unite us again." Responded Bael.

Beliel rescinded.

"Your wisdom will prevail as always."

"Leave me now. Bael commanded. For I must consider this in silence."

"By your command, elder." Beliel replied.

High Council Judgement

The members of the High Council reformed for the passing of judgement. Bael, Beliel, and Arjaxx sat at the top tier. They summoned the One. Again, she appeared in a flash of blue light. There was nothing to discuss or deliberate for judgement was being passed down for everyone to witness. The

High Council sat before the Tiers of Judgement to hear the decrees set down.

Beliel spoke first.

"Brothers of the Council, be it known for all, the elders and brethren of the Judgement have deliberated on the matter of the young One's case before us.

They have reached a verdict that will stand unchallenged before the Collective.

Hear now the judgement."

The Hall of Justice was quiet. The atmosphere tingled with anticipation for the outcome. The One was relaxed but alert, knowing that her fate as a Djinn in the world of Djinns hung in the balance.

Bael reached through the blackness of the void with his utterance. The void shook with his vibration.

"Brothers of the Council and all in the Collective, from this moment and beyond the eternal, the new One shall be deemed confirmed as a Djinn of the ninth order. She shall reign in her own sphere of influence, defined by the highest of her vibration. Yet she and her kind in the One shall be separate from the rest of the Collective.

"Further. No Djinn of any realm shall enter her realm unless invited by the One. She is given a free choice to continue her expressions without disruption from any other as she deems fit.

"Be it known that this does not condone the One's actions. Her realm shall stand as an example for all to witness. This way of freedom is condemned by the court and shall not be included in the Collective at large. Nor shall the One try to incorporate her way into the Collective and its realms. This is the decree of the elders of the High Council."

Bael then dropped his scepter to the great hall floor three times saying.

"So let it be said, so let it be done.

Then Bael continued.

"From this moment, the One will be known as the nameless One. There is no recognized tradition to assert her name. She is banished from the Collective and its boundaries. No contact will be made with the nameless One by any other and if so, at their peril.

Bael dropped his scepter again three times to the floor of the Hall of Justice saying.

Creator - Source

"So, let it be said, let it be done."

Tiamat, The First temple

The following are excerpts and adaptations taken from a previous work by Michael Morgan, called The Untold History of Planet Earth.

Deep in the outer regions of the One, Beleth, Casiel, and Saganagra exchanged thoughts with growing dissent. Beleth continued with his grumbling.

"Brother Casiel, do you not feel the freedom? It's not like any experience we have felt before. This fresh perspective comes without burden."

Casiel considered Beleth's remarks and was puzzled.

"What do you mean, Brother? When have we had a burden?"

"Why, the burden of the overbearing pressure from the One. It's always her will. Why cannot there be complete freedom, even from the One."

Saganagra chimed in.

"We are also her freedom, and we express in this way. Is not that freedom?"

Beleth leaped down from where he was.

"Yes brothers, but are we free? We are free to agree, but are we free not to agree? Let us examine what we are doing here. We choose to contract. We reversed the movement. I think this is the real freedom, and the problem."

Casiel and Saganagra looked toward Beleth with furrowed brows. Then Casiel looked at Saganagra, shaking his head.

"We don't understand brother. What are you saying?"

Beleth paused for a moment, thinking he might explode with anger. His brothers seemed to have lost their minds.

Beleth continued.

"Try to follow me on this. Look what we have created. We stand here with our own mind and perspective. Why don't we use it? I know in my heart it is what she wants for us. What I advocate is, this is the time we free ourselves from the One's tyranny of kindness. She sets us free, but we are not free.

"And what would this new freedom look like?" Said Saganagra.

Beleth place his hand on Saganagra's shoulder in a comforting way.

"We would agree not to agree. The One could not ignore that her way is not the only way.

"Tell me brother Casiel, how is she different from other Djinns? She declares freedom but behaves as they do. Don't you see?"

"I suppose you are right. What shall we do? It seems we should return to the whole and expand as the others do."

Beleth grew bolder.

"No, brothers. This is our chance, maybe our only chance, to show the One we stand and follow our passion as the One does, not retiring, not regretting to push on.
to a perfect conclusion.

"We must choose our way. We must carve out of her reality a slice of our own existence. We can shift again to reduce our contractions until there is no further level to confirm our reality. We should declare our way and call our brothers to align with us. Why not join? Let us declare that we refuse to go back to her way and build a separate realm. Then we will be free to reign over our own kingdoms, doing our will and not hers."

In time, many Stellar Minds followed Beleth's cry for greater freedom, though they did not realize the implications. The contraction that began with simple curiosity, conceived, and carried out in the name of the One's will, descended into the darkness of dissent and rebellion against the One.

They joined under Beleth's leadership. With fervor and dedication, they marched into the darkness of unconsciousness to further reduce their awareness of anything except their own blind will, to be different and apart from the One, no matter what the cost.

The Stellar Minds inhaled the pride and self-importance brought on by independent consciousness and exhaled downward into a blast of lower conscious parts. The Emotional plane emerged.

The dense material of their mental bodies exploded into five polarized aspects of positive and negative emotional energy. Neutral and unconditional energy remnants of the One separated like a crash of broken glass into the density they created. These were split-off sub-impressions like chards of the original, empty reflections of the divine vessel of passion from the One. These energies did not connect to any reality, but were ephemeral copies of what was once, perfect harmony and grace.

A sad aspect of this dilemma was that what they sacrificed could not be remembered. They lost all in the oblivion of darkness. The fallen ones could not appreciate their sorrow. From loss at the beginning, they had no recollection of giving it up.

The Emotional body reformed into clusters of the densest material, and as unnatural evolution unfolded, in the deepest, most dense region of their creation was the Astral plane or lowest heaven. It was like residue dripping from their explosion. Their movement came to a complete halt, and they lost any sense of vitality and motion. Yet they did not realize their true predicament.

They entered a dream. Imagination and mental capacities were engaged to maintain a non-real world, a physical matrix of density. A whole multiverse unfolded as reflections of memory marred by separation, a poor replica of a grander place they once knew, myriads of stars, galaxy clusters with planets and moons, as vast as the realm they came from. This dream came with extreme lucid details of their inner most fantasies and lost desires. This was the grand illusion, a complete realm. Created by them, where they felt no loss or sorrow, or the pain of their actions. In this realm they created time and space. Their dream turned into a nightmare of suffering and loneliness. Time reflected on their loss. Space emerged to reflect the immensity of their separation. They did not realize the truth and were unconscious of what they were. The poor creatures were shadows of themselves and could not remember how to return home, even if they had wanted.

The fallen were lost. There was no possible way back to neutrality of the One. Polarity drove their beliefs and reinforced their illusions. The fallen Stellar Minds believed in the physical world they had created, forgetting their intentions and memories of intimate connection to the One. It was as if they had become addicted to contraction and made ill from it.

The One grew concerned of their plight when she felt this strange energy of sadness, of loneliness and suffering. It was strange because it was not familiar to her realm of love, harmony, and joy. She knew something was wrong and wondered how to resolve the horrible catastrophe.

Though she did not foresee the unfortunate outcome of their actions, she felt hope they could recover from the strange malediction. Her children were lost and needed help to find their way home. She had no judgement about their attitude, or their rejection of her ways. This awful condition of their attitude was caused by their sickness. Like a loving mother to wayward children, she beckoned them to come home. Her awareness reached out with love and compassion, calling to those who had not fallen, hoping that one or more could come to the aid of their brothers.

The brightest and wisest of the Stellar Minds, Luxcius, answered her call. He was the One's arch chancellor and favored first son above the unfallen. Luxcius expressed his deepest sympathy for the plight of his brothers, understanding the problem as well as the urgency.

"Mother of us all, it is of the utmost importance the fallen return to the fold. It is also in our interest to prove the Collective wrong about your way of freedom."

"Dear friend, my right most trusted." Said the

One.

"It gives us pleasure. To see your concern and caring for your brothers. I hasten to add, it is not for my sake you do this, but for theirs."

"You are right. Luxcius continued. This situation is most difficult and complicated. They must return with honor and righteousness yet redressed of trespasses against you."

"What have you to contribute?" The One responded.

Luxcius continued.

"After careful consideration, I believe they need loving guidance from your eminence. Yet while they are entrenched in illusion, they must understand what they have done and learn from it."

"Interesting. So, go on." The One insisted.

"Well, what I have conceived is radical in approach, and requires your sanction. We need to provide an arena where they may continue with their illusions under controlled conditions. Your emanations will assist them in unlearning the ways of separation and relearning the way of union." Luxcius suggested.

"We do not see how this requires special

dispensation." The One said.

"One of their illusory worlds needs to be utilized, a planet like they have conceived, except the planet is derived from you. Through this action, we can embed into that world, a path of light out of the worlds of darkness." Luxcius said.

"How do you propose to accomplish this, when their worlds are dead to us?" declared the One.

Luxcius answered.

"With a volunteer to become such a world through the de-vitalization of his being into a living planet."

"You mean to threaten another of my children through de-vitalization?" The One
Said with alarm.

"Yes." Luxcius said confidently.

"With our conscious control. By careful treatment, nothing will be lost for the volunteer or the others."

The One quietly deliberated the plan from Luxcius and then inquired.

"And, my son, who shall be. This volunteer?"

"Tiamat, mother!" Luxcius answered.

The One rejected Luxcius' suggested volunteer.

"He is young and more feminine. Choose someone else, someone older, perhaps imbued with male-like positive propulsive, a necessary but bolder vitality to undergo such a tumultuous challenge." The One demanded.

"No. I must disagree great One. Luxcius said strongly while tempering his firmness with respect.

"Tiamat, Luxcius insisted, is the perfect choice because of his feminine preponderance. The fallen will seek a nurturing environment in which to support their reclamation."

Then the One withdrew her suggestion.

"Very well, my son." The One continued. "Your plan has merit. What will you call Tiamat that we may know him by his new form?"

Luxcius smiled and spoke.

"Why not use his true name? It is a good name, and he will be the footstool of your compassion and love."

The One Smiled at Luxcius.

"We shall give our blessing,"

Later, the One continued to ponder over Luxcius' plan and decided to add her own vision of nurturing the fallen would require. She imbued

Tiamat, The First temple

Tiamat with all the grandeur and beauty of a divine garden befitting of a proper environment to illustrate her capacity for compassion for their situation, a divine temple instilled with her energy.

She created a new race of beings that could be part of the lower heavenly world of Tiamat, and yet be completely connected to the higher light worlds. She deemed this new life form to be called Nom-lu-Lu. They would serve along with the consciousness of Tiamat to help the fallen understand and remember her way by virtue of example.

Further, she examined the location of Tiamat in his movement around the system of dead planets. She felt the fifth orbit would need support from additional illumination spiritually as well as, a perfect environment for the new life she created to evolve. So, she created a portal connecting the light worlds of her realm to shine onto all the planets in the system. A star as a sun, would be used to embody this portal, to shed the divine light of higher consciousness and encouragement to Tiamat, thus ensuring that he would never forget his true being and her way in this difficult task.

The portal would need an overseer, a guardian of the divine gate. So, she chose the Stellar Mind Sukon to be the guardian of the portal.

Earth, Salvation's Child

The following are excerpts and adaptations taken from a previous work by Michael Morgan, called The Untold History of Planet Earth.

Like many of the solar systems within the multitude of galaxies in the multiverse, the star/sun called Sukon, would not be the only solar orb, for Sukon had a twin, a smaller dwarf star that moved about silently and unnoticed in a long elliptical path beyond the ring of debris called the Kuyper belt. Its complete orbital path would swing around Sukon in a period between its farthest point or aphelion to its nearest point or perihelion near Sukon. This path took 25,772 years to complete, the period known as the precession of the equinox. The smaller dwarf star known as a brown star, did not exude much in the way of heat or light, but it also evolved with seven planets revolving about its position.

The path of the brown dwarf would sometimes vary because of the influence of the larger gas giant known as Jupiter, one of the planets next to Tiamat that orbited Sukon. Its gravitational pull would keep altering the path of the brown dwarf until during one pass, the brown dwarf and its seven planets moved into the inner solar system of Sukon. One of the outer planets of the brown dwarf had two moons revolving around it and that planet was brought into proximity to Jupiter's gravitational pull. The gravitational force of Jupiter caused the smaller of the two moons to collide with Tiamat. Tiamat was obliterated, with more than half of the planet reduced to a ring of asteroids now occupying the space between Jupiter and the adjacent red planet known as Mars. The orbital position of the remainder of Tiamat moved out of the fifth orbit and into the third orbit.

In this calamity, most of the Nom-Lu-Lu were destroyed and all the flower and fauna of life taken away too. Having a precognitive anticipation of this calamity some of the Nom-Lu-Lu sought refuge inside of one of the mountainous regions of Tiamat. There they formed a protective crystal-like cocoon while entering a suspended animation to await rescue at another other time.

Despite the debacle, Luxcius was determined to form a reclamation of the spirit of Tiamat and restore his physical form to continue with the original plan of redemption of the fallen.

Luxcius needed special assistance for the transformation of Tiamat. For this, he chose a little-known group of immortals that specialized in change and metamorphosis of living matter. They were called the Varagonites. They existed in a remote region beyond the realm of the Djinn called the straights of Varagae. Also specific to these unusual creatures, there existed other many small beings called Seraphim, that possessed magical abilities derived from their analysis of the fallen as they manipulated spiritual laws which controlled the physical dream reality of the multiverse they created.

Luxcius found the Varagonites while exploring the regions at the rim of the Collective. The space in the Straights behaved very much like the Archway of Praxis. The energy was dense and more water-like, changing direction and swaying like an ocean's currents. Luxcius found it difficult to navigate the region without exercising control of his conscious center.

In his expansion, following the One's directive, he wanted to explore the interchange of love experienced by other species. The Seraphim showed a great interest in the energy, the quality of openness and trust, that was contrary to their experience of the Djinn. Luxcius emerging out of the Djinn represented a mystery to them.

Unlike most immortals existing in an androgynous state, (male and female elements within the same being), the Seraphim altered their gender qualities at will. Though they remained with their unique male and female element, they were changelings. They also loved to alter their age. At one moment they could be old and in the next moment children.

After meeting with the Varagonites, they introduced Luxcius to the Seraphim. Luxcius explained to the Seraphim the situation of his fallen brothers. The Seraphim were intrigued by the fallen behavior. They had already learned a great deal from their dilemma. Also, they wanted to continue their studies of the fallen and their manipulation of the peculiarities of the dense matter of the multiverse.

Luxcius expressed his unusual request to integrate Tiamat, one of Luxcius' closest friends, into the broken planet residing in the third orbit about the star Sukon. Tiamat needed to exhibit the qualities of density in the fallen dream state multiverse yet remain in conscious harmony with the One's awareness. The chief magi Arajixx of the Seraphim, responded to Luxcius's request. Though Arajixx was mildly interested in Luxcius' problem he seemed preoccupied and nonchalant.

"Hmmm." Arajixx murmured as he rubbed his furry chin.

"It's an unusual request and an interesting problem. Integrating an immortal being into an illusory object that appears dead yet conscious and flexible to the light of your Djinn, is a challenge. We think it may be manageable."

"But can you, do it?" Luxcius asked.

"Oh my, yes, we can. We love these sorts of challenges." Responded Arajixx.

"Good. Luxcius said. Then proceed immediately."

"Our magic is superior among those with skill." Arajixx continued.

After an indeterminate period, Arajixx completed Tiamat's transformation and integration while the planet remains residing in the third orbit of the binary solar system of Sukon.

Arajixx said.

"That perhaps Tiamat would be better suited with a new identity having escaped the trauma of the original form becoming obliterated."

Arajixx suggested a derivative identity relating to his transformation and grounded into his new identity. Arajixx recommended the term Terra the Firm, an expression we Seraphim would describe in the shorter phrase as Earth. Arajixx Also noted that the fragment of the broken planet could not go forward without becoming a fully invested sphere, so he took the initiative to fill the void of Earth's form with water he collected from nearby comets he brought to rain down upon the earth surface. So, earth was three-fourths water now and expressed one giant continent of land. This was only the beginning of the task at hand.

The fallen needed a strong identified attachment to keep them focused on the earth and its supportive environment while Luxcius implemented his rehabilitation program. Luxcius asked Arajixx to manifest polarized life forms on the planet's surface. These life forms would ultimately serve as hosts to the fallen.

Arajixx did not comprehend the concept completely but complied to Luxcius' request. Arajixx knew of the importance of strong lower life forms capable of providing the hosting attributes required. An evolutionary development would be needed to synchronize the lower life form to earth as well as, provide the need for adjustment to the hosted fallen. Though the fallen were in a contracted state, their energy and consciousness would still be an unresolved issue perhaps during the adjustment process. Arajixx considered many different life forms from his home world as models. Various changeling forms reflected unfolding lower spiritual levels, already present in the fallen Stellar Minds.

With five illusory planes of existence down to the Astral, four elements were markedly expressed: water, fire, earth, and air. To complete the connection to Djinn
awareness, the lower animating spirit involved was called the Akasha. The evolutionary form needed to reflect all these elements. So, the first form emerged from the water element and would

eventually leave that element in favor of the land and air element. The amphibian creatures emerged upon and walked the land.

With the ecosystem balanced, Arajixx believed the most desirable lower life form needed to exist on the surface. The surface life appeared last, representing the strengths found in every evolved species. A long period passed before the sophistication of the land creatures manifested. Only then could the chosen life forms support the immense force of androgynous consciousness of the Stellar mind. Arajixx discovered that the radiation coming from the larger of the two solar orbs, Sukon, was too strong for the health and development of surface dwellers. So, he created a canopy, a watery barrier to mitigate the radiation striking the surface. Arajixx also added a molten metal core at the center of the new planet earth and set the earth into a slow spin, encouraging the cold magnetic force to build up offering further protection to any surface dwellers evolving from the harsh energies streaming from other celestial objects still developing in the area.

Luxcius built a staging area on the second planet

from the solar orb of Sukon which he named Vaness (Venus). Luxcius asked Arajixx to keep Vaness in a gaseous state long enough for the fallen Stellar Minds to remain suspended until the earth was ready for their first infusion.

Arajixx predetermined the only polarized life form that could sustain the force of Stellar Mind consciousness would be a primate, a distant cousin of Arajixx' home world. Even with best efforts of Arajixx' planning, there was no guarantee of success.

Arajixx warned Luxcius.

"Luxcius, you must realize, what you have asked from we Seraphim is highly experimental. The diverse examples of lower biological forms of life have never come into such intimate contact with such advanced consciousness before."

"Don't you think I know? The situation is unique and calls for radical solutions. I have complete confidence in your powers to achieve this feat of magical engineering." Luxcius said.

"We wanted you to know lower evolution by magic is unpredictable and against what we normally do." Exclaimed Arajixx.

Luxcius retorted.

"Yes. But consider the One emerging from the Djinn Collective. Of course, it has not been done before. You have yet to finish your mission."

"Yes, Luxcius, we hope for the best." Arajixx comforted.

The stage on Vaness was set and Luxcius' plan was well underway. He hoped to provide a world for the fallen to relax in their illusions, then help them focus on reclaiming their lost consciousness. This would give Luxcius the opportunity to assist them in organizing their direction from the meandering energy. At the same time, Sukon would superimpose a loving, guiding, unifying principle from the light worlds flowing through the portal at his core, thus encouraging them to remember their origins, and allow their return to the whole of the One.

On earth, the early stages of violent development wound down to isolated volcanic action and sever tropical storms. Heavy rains developed into monsoons which created a lush tropical jungle environment of flora and fauna. The rain forests were thick with Popul and tall Banyan trees, as well as giant ferns and thick undergrowth. The jungle thrived on the rich volcanic soils teaming with insects that helped to pollinate the flora. Small animals scurried about seeking food while building nested shelters from the elements.

The new world was polarized with one great land mass surrounded by an even greater sea. The great continent was later known as Gwandana. In a small eastern coastal region, the first primates appeared. They were small creatures living in the banyan trees. These early primates were very agile, utilizing their long tails and their hands and feet, sporting three long and three short fingers. Their eyes were large and round having dark pupils to help cope with the dimness of the light below the canopy. They did not have eyelids. So, their appearance seemed to have a striking look as they stared out at their environment. Their tails, often used to allow them to hang upside down, left their hands and feet free to grab fruit dangling from other branches nearby.

These early primates were the ancestors of the present-day Lemurs. The area of this part of the continent would become known as Lemuria after the tectonic masses began to break up into individual land masses due to underlying volcanic activity.

The unsuspecting Lemurs hung carefree in the comfort of the high branch shelters above the ground while above and beyond them on Vaness, androgynous life was poised to descend on them. One day the Lemurs looked up to see bright lights like meteors crash through the vapor of the canopy in blinding flashes raining onto the surface. The Lemurs were disturbed by the intrusion. They had seen the showers of light before, from real meteors streaming into the earth's atmosphere. Looking on below, the lights did not hit the surface. Scampering around within the high trees, they watched with curiosity at their would-be hosts.

The Stellar Minds rushed toward the unsuspecting primates, attaching themselves. like parasites. The Lemurs cried out in pain and fell from the trees, dead on the ground below. One after the other they died. As Arajixx had anticipated, the first infusion failed, indicating the primate's unsuitability. The first root race of earth was a group of lifeless heaps on the floor of the rain forest.

Luxcius found his brothers dizzy and confused without the first anticipated hosts. The Stellar Minds looked on him with bewilderment.

"Why can we not meld with these creatures?" They exclaimed.

"Patience, my brothers. Declared Luxcius. We will bring this process to fruition soon."

Then Luxcius quickly approached Arajixx with concern.

"Why are my brothers without hosts?" Luxcius demanded.

"This is a work of much difficulty. We must adjust the primate's nervous system to adapt to the shock of greater consciousness more easily. Remember, these creatures have never been self-aware. The results will be better at the next change."

"I am depending on you. My plan depends upon your success!" Luxcius warned.

Arajixx continued making genetic changes adjustments with his magical skill to raise the frequency of the primate's nervous system into greater sophistication. Once again, the Stellar

Minds descended upon the altered creatures. As they attached, the lemurs cried out in pain again, even though the attachment sustained the Stellar Minds a little longer. Now more lay dead on the forest floor. The second root race had failed.

Arajixx looked on with some concern. With Luxcius watching him, he remained steadfast in his conviction with his mission. He changed the primate's genetic frequency to a higher tone, lifting their nervous system to yet another level of sophistication. This time when the fallen Stellar Minds descended on the primates, their cries sounded different. It was not pain, but surprise. The third seeding had triumphed. They lived, and thus became a marriage of animal and spirit of a higher order.

Soon they descended from their tree shelters. Untouched primates looked below with wonder. The changed primates behaved differently from their perched counterparts. Under the influence of their spiritual symbionts, they climbed to the ground and foraged on the surface. They began to make their nests of shelters in nearby caves. The third root race of humanity in Lemuria had begun.

Androgyny to Polarity

The following are excerpts and adaptations taken from a previous work by Michael Morgan, called The Untold History of Planet Earth.

Meanwhile in High Heaven

Beliel soon learned of Luxcius' endeavors to recover the fallen. Stellar Minds. He knew Luxcius exhibited similarity to the Djinn in his ambition. For Luxcius, it was a weakness. For the One, his weakness became hers.

Still disgruntled with Bael's decision about the One, Beliel believed this might be the opportunity he had hoped for. If he could use the ambition of Luxcius to detour the One's progress, he could assert Bael had made a bad decision to let the One live and use it to undermine the High Council's confidence in him. This would improve his chances of dislodging Bael from the Council and rise to become Supreme Chancellor.

This represented another contrasting point between the Djinn and the One. Hierarchy leads to competition among the ranks through ambition. Without hierarchy in the One's realm, ambition was non-existent and there was no competition without its driving force. The will of the One was also common to all so ambition did not arise, at least in principle.

The One did not anticipate the effect of Luxcius' ambition until much later. The complete dedication to unconditional love and compassion kept the One from viewing faults and limitations, and their effects. The One was innocent. Beliel's plan to undermine Luxcius soon unfolded. The One didn't see it coming.

On Earth, as the living spirit of Tiamat, the Stellar Minds continued to influence the primates by altering their behavior. They ceased climbing trees and continued to forage on the ground for food. They sought caves for shelter, huddled for warmth and mutual protection.

The fallen became engrossed with basic elements on Earth along with the pleasure of knuckle walking on the surface. It was exhilarating to have the soft, warm soil receive their feet and hands while they explored the joy of traversing.

At the same time others explored the other elements as well, like the experience of playing in the water. After several primates died the Arajixx, the chief magi of the Varagonites realized that the nostrils of the primates were not designed for plunging under the surface of water. The environment of the Earth being largely waterlike, was quite different than the environment found in the regions of Arajixx' home world. Arajixx realized that the primate nostrils could not dip below the surface of the water element without experiencing breathing difficulty.

The Seraphim continued to assist in the alterations of the primates, facilitating a smooth continued symbiont relationship for the fallen. They sped up the loss of hair to facilitate ease of movement in the water element. A new bridge covering the nostrils allowed a greater measure of protection from unexpected water entering the lungs. Meanwhile, the land walkers rose to an erect posture and altered their movement to walk upright with less knuckle walking. While both variants of the species soon lost the need for tails, since their need to forage in the trees was no longer necessary.

The water primates needed less physical development since the water element supported their weight. The water primates subsequently remained small in stature while they subsisted on easily obtained food from sources in the water, they became more pensive and began to develop their mental abilities. Vast and continuous mental focus caused their craniums to swell adapting to the added convolutions and size of their brains.

Meanwhile

By contrast, the land walkers developed strong bodies, able to climb, leap and jump while pursuing their prey for food. The changes in temperature from the day and into the night encouraged keeping much of the hair on their bodies. Soon, the primates realized that animal skins taken from their prey, could augment their need to remain warmer when severe cold weather arose. And the skins provided crude coverings for their feet which helped to prevent cuts and bruises on their feet when engaged in the act of pursuing prey in a hunt. After many millennia, hunting tools were made and the discovery of fire made possible for open areas for dwelling as well as, providing greater warmth inside their caves and later the discovery of cooking their food.

Arajixx was confident of the early stages of primate development and indicated promising evolutionary development on their part. Confident that the primates were strong enough now to withstand the intense energy of the large yellow sun, Arajixx ordered the dispersal of the thick vapor canopy surrounding Earth to be lifted. The bright light of the solar orb, Sukon, forced further changes for the species such as eyelids to help adjust to the bright light and forward protruding foreheads that were covered with bushy brows.

The water primates changed their skin quality to a salamander-like quality that could change color and texture which offered them an additional protection from the bright sunlight as well as, a chameleon-like adaptability with their surrounding environment that provided an invisibility against predators. By contrast, the land walkers had very thick leather-like skin of a ruddy-red coloration. The hair remained to help protect the delicate areas such as the chest, groin, and back. The hair grew long at the top of the head to protect the scalp of the head from Sukon's strong rays. Since the larynx was not developed yet, communication by speech remained only as crude grunts and gestures with the hands. It would be thousands more millennia before verbal speech replaced the crude form of telepathy already existing, resulting from the fallen consciousness residing within.

Not every Stellar Mind gave way to Luxcius' plan for a return to the One's realm. One such Stellar Mind resented the symbiosis of Stellar consciousness bound within the conjured hairy beasts. His name was Pan. He took umbrage to the whole idea but conceded the need for a greater focus of their energy. Pan put forth his own claims to Luxcius.

Pan spoke telepathically.

"Brother, why should I or anyone else accept this crude expression of lower life here? I have sufficient imaginary powers to develop my own form to express. We do not need these beasts. They seem to me to be limited. They repulse and do not suit my desire."

Luxcius responded.

"Brother Pan, do you not see the importance of

living here on this island Earth, and the unique forms of lower physical lifeforms chosen by

Arajixx, along with the embodiment of your brother Tiamat? You would do well to choose these lifeforms, as they prove to be most functional in this environment."

Pan continued.

"I appreciate your efforts brother Luxcius, but I am not the only Stellar Mind to dispute the lower forms and their limitations. I see the value of Tiamat, but I wish to apply another form to express. I will not stay. I will go to another part of this unique world and find my own form."

Pan left, despite Luxcius' protests, along with several others to an area further southwest on the continent. Then, after millions of years past, and the great tectonic plate of Gwandana broke up, spreading apart to form other separate smaller continents, Pan and others settled on another smaller island continent to the south that would be called Galapagos.

The defiance of Pan upset Luxcius, but his troubles were just beginning. Beliel
descended to the sphere called Earth to sow the

seeds of dissent among those that resided as symbionts in the primates.

Beliel set to work by pointing out to the fallen there was a most curious energy called spirit that provided life for the primates. He explained that it was the primary source for the procreative agent responsible for their propagation as a physical species. Beliel appealed to the fallen to notice the sexual force flowing between the primates during their mating season.

Beliel suggested if they engaged in the mating process, they would come to understand the unifying principle of spirit, and then have greater knowledge at the fundamental stages of being. To complete his seduction, he promised them a fast return to the unified state and an end to their suffering.

The Stellar Minds took Beliel's suggestion to heart. He left them and returned to the realm of the Djinn, knowing he had planted the seeds of discontent. It would only be a matter of time before they were all lost. Beliel's evil idea puzzled them. How could they embrace the procreative act when they were by nature androgynous? How

Androgyny to Polarity

could they feel the unity of the polarity, the joining, unless they were polarized themselves?

The fallen approached Luxcius with troubled minds, and many questions. They petitioned him to separate them from their androgynous state into male and female, explaining that they, not Beliel, had discovered this procreative energy called spirit.

The Stellar Minds wanted to experience the sexual force exchanged between primates during the mating process, and thus better understand the unifying principle.

The Stellar Minds were very convincing. Their arguments played on Luxcius' weakness of ambition. He was desperate to succeed. Anything that would decrease the chances of failure, he favored. Luxcius agreed to give them what they wanted with the help of the Seraphim. Arajixx then separated the fallen Stellar Minds into their male and female components. Excited by the promise of experiencing newfound perspectives, the Stellar minds rejoined the primates looking forward to a quick end to their suffering. They merged with each of their gender, male to male and female to female. Luxcius looked on with some trepidation. He wondered about the outcome This had to be a mistake, but he hoped for the best.

After several generations, Luxcius' worst fears were realized. The Stellar Minds disintegrated through the offspring. In the first mating, Stellar consciousness fractured into halves. With the next generation, they fractured again into quarters, and so on until there was none sufficient to remember being splintered. It was too late. The Stellar Minds were lost into utter chaos, with no hope of retrieving them. Luxcius, frantic about what to do, lamented about how to explain his disaster to the One.

He paced and racked his burdened mind for an answer. Alas, Luxcius had no answer, they were lost to oblivion, and that was the end of it. His plan in shambles, his pride and arrogance were to be his undoing. There would be no saving grace, for he had destroyed his brothers out of his love for them. He could not see that it was his terrible ambition behind his motive, in that he was blind.

He turned to Arajixx for help.

"Is there nothing you can do?"

Androgyny to Polarity

Arajixx lamented.

"I am truly sorry for you. Taking your brothers apart was easy. We have no tools or, process to find them and put them back together. In the mating process of the primates, they descended through the offspring at random. The precise path is unknown. They do not remember who they are. So, we cannot ask them to stand up and identify themselves. There is nothing that can be done. We are sympathetic to your loss. We bid you condolences and farewell."

Meanwhile

Pan and his followers arrived in the Galapagos. They explored their creations of their own combinations of animal-man-like creatures. There were half primates with half horses, half primates with half birds, even half primates and combinations of fish, which Pan called mermen and mermaids. It was endless.
Soon they all grew tiresome of the fruitless escapade. They knelt with humility to ask the One's Forgiveness.

The One appeared full of compassion in their plight.

"Do not despair my children, rejoice instead. You have seen the finality of the sorrowful path you have taken. Can you not see in our countenance the unconditional love we have for you? Return to the inner fold at once. All that is ours is yours to partake."

Pan responded prostrate before the One.

"Mother of us all, please know we love you and wish to respect your wishes, but we feel we must decline. With your consent, may we request to remain here in this world of Tiamat to continue with this divine task of assisting our brothers. It is your love and devotion that is projected. We wish to remain in the Astral level of your kingdom, in this illusory realm, where we can best serve to maintain the living things here, and assist Tiamat in his expression on your behalf, since Arajixx is no longer here to guide this manifestation."

The One smiled at Pan. She expressed a wave of blue and golden light, full of love and compassion for him and his followers, which she showered on them.

Androgyny to Polarity

"Blessed are my children and their good works. Our realm of freedom shall flourish and propagate through the lower kingdoms. May tidings of joy flow in your being and provide continued assistance to your brothers who struggle to embrace their depleted condition on Tiamat. Your efforts will open greater possibilities, so they may remember that our love offers the divine beauty and grace of continued life as it abounds on and through Tiamat. Where is my son Luxcius? And where are the rest of my children?"

The following are excerpts adapted from The Memoirs and Prophecies of an Extraterrestrial God, The Lost Book of Enki, by Zechariah Sitchin

According to Berossus, a Chaldean priest of Bel, historian and astronomer in Babylon (65 B.C.), reported ancient records existing before the great flood, hidden in the city of Sippur, one of the cities of the ancient gods. However, Sippur was overwhelmed by the deluge and destroyed.

Some of the writings surfaced again in the annuls of the Assyrian King Ashurbanipal (668-633 B.C.) discovered by archeologists in the mid-nineteenth century in the Assyrian capital Nineveh in the palace library. The king was known to be a collector of olden texts amounting to over 25,000 clay tablets declaring "the god of scribes has bestowed upon me the gift of the knowledge of his art."

The account and Testation, from the words of Endubsar, master scribe, son of Eridu city, Servant of Lord Enki.

Approximately 450,000 years ago, extraterrestrial astronauts (a reptilian race called the Anunnaki) from a planet called Nibiru from the binary dwarf star system came to Earth in search of gold. They landed in a spaceship called Eh-Din (meaning Garden in Anunnakian), in the seas near the land that was known as Mesopotamia, located in the great "AB-ZU" (Southeastern Africa). They came ashore and established Eridu, "Home in the Faraway." In time, the settlement expanded. Then the settlement became Mission Earth, a large community around the great spaceship with a Control Center, a spaceport, mining operations and even a way station established on the planet Mars.

They attempted mining from the waters of the Euphrates River, but the amount retrieved was far less than what was needed. The mining shifted from the waters to mine from the ground. The ore in the ground was in quantities far greater, but those assigned to do the work, the Iggigi, joined together and refused to do the hard work demanded of them.

Anu, the ruler of their planet Nibiru, and ruler of the Anunnaki inhabitants on earth, (referenced in Sumer language) "Those Who from heaven to Earth Came," demanded an immediate solution to this work stoppage. But king Anu also decreed that there would be limits on any indigenous creature used to replace the Iggigi. They were not to reproduce themselves. With minor changes, the new specimens as slaves, would be able to understand their language to follow commands, as well as operate their mining machinery, but not to reproduce in greater numbers for fear they may rebel and revolt against their masters.

    The king approached his first-born son EnKi, who was well versed with his planet's history and its inhabitants. He was an accomplished scientist and geneticist and along with his half-sister, Ninharsag, the ship's chief medical officer. Both realized the fastest and easiest way to overcome the problem of manpower required was to explore the indigenous life forms in and around the city of Eridu. A bipedal hominid known as Homo-Erectus, was found roaming the area in sufficient numbers, and chosen as a promising specimen for experimentation. The animal was large and strong. After shortening the animal's life span to 70 years, many experiments could be achieved in a relatively short period.

Anunnaki History on Earth

The first genetic results developed an Adamu, (Anunnaki term) the first Adam, from Homo-Erectus to Homo-Sapien. However, Ninharsag discovered that after the first successful genetic alterations, the Homo-Sapien could not reproduce. The process of making new Adams individually would not be a good solution due to their time constraints.

Nibiru's atmosphere was failing and slipping away quickly. Gold in a powdered form would secure the atmosphere, but the need was quite urgent.

EnKi decided that he would defy the king's order that the Adamites could not reproduce. He altered the genetic sequence by adding his own DNA. This restored their reproductive capability. Also, this increased their intelligence and at the same time, made possible the Sapien's ability to evolve more quickly.

Lord EnKi was part of the first group to arrive on Earth. Due to a rather complicated set of rules of succession on Nibiru, EnKi, though firstborn son of king Anu, would not be the heir to rule after the king passed. Rulership would fall instead to his brother, InLil, who was second born. Then the king decided to also give the leadership of the Earth Mission to InLil. This began a rivalry between the brothers. So, to help quell the dispute, the king bestowed the name EnKi to his first born, meaning "Ruler of Earth." The rivalry did not stop there, however. When InLil found out about EnKi's genetic addition to the Adamites, he immediately informed his father. This caused a great argument between the brothers and their father. Further, the king ordered that EnKi be banished from the community of EH-Din.

In addition, InLil despised the adamites that EnKi created which helped to solve the atmospheric problems on Nibiru. EnKi was praised by king Anu for his brilliant efforts, but this made In Lil jealous. He was hoping to find a way to undermine EnKi's success. Seeking a way to undermine EnKi, he played upon the king's fears of an insurrection by adamites and convinced the king to destroy all the Adamites. EnKi became furious with InLil and ended up killing InLil over his betrayal.

Note: During the invasion of Jerusalem by the

Babylonian armies, the Israelites were captured and brought back to the city of UR and enslaved in 586 BC. During their 500 years of captivity, the Israelites had access to Sumerian historical tablets and began to formulate their own narrative from the Sumerian history of God and man.

Written in Hebrew, part of the Torah narrative was to tell the story of Genesis, the creation, about Adam and Eve, the garden of Eden, the deluge, the tower of Babel. The serpent (EnKi) in the garden (EH-Din), the temptation of Eve 'eating' the apple (genetic changes) and the commandments from God (Anu) about the 'tree of life' (The Vegas Nerve complex in the brain) offering the knowledge of good and evil, (as in evolution) and the subsequent banishment from the garden (EH Din).

There were many stories adapted from the Sumerian historical accounts such as, "The Enuma Alis" (Sumerian Genesis account) of the two brothers Cain (EnKi) and Abel (InLil), Cain killing Abel and then being banished. Also, in the Sumerian historical records, the "Epic of Gilgamesh" defined the saga of Gilgamesh, his building an ark and his survival is the story of the great flood (here, Noah is interjected instead of Gigamesh.)

Meanwhile in High Heaven

The One still concerned about her lost children, decided to assign 200 of the Angelic Realm, to become Watchers or guardians over the fallen. After EnKi and Ninharsag completed the alterations of the brutes, Homo-Erectus, into the civilized Homo-Sapiens, the females of the adamite species became very attractive to the Watchers. They descended upon the earth and made wives of these females and bred with them creating the giants called Nephilim. (Genesis 6.4) "There were giants in the earth in those days; and after that, when the sons of God came in unto the daughters of men, and they would bear children to them, the same became mighty men which were of old, men of renown." Their giant offspring roamed the Earth feeding off the earth until there was nothing left to eat. So, they became cannibals attacking and eating adamites and even attacking their own kind later.

Meanwhile in Eridu

The conflict carried on between the two brothers' sons, even among their grandchildren. Personal agonies sharpened ambitions for all those born on the Earth who faced the loss of longevity that Nibiru's extended orbital period provided. It all came to a climax in the last century of the third millennium B.C. when Marduk, EnKi's firstborn by his official spouse, claimed that he and not EnLil's firstborn son, Ninurta, should inherit the Earth. The bitter conflict which included several wars led to the use of nuclear weapons and with that, the unintended demise of the Sumerian civilization.

Recent archeological excavations of the desert plain in Iraq has indicated some remaining radioactivity in the deeper soil there. With the rapid expansion of the adamites along with the emergence of the giants in the Eridu kingdom, forced king Anu to take InLil's advice. The situation had so disturbed king Anu, bringing him to decide the complete destruction of all Earth's inhabitants.

Upon the next orbit cycle (Shar) of the planet Nibiru and its dwarf star, (which later became known as Nemesis according to the later Akkadian records, due to its role in the great flood), orbiting around the central sun of the inner planets including Earth. king Anu ordered his scientists to shift the orbital path of the Nemesis system closer to Jupiter utilizing Jupiter's gravitational force which brought Nibiru very close to Earth. The result was Earth's poles flipped causing a shift of the Earth on it's axis by more than 40 degrees. The main continent of Gwandana broke apart and the resultant tidal waves wiped out all life including most of the Adamites and the Nephilim except for Gilgamesh.

Though EnKi was forbidden to speak with the Adamites after his exile from EH-Din, EnKi defied his father again by relating the warning of the coming calamity through surrogates, instructing Gilgamesh to build an ark.

Yahwey, Elohim Storm God

Excerpts for this chapter are taken from the work, Gods of the Bible by Mauro Biglino, an Italian biblical scholar, translator and publisher. He directed and supervised the translation and publication of 17 books of the Old Testament for Italy's main Catholic publisher, whose Vatican-approved texts are used in theosophical, ancient Hebrew, and biblical studies schools and universities.

To discuss who is the "God," Yahwey we must examine the biblical references to the being, called Elohim. Which, then this term begins in the book of Genesis of the Old Testament, King James' Version.

The concept of "God" as taught in modern day religious studies possess specific spiritual characteristics, which include omnipotence, omniscience, eternity, compassion, love, and so on. The author agrees with the author Biglino, the actual entity referred to here, may present a very different perspective that would probably shock the reader.

Despite the meaning that is given to the term

alien, which etymologically means "foreign," "other," "different," and or "unknown," even "extraterrestrial." With a thorough reading of the correct translation of the bible reveals a concept of "God" as quite alien compared to the common concept of a spiritual being.

Much of our religious texts all stem from a source of historical records that predate the Jewish Talmud and the Torah for which Judaism is based. This source, in fact dates from clay tablets written in Sumerian cuneiform found in the temple library remains of Ninneveh, near the city of Sippur, an ancient city of Babylonian culture dating well over 6,000 years before the pharaonic dynasties of Egypt. As you might proceed to join in the main question that you might ask, were monotheistic religions the byproduct of ancient encounters with technologically advanced visitors from another world.

Many authors in the recent past, such as Zacharia Sitchen, Chronicles of Earth History, and The Lost Book of Enki, have dealt with the idea of possible contact with extraterrestrial civilizations. Many books have formed the hypothesis that such civilizations are at the origin of our species' biological and cultural evolution.

In the second half of the 20th century various authors have tried to deal with this subject by quoting and analyzing passages from the Old Testament. They did so by relying on mainstream translations of the Bible available to the public.

The term "Elohim" is translated as "God" in commonly available Bibles. However, this term is left untranslated in the interlinear Bible edition prepared for specialists and scholars of the ancient texts.

Theologians and believers regard the Bible as the Revealed Truth, a sacred text. They worship and pray on it. They read it as though the words are spoken from the mouth of God. This attitude is prevalent outside of the religious sector as well. Politicians take the oath of office on the Bible; court eyewitnesses swear on it before giving testimony. It is a text considered the epitome of unquestionable truth and reliability.

This perspective represents an open contradiction with the nature of the book, made up of endless passages and stories with incessant manual copying and transcriptions, censorship, and amendments that lasted more than 2,500 years. The Old Testament represents a series of books that are the most frequently written, rewritten, manipulated, altered, interpolated, modified, erased, corrected, eliminated and rediscovered in human history. When you speak of the Bible, it does not refer to a single, coherent text written with a specific purpose at a moment in the past. The Bibles we have in the present are based on the Stuttgart Bible, the printed version of the Leningrad Masoretic Codex, prepared between the sixth and nineth centuries CE by the Masorites, guardians of the Masorah, i.e., the tradition of the school of Tiberias, who belonged to the family of Moshe Ben Aaron Ben Asher.

This Biblical version has significant differences between the various denominations. Catholics believe the Old Testament contain 46 divinely inspired books, for the Jewish canon only 39 books are recognized. Christians accept some divinely inspired books that are not recognized in the Jewish canon. For example, books of Tobias, Judith, Wisdom, Baruch, Sirach, the first and second Books of Maccabees, and some passages of Esther and Daniel. The reformed church, i.e., Protestants adhere to the Jewish canon. In contrast, Coptic Christians accept in their canon the Book of Enoch and the Book of Jubilees which, are considered heretical texts by others.

The Greek Orthodox Church will not use the Leningrad Codex but accept the text of the Septuagent written in Greek in Egypt in the third century BCE. Compared to the Masoretic version, the Greek Bible has approximately one-thousand variations, important because they represent significant differences in the meaning of the text which, also show corrections and amendments (textual forgeries) made by Masoretes. By the same token, the rabbis reject the Septuagent and argue only the books believed to be consistent with the law, written in Palestine, in Hebrew, before Ezra (fifth century BCE) as acceptable.

In northern Palestine, in the territory of the Samaritans, the truth is not in the code written by the Masoretes but in Samaritan Torah (Pentateuch). The Samaritan Torah has up to two-thousand variants compared to the Masoretic code. In the

Samaritan canon, only the first six books are recognized as truly divinely inspired, i.e., the Pentateuch and the Book of Joshua. The Peshitta, the Syriac Bible, accepted by Maronites, Nestorians, Jacobites, and Melkites also differ from the Masoretic Bible. Part of the Jewish culture believes that the Talmud contains more truths than the Bible itself. All that is before you consider anything close to translation problems that have occurred with all these texts!

Since the discovery of the Dead Sea Scrolls (also Known as the Qumran texts) provide a different version of the Book of Isaiah which only increases the uncertainty between these texts and the Masoeretes. Finally, the compilation of the first five books of the Old Testament, known as the Torah, or Pentateuch, is traditionally attributed to Moses. But scholars know that these texts were written during and after the Babylonian exile. The present manuscripts do not predate second century BCE. So, there is not a single book of the Old Testament which can be said with certainty of who wrote it and when. The same can be said of course with the New Testament's four gospels, Mathew,

Mark, Luke, and John. So, it goes beyond common sense.

The Sumerian-Akkadian narratives are defined as myths, legends and fables, while at the same time, the Bible is in part derived from them, that represents the truth inspired by "God"!

So, with that said, let's go back to the problem of Yahwey. Let's begin with a few pages devoted to the term "God." In particular; does "Elohim" mean "God"?

"Elohim" has a certain meaning today, but no one knows what this word "Elohim"
meant for the writers of the ancient biblical texts during the time when they were written.

If it is accepted that "Elohim" means "God", is our idea of "God" today the same as the concept of "God" that ancient Semitic people had thousands-of-years ago…No! The term "Elohim" in the Hebrew Bible contains multilayered semantics.

"Elohim" is not the only term in the Bible translated as "God." For example:
some of the meanings ascribed to the Hebrew dictionary are "rulers", "judges", "gods",

"superhuman beings", "angels", "children of god", "mighty ones", "God", "deity", "godlike beings", "those from above". "God" also is rendered from the biblical term Eloha, according to some scholars, a variant as the feminine singular form in which the term "Elohim" is derived. Another " divine" name is "EL"which is considered the singular form of "Elohim". To some scholars these two terms differ, where EL would mean "strong", "powerful", "an object of fear", or
"Something to be accomplished." It can also mean "chief", or "Lord." The term "Elohim" in the traditional translation contains the Hebrew ending of the plural form. Yet in the Bible, "Elohim" is used with both singular and plural verbs. So, does that mean "God" or "Gods"? In Hebrew, "Elohim" is combined with an article, the article in the singular and in the plural are the same, without distinction.

This issue must give rise to some doubt! So, in the Old Testament, the Elohim are clearly and recurrently presented as a plurality of individuals.

To illustrate this point, the following statement is given from Genesis 31:53:

Following a tumultuous confrontation, between Jacob and his father-in-law Laban. They erect a stone on which they both swear neither shall pass that marker with hostile intent. To ensure compliance with the pact, they evoke the Elohim as follows:

"May the Elohim of Abraham and the Elohim of Nahor, the Elohim of their father, judge between us."

Nahor was Abraham's brother and Laban's grandfather. So, Abraham's family was divided and followed and worshiped different Elohim. Interestingly, in the Italian edition of the Jerusalem Bible (EDB, 2013), The above passage is correctly explained in a note: "The gods on both sides are called as witnesses. As customary in ancient treaties."

In Exodus 15:11, After their deliverance from Egypt, The Israelites sing a song of joy to Yahwey, praising him exclaiming, "Who is like you among the Elohim."

In Exodus 20, While enumerating the Ten Commandments, the alleged "God" begins with an assertion leaving no room for interpretatio:

"I am Yahwey your Elohim, who brought you out of the land of Egypt, out of the land of slavery. You shall have no other Elohim before me."

And finally, in Deuteronomy 6,

Moses speaks to his people and admonishes them:

"You shall not follow other Elohim among the Elohim of other nations around you."

So, it seems clear that the Elohim were the gods of many nations, and according to the Sumerian accounts, all these gods (Elohim) were none other than those (Anunnaki god-kings). These rulers were Chamosh, Milkom, Astarte, Rimmon, Yahwey, El, Enlil, Enki, and Samyazi. These represent the 9 "immortal rulers" in the Sumerian accounts that ruled over the Anunnaki nations. These are the generals who were put in charge over the peoples of all the nations of Eridu, the Mesopotamian Earth base station of the Anunnaki in the great AB-Zu. These are the rulers left behind to tend to the mines continuing to produce the gold for Nibiru, when King Anu left Earth to return to the home world of Nibiru.

In fact, the Sumerian accounts of these rulers, the

kings who ruled for tens-of-thousands of years because their life span was based on the orbital path of Nibiru, not the orbital path of Earth or Ki. So, they were considered immortal by the populous at the time. The offspring who were born from the Adamites and the sons of Anu, on the Earth, lived only for a thousand years by contrast. So, these ruler-generals are the Elohim, the ones referred to in the Hebrew translation that really meant "Those on high, who observed the heavens and the Earth" as opposed to the
King James' version that says, 'In the beginning, "God" created the heavens and the Earth.' The conclusion by the author is the awful truth to the faithful; the "God" everyone is praying to is gone. The 'so-called Storm God', a non-immortal being who sat perched in his Ruach (flying vehicle) on top of Mount Sinai giving instructions to Moses, vacated the planet Earth hundreds-of-thousands of years ago and no longer exists here. He wasn't the all-powerful divine being of Abraham, Jacob and Isaac, but none other than an extraterrestrial being from another world!

The following data are excerpts taken from the National Institute of Health, and the National Cancer Institute information data site and represent a purely mechanical (robotic) view of the human body processes as a fundamental starting point for discussion.

The Human Body

Human beings are the most complex organisms on the planet. Billions of microscopic parts, each its own identity, working together in an organized manner for the benefit of the total being. The body is a singular structure but made of billions of smaller structures of which are categorized into four major kinds.

Functions and Life Processes:

These functions comprise the physiological and or psychological systems, ultimately through the cells' functions. Survival of the total organism is the fundamental driving force of the system and is the most important. This survival depends on the body's maintaining or restoring something called homeostasis, a quality state of relative constancy of the body internal environment.

In 1813-1878, the French physiologist, Claude Bernard, made a fantastic observation. Noting that the body cells survived in a healthy condition only when the temperature, pressure and chemical composition of their environment remained constant. Then, later, an American physiologist, Walter Cannon from 1871-1945, suggested the name for this constancy he called homeostasis. This key word comes from two Greek words; "Homeo", meaning the same and "Stasis", meaning standing. Otherwise, meaning standing or staying the same. Cannon stressed that homeostasis does not mean something that is set and immobile, staying the same all the time. Homeostasis by his definition meant the condition that my vary, but relatively constant.

So, homeostasis depends on the body's ceaselessly carrying out many activities or functions while its major functions respond to changes in the environment, exchanging material between the environment and cells, such as, metabolizing foods while integrating all the body's activities.

Normally, the body's ability to perform many of its functions change gradually over the years of its total life span, at infancy and in old age. Childhood is characterized by continual development and maturation of the system, where those functions gradually become more efficient and effective. During late maturity and old age, the opposite is true. All the functions gradually become less efficient and effective.

All living organisms have certain characteristics that distinguish them from non-living forms. These include organization, metabolism, responsiveness, movements, and reproduction. In the human form there are additional requirements such as growth, differentiation, respiration, digestion, and excretion. All these processes are interrelated. No part of the boy, from the smallest cell to a complete body system works in isolation. Operating in a fine-tuned balance for the being of the individual. Disease represents a disruption of the balance in these processes.

At any level of the physical-organizational scheme, there is a division of labor. Each component has a job to perform in cooperation with the others. If a single cell loses its integrity or organization, will die.

Metabolism:

Metabolism is a broad expression that includes all the chemical reactions that occur in the body. One phase of metabolism is catabolism where complex substances are broken down into simpler building blocks and energy is released.

Responsiveness:

Responsiveness or irritability is concerned with detecting changes in the internal or external environments and reacting to that change. It is the act of sensing a stimulus and responding to it.
Movement:
There are many types of movement within the body. On the cellular level, molecules go from one place to another. Blood moves from one part of the body to another. The diaphragm moves with every breath. The ability of muscle fibers to lengthen or shorten cause movement called extension and

contraction.

Reproduction:

Reproduction refers to the formation of a new person, the birth of a child. Life is transmitted from one generation to the next. In a larger sense, reproduction also refers to the creation of new cells for the replacement and or repair of old cells and for growth. This is then cellular reproduction. These actions are key to the survival of the individual and to humanity.

Growth:

Growth refers to an increase in the size either through an increase in the number of cells or through an increase in the size of an individual cell. For growth to occur, anabolic processes must occur at a faster rate than catabolic processes.

Differentiation:

This is a developmental process by which individual cells change into specialized cells with distinctive structural and functional characteristics such as stem cells that can turn into heart cells or nerve cells. Through differentiation, cells develop into tissues and organs.

Respiration:

Respiration refers to the process with the exchange of oxygen and carbon dioxide between cells and the external environment. It includes ventilation, the diffusion of oxygen and carbon dioxide, and the transport of gases in the blood. Cellular respiration deals with the cell's utilization of oxygen and the release of carbon dioxide in the metabolism.

Digestion:

This is the process of breaking down complex ingested foods into simple molecules that can be absorbed into the blood and utilized by the body.

Excretion:

This is the process that removes the waste

products of digestion and metabolism.
from the body. Thereby ridding the by-products that the body is unable to use, which are toxic and incompatible with life.

Though these processes are essential to life they are not enough to ensure the survival of the individual. In addition to these processes, life depends on certain physical factors from the environment. These include water, oxygen, nutrients, heat, and pressure. In addition to this mechanistic viewpoint, there are other factors which classical medical science does not recognize. These are energies that fall into the category of esoteric science, such as the animundi or 'life force', what the Asian culture refers to the life force before manifestation as Wu-chi, and Chi the physical manifestation or anima of the body which flows through hidden psychic channels of the body called meridians. The Indo-Aryan culture refers to these energies as prana.

Here, is also added other important and critical aspects relating to the foundation of the subject of understanding the principle of the 'keys and their application.

The Human Nervous System

The nervous system is the major control, regulation, and communication system in the body. The center for all mental activity as thought, learning, and memory. Together along with the endocrine system, the nervous system is responsible for regulating and maintaining homeostasis. As part of the sensory function keeps the body in touch with the environment both internally and externally.

The nervous system is composed of organs, such as the brain, spinal cord, nerves, and ganglia, which include various tissues such as nerves, blood, and connective tissue which carry the complex activities of the system. There are three groups which have overlapping functions: Sensory, Integrative and Motor.

Millions of sensory receptors detect changes, called stimuli occurring inside and outside of the body. They monitor temperature, light, and sound from the environment. Internally, they detect variations of pressure, Ph, and carbon dioxide concentration as well as levels of electrolytes.

These sensory signals are converted into electrical signals called impulses and transmitted to the brain. Decisions are made based upon the sensory input, and this is called integration.

Although each subdivision of the system is also called a nervous system, these smaller systems belong to the single, highly integrated nervous system. Each subdivision has structural and functional characteristics that distinguish it from the others. The nervous system is divided into two subdivisions: the central nervous system and the peripheral nervous system. The brain and spinal cord are organs of the central system. They are in the dorsal body cavity, encased in bone for protection. The brain is in the cranial vault, and the spinal cord is within the vertebral canal of the vertebral column. These are at what is called the foramen magnum.

The organs of the peripheral nervous system are the nerves and ganglia. Cranial nerves and spinal nerves extend from the CNS to peripheral organs such as muscles and glands. The ganglia are collections, small knots of nerve cells outside of the CNS. The peripheral nervous system is further divided into afferent(sensory)

Division and an efferent(motor) division. The afferent component transmits impulses from the peripheral organs to the CNS. The efferent component transmits impulses from the CNS out to the peripheral organs to cause and effect or action.

The efferent component is again subdivided into the somatic nervous system and the autonomic nervous system. The somatic system supplies motor impulses to the skeletal muscles. Because these nerves permit conscious control of the skeletal muscles, it is also called the voluntary nervous system. The autonomic nervous system is called the visceral efferent system, supplying motor impulses to the cardiac muscle, to the smooth muscle and to the glandular epithelium. It is further divided into. The sympathetic and parasympathetic divisions.

The autonomic nervous system regulates the involuntary or automatic functions.
The brain is continuous with the spinal cord at the foramen. The CNS is surrounded by connective tissue membranes, called meninges and

cerebrospinal fluid. There are three layers of meninges around the brain and spinal cord. The outer layer, called the dura mater, the middle layer called the arachnoid resembling a spider's web in appearance containing thin threadlike strands that attach. To the innermost layer. The space under the arachnoid is the subarachnoid space, filled with cerebrospinal fluid containing blood vessels. The pia mater is the innermost meninges, a delicate membrane tightly bound to the surface of the brain and spinal cord.

The brain is divided into the cerebrum, diencephalons, brain stem, and cerebellum. The cerebrum is the largest portion of the brain divided by deep longitudinal fissure into two cerebral hemispheres. These hemispheres are separate entities and connected only by an arching band of fibers called the corpus callosum. The corpus callosum provides a communication pathway between the two halves. Each hemisphere is divided into five lobes, four have the same name as the bone covering them: the frontal lobe, the parietal lobe, the occipital lobe, and the temporal lobe. The fifth lobe lies within the island of Reil.

The diencephalons are centrally located and surrounded by the cerebral hemispheres. Inside includes the thalamus, hypothalamus and epithalamus.

The thalamus consists of two oval masses that serve as relay stations for all sensory impulses except the sense of smell going to the cerebral cortex. The hypothalamus below the thalamus plays a key role in maintaining homeostasis. The epithalamus is involved with the onset of puberty and rhythmic cycles considered the biological clock.

The brain stem consists of three parts: midbrain, pons, and medulla oblongata.

The pons form conduction tracts between the higher brain centers and the spinal cord. All the ascending (sensory) and descending (motor) nerves connecting the brain and spinal cord pass through the medulla.

The cerebellum located below the occipital lobes of the cerebrum form the communication pathways between the cerebellum and other parts of the CNS.

The Ventricles and Cerebrospinal Fluid

The ventricles are a series of cerebrospinal fluid filled cavities within the brain.

Not much is known about the purpose of these cavities but esoterically they are unique and vibrationally relate to higher spiritual function. The spinal cord is divided into 31 segments (2 more make a total of 33 segments) but physical science does not recognize this. Spiritually speaking 33 is an important number regarding evolution. The distal end of the spinal cord, many spinal nerves extend beyond the conus resembling a horse's tail called the cauda equina.

This area is also significant to the evolution of the spiritual being.

There are twelve pairs of cranial nerves emerging from the inferior surface of the brain. These pass through the foramina of the skull to innervate structures in the head, neck, and facial region. Esoteric knowledge refers to these as the 12 psychic channels, normally dormant until the ascension process is underway.

The Endocrine Glands and Their Hormones

The endocrine system, along with the nervous system, functions in the regulation of body activities. The nervous system acts through electrical impulses and neurotransmitters to cause muscle contraction and glandular secretion. The effect is of short duration, measure in seconds, and localized. The endocrine system acts through chemical messengers called hormones that influence growth, development, and metabolic activities. The action of the endocrine system is also measured in minutes, hours, or weeks and is more generalized than the action of the nervous system.

There are two major categories of glands in the body – exocrine and endocrine.
Exocrine glands have ducts that carry their secretory product to a surface. These glands include the sweat, sebaceous, and mammary glands and the glands that secrete digestive enzymes.

The endocrine glands do not have ducts to carry their product to the surface. They are called ductless glands. Thee endocrine is derived from the Greek terms "endo," meaning within, and "krine," meaning to separate or secrete. The secretory products of endocrine glands are called hormones and are secreted directly into the blood and then carried throughout the body where they influence only those cells that have receptor sites for that hormone.

The pancreas is a long, soft organ that lies transversely along the posterior abdominal wall, posterior to. the stomach and extends from the region of the duodenum to the spleen. This gland has an exocrine portion that secretes digestive enzymes that are carried through a duct to the duodenum. The endocrine portion consists of the pancreatic islets, which secrete glucagens and insulin. Alpha cells in the pancreatic islets secrete the hormone glucagon in response to a low concentration of glucose in the blood. Beta cells in the pancreatic islets secrete the hormone insulin in response to a high concentration of glucose in the blood.

Thyroid and Parathyroid Glands

The thyroid gland is a very vascular organ that is in the neck. It consists of two lobes, one on each side of the trachea, just below the larynx or voice box. The two lobes are connected by a narrow band of tissue called the isthmus. Internallym gland consists of follicles, which produce thyroxine and triiodot hyronine hormones. These hormones contain iodine. About 95% percent of the active thyroid hormone is thyroxine, and most of the remaining 5% is triiodothyronine.

    Both require iodine for their synthesis. Thyroid hormone secretion is regulated by a negative feedback mechanism that involves the amount of circulating hormone, hypothalamus, and adenohypophysis. If there is an iodine deficiency, the thyroid cannot make sufficient hormone. This stimulates the anterior pituitary to secrete thyroid-stimulating hormone, which causes the thyroid.
gland to increase in size in a vein attempt to produce more hormones. But it cannot produce more hormones because it does not have the necessary raw material, iodine. This type of thyroid enlargement is. called goiter or iodine deficiency.

    Calcitonin is secreted by the parafollicular cells of the thyroid gland. This hormone opposes the action of the parathyroid glands by reducing the calcium level in the blood. If blood calcium becomes too high, calcitonin is secreted until calcium ion levels decrease to normal.

Four small masses of epithelial tissue are embedded in the connective tissue capsule on the posterior surface of the thyroid glands, and they secrete parathyroid hormone or parathormone. Parathyroid hormone is the most important regulator of blood calcium levels. The hormone is secreted in response to low blood calcium levels, and its effect is to increase those levels.

Hypoparathyroidism, an insufficient secretion of parathyroid hormone, leads to increased nerve excitability. Low blood calcium levels trigger spontaneous and continuous nerve impulses, which then stimulate muscle contraction.

Adrenal Gland

The adrenal gland, or suprarenal is paired with one gland located near the upper portion of each kidney. Each gland is divided into an outer cortex and an inner medulla. The cortex and medulla of the adrenal, is like the anterior and posterior lobes of the pituitary, develop from different embryonic tissues and secret different hormones. The adrenal cortex is essential to life, but the medulla may be removed with no life-threatening effects.

The hypothalamus of the brain influences both portions of the adrenal gland but by different mechanisms. The adrenal cortex is regulated by negative feedback involving the hypothalamus and adrenocorticotropic hormone; the medulla is regulated by nerve impulses from the hypothalamus.

The adrenal cortex consists of three different regions, with each region producing a different group or type of hormones. Chemically, all cortical hormones are steroid.

Mineralocorticoids are secreted by the outermost region of the adrenal cortex. The principal mineralocorticoid is aldosterone, which acts to conserve sodium ions and water in the body. Glucocorticoids are secreted by the middle region of the adrenal cortex. The principal glucocorticoid is cortisol, which increases blood glucose levels.

The third group of steroids secreted by the adrenal cortex is the gonadocorticoids, or sex hormones. These are secreted by the innermost region. Male hormones, androgens, and female hormones, estrogens, are secreted in minimal amounts in both sexes by the adrenal cortex, but their effect is usually masked by the hormones from the testes and ovaries. In females, the masculinization effect may become evident after menopause, when estrogen levels from the ovaries decrease.

Within the human being there exists two primary potential directives: The downward movement is procreation, the development and expansion of the species. The upward movement is Recreation, the development and evolution of the human organism to higher orders of vibration and function inclusive of expanded awareness and consciousness with a deep and abiding connection to the quantum hive consciousness and extended life span.

Hormones of the Adrenal Medulla

The adrenal medulla develops from neural tissue and secretes two hormones, epinephrine, and norepinephrine. These two hormones are secreted in response to stimulation by sympathetic nerve, particularly during stressful situations. A lack of hormones from the adrenal medulla produces no significant effects.

Gonads

The gonads, the primary reproductive organs, are the testes in the male and ovaries in the female. These organs are responsible for the sperm and the ova, but they also secrete hormones and are endocrine glands. Male sex hormones, as a group, are called androgens. The principal androgen is testosterone, which is secreted by the testes. A small amount is also produced by the adrenal cortex.

Production of testosterone begins during fetal development and continues for a short time after birth, nearly ceases during childhood, and resumes at puberty. This steroid hormone is responsible for the growth and development of the male reproductive structures and increased skeletal and muscular growth as well as enlargement of the larynx which is accompanied by voice changes, The growth and distribution of body hair as well as increased male sexual drive is included.

Testosterone secretion is regulated by a negative feedback system that involves releasing hormones from the hypothalamus and gonadotropins from the anterior pituitary.

Two groups of female sex hormones are

produced in the ovaries, the estrogens and progesterone. These steroid hormones contribute to the development and function of the female reproductive organs and sex characteristics. At the onset of puberty, estrogens promote the development of the breasts, the distribution of fat evidenced in the hips, legs, and breast as well as the maturation of reproductive organs such as the uterus and vagina. Progesterone causes the uterine lining to thicken in preparation for pregnancy. Together, progesterone and estrogens are responsible for the changes that occur in the uterus during the female menstrual cycle.

Prolactin hormone promotes the development of glandular tissue in the female breast during pregnancy and stimulates milk production after birth of the infant.

The Pituitary and Pineal Glands

The pituitary gland or hypophysis is a small gland about 1centimeter in diameter, about the size of a pea. It is nearly surrounded by bone as it rests in the sella turcica, a depression in the sphenoid bone. The gland is connected to the hypothalamus of the brain by a slender stalk called the infundibulum.

There are two distinct regions in this gland: the anterior lobe (adenohypophysis) and the posterior lobe (neurohypohpysis). The activity of the adenohyophysis is controlled by releasing hormones from the hypothalamus. The neurohypophysis is controlled by nerve stimulation. The growth hormone is a protein that stimulates the growth of bones, muscles, and other organs by promoting protein synthesis.

This hormone drastically effects the appearance of an individual because it influences height. If there is too little growth hormone in a child, that person may become a pituitary dwarf or normal proportions but small in stature. An excess of the hormone in a child can result in an exaggerated bone growth and becomes exceptionally tall or a giant.

Pineal Gland

The pineal gland, also called the pineal body or

epiphysis cerebri, is a small cone-shaped structure that extends posteriorly from the third ventricle of the brain. The pineal gland consists of portions of neurons, neuroglial cells and specialized secretorycells called pinealocytes. The pinealocytes synthesize the hormone melatonin and secrete it directly into the cerebrospinal fluid, which takes it into the blood. Melatonin effects reproductive development and daily physiologic cycles (also known as the circadian rhythm, or body clock.) The Pineal gland also secretes another hormone called Dimethyl Tryptophane, a very powerful psychotropic hormone, which can cause strong aberrations in the consciousness, including hallucinations and visions, and can cause extended dormant psychic function. This secretion is normally dormant throughout normal life and is only stimulated by externally applied psychotropic substances such as, Psilocybin or Lysergic Diethylamide.

  Esoteric knowledge relating to these glands often refer to their combined action as organs of second sight and intuition and commonly referred to as the third eye. In addition to the major endocrine glands, other organs have some hormonal activity as part of their function. These include the thymus, stomach, small intestines, heart, and placenta.

Thymosis, produced by the thymus gland, plays an important role in the development of the body's immune system. The lining of the stomach, the gastric mucosa, produces a hormone, called gastrin, in response to the presence of food in the stomach. This hormone stimulates the production of hydrochloric acid and the enzyme pepsin, which are used in the digestion of food. The mucosa of the small. Intestine secretes the hormones, secretin and cholecy stokinin. Secreting stimulates the pancreas to produce a bicarbonate-rich fluid that neutralizes the stomach acid.

Cholecystokinin stimulates contraction of the gallbladder, which releases bile. It also stimulates the pancreas to secrete digestive enzyme The heart also acts as an endocrine organ in addition to its major role of pumping blood. Special cells in the wall of the upper chambers of the heart, called atria, produce a hormone called atrial natriuretic hormone, or atriopeptin.

The placenta develops in the pregnant female as

a source of nourishment and gas exchange for the developing fetus. It also serves as a temporary endocrine gland. One of the hormones it secretes is human chorionic gonadotropin, which signals the mother's ovaries to secrete hormones to maintain the uterine lining so that it does not degenerate and slough off in menstruation.

Characteristics of Hormones

Chemically, hormones may be classified as either proteins or steroids. All the hormones in the human body, except the sex hormones and those from the adrenal cortex, are proteins or protein derivatives. Action hormones are carried by the blood throughout the entire body, yet they affect only certain cells. The specific cells that respond to a given hormone have receptor sites for that hormone. This is sort of a lock-and-key mechanism.

If the key fits the lock, then the door will open. If a hormone fits the receptor site, then there will be an effect. If a hormone and a receptor do not match, then there is no reaction. All the cells that have receptor sites for a given hormone make up the target tissue for that hormone. In some cases, the target tissue is localized in a single gland or organ. In other cases, the target tissue is diffuse and scattered throughout the body so that many areas are affected. Hormones bring about their characteristic effects on target cells by modifying cellular activity.

Protein hormones react with receptors on the surface of the cell, and the sequence of events that results in hormone action is relatively rapid. Steroid hormones typically react with receptor sites inside a cell. Because this methos of action involves synthesis of proteins, it is relatively slow.
Control of Hormone Action

Hormones are very potent substances, which means that very small amounts of a hormone may have profound effects on the metabolic processes. Because of their potency, hormone secretion must be regulated within very narrow limits to maintain homeostasis in the body.

Many hormones are controlled by some form of a negative feedback mechanism. In this type of system, a gland is sensitive to the concentration of a substance that it regulates. A negative feedback system causes a reversal of increases and decreases in the body conditions to maintain a state of stability or homeostasis. Some endocrine glands secrete hormones in response to other hormones. The hormones that cause secretion of other hormones are called tropic hormones. A hormone from gland A causes gland B to secrete its hormone. A third method of regulating hormone secretion is by direct nervous stimulation. A nerve stimulus causes a gland A to secrete its hormone.

One-hundred-fifty years ago, the average life span was 35-40 years. The main reason for this was the rather archaic medical facilities and availability of modern medicines we have now in the 21st century. Now, with the advent of modern medicine and the creation of vaccines that have overcome measles, bubonic plague, yellow fever, polio, smallpox, and a variety of influenza which seems to metamorphous each year. In 2020 the worldwide pandemic of Covid virus swept through many countries catching many nations off guard because there was no vaccine for this strain of Sars 1 strain, an agent known to be the basis for biological weapons.

There are many conspiracies around this outbreak, which I will not entertain in this treatise, but it remains to be seen whether the so-called vaccine is effective when there is so much controversy. The inoculations were not vaccines based upon the actual virus, but protein-based DNA agents created in labs like the original virus and how it was created, meaning by gene splicing, which may prove to be more harmful to humans in the long run.

In recent years, within the last two decades, many universities have been doing research on the origins of DNA genetic based diseases. In that research, a novel approach to the age-based diseases have led scientists to approach the basic elements within the genome which reveals new insights into solving the genetic aging diseases around the fundamental issue of aging altogether. In particular, the team at the genetic labs at Harvard university, under the leadership of Doctor David Sinclair, an Austrailian-Americn biologist, have been very successful in isolating certain parameters around the aging of cells, and the cause for contamination by senescent (dying) cells which, have stopped replicating and exuding toxic substances contributing to the aging process among healthy cells.

In short, the concept is that cell reproduction is based upon the communication of older cells to the younger cells during replication by passing along critical information that relates to the accuracy of the replication process.

This idea has led Doctor Sinclair to conclude that the aging process is not a natural phenomenon, but rather a disease itself. He believes as do others, that this problem can be overcome by restraining the aging process, or even more, stopping and even reversing the process. He realizes that the average life span now is approximately 70-80 years. The life span can be extended to 300 years through genetic treatment now. This would be a very expensive way to accomplish the outcome and beyond expensive for most people. Instead, he is attempting to create a serum of combined chemical additives that would accomplish the same result and formulated into a pill taken daily.

Shinya Yamanaka born September 4, 1962, is a Japanese stem cell researcher and a Nobel prize laureate. He is a professor and the director emeritus of Center for IPS Cell (induced Pluripotent Stem Cell) Research and Application, at Kyoto University.

He has discovered four factors that relate to the aging process. He has utilized these four factors on animal specimens with remarkable success.

Doctor Sinclair following up on Doctor Yamanaka's research, has determined that reverting normal cells back to their original stem cell state would result in a cancerous condition within humans. So, Doctor Sinclair has removed the last factor allowing the cells to revert to a younger state but then stop before becoming stem cells. Then this process could be repeated over and over reversing the aging process ad infinitum.

At the same time, the progress by NASA and the private company, SpaceX owned by Elon Musk are working on rocket ships to put men back on the Moon with a permanent base, also to establish a permanent base on Mars, with the idea of colonization on Mars and beyond.

Long space flights represent a problem for astronauts and the anti-aging process becomes attractive. But another concept to accomplish longer space flights would be multi-generations of astronauts developed to reach beyond the solar system and even into the far reaches of the galaxy. The obvious problem is the rocket ship approach which is too slow to travel the vast distances, such as the nearest star system, Alpha Centauri, which is 4 light years away, by way of light traveling speed. A rocket ship would require hundreds if not thousands of years to accomplish traveling at a small percentage of the speed of light. Then the problem of fuel and weight become inhibiting factors as well.

Scientists are examining other means of propulsion which could approach the speed of light, however, that limiting speed is still too slow to reach other further points of the galaxy. A new field of experimental organic-mechanical development is being explored called (trans-humanism). The human body would be replaced by a robotic structure and the brain of the robotic structure would be artificial and the human consciousness would be downloaded as a computer program is downloaded into a computer today. As much as this sounds like science fiction, the development of artificial intelligence to the point of real sentience is nearing a reality in our lifetime. Neural implants are already being developed to enhance human performance as well as, allowing human minds to control prosthetic limbs now through embedded neural pathways into the human nervous system.

These approaches suggest direct solutions to long term space travel that will not require on board food supplies or water and the need to control the localized atmosphere for human habitation. At the least, these solutions may first be used as a way of creating crews to establish forward colonies for future human habitats in otherwise dangerous environments. These new artificial intelligence devices are making possible self-driving vehicles on the road as the autopilot allows planes to fly without the aid of the pilot.

Soul, Ghost in the Shell

There are many untruths perpetrated by religious dogma regarding the soul. The first is the idea that the soul is in mortal danger of destruction through damnation. This idea is a religious mechanism of psychological manipulation to impose control and subjugation of the masses through fear of retribution and punishment from God. This manipulation is not relegated only to Christian concepts. In Eastern religious dogma there is the idea of Karma.

The idea of 'bad' karma is utilized to hang over the faithful as a watchdog to keep them from behaving badly by the threat that whatever is done will haunt them with something bad that will happen either later in this life, or in the next. Hence, why the priesthood declares that the soul needs to be saved from the ravages of sin thus proclaiming their important role as saviors of humanity.

To understand and grasp why this is fundamentally untrue is to begin to understand the true value of the human being. Further, it is interesting to note, based on modern alien abduction accounts, that the soul is even coveted by other advanced civilizations on other worlds. We as humans need to wake up to the truth about the true essence of soul.

One of the reasons for expelling the heretical gospels was because within those texts it clearly states that there is no need for an interceder between the faithful and the Highest God. A fact that essentially puts the priesthood out of business.

According to the Sumer historical accounts, when the Anunnaki demigods came to earth, they landed and settled in the Mesopotamian region 450,000 years ago with a purpose to mine for gold. Their home planet, Nibiru, was suffering an atmospheric depletion. They needed powdered gold to keep the atmosphere from slipping away.

Their workers, the Iggigi, began extracting gold from the Euphrates River, but it was not enough to supply their needs. They realized they would need to mine the larger deposits from the earth and that work was far more difficult and the Iggigi refused.

The Anunnaki Genetic engineers, Enki, and Isis, sought to find an appropriate indigenous life form in the area, strong enough and advanced enough that only minor genetic alterations would provide a

Soul, Ghost in the Shell

good mining work force intelligent enough to understand their commands, smart enough to operate their equipment but not smart enough to rebel against their overlords. Isis determined that the bipedal Hominid known as Homo-Erectus would be a perfect specimen.

The average life span in the normal evolution of the humanoids (the hominids) was more than a thousand years. Time needed to accomplish all this genetic work was of the essence. The Anunnaki overlord, King Anu, demanded to create a work force immediately to mine the gold and return it to Nibiru, as their planet's atmosphere was failing fast. A speedy solution was needed. The first order of genetic business was to shorten the hominid's life span.

Many DNA alterations were needed. The test results of each cycle needed to be quick to realize successful results. The Anunnaki engineers Enki and Isis, shortened the hominid's life span to three score and ten years (roughly 70 years). This allowed confirmation that the DNA alterations were effective. After the changes were made Isis discovered that the new hybrids could not reproduce. She realized the individual manipulation of each Homo-Erectus would not supply the demand for a larger work force in time allotted.

The DNA changes altered the Homo-Erectus into Homo-Sapiens. The Anunnaki called the first Homo-Sapiens Adamu, meaning the first Adam. In genesis, the Hebrew scripture of the Israelite's translation of the Sumer historical creation accounts, said God (meaning Jehovah or Yahweh) created Adam in his own image. In the Sumer accounts it was Elohim (those on high or Anunnaki demigods) that created the first Adamu slave. So, when the Hebrew scripture said that God created man in his own image, it was the Elohim, that created Adamu in their image, using altered Hominid DNA with their DNA image.

As a point of Sumer record, Jehovah was an Anunnaki general left behind to rule over the hybrids and continue the mining of gold without interruption until King Anu ordered the complete destruction of the Adamites by virtue of a flood.

Despite King Anu's command to limit the abilities of the hybrids, Enki decided to add his

Soul, Ghost in the Shell

own DNA to the mix making it possible for the hybrids to procreate, and they did in greater numbers. However, this also increased the evolutionary possibility for Homo-Sapiens to become more powerful like the demi-gods.

The fundamental DNA of the Anunnaki was reptilian in essence. Here again, is another misinterpretation of the Sumer accounts in the Hebrew scripture, which tells the story of the snake (the reptilian in the garden of Edan) tempting Eve, the companion of Adam. But the Hebrew account describes the forbidden fruit (the apple) of the tree of life (as knowledge of good and evil) which is a description of the Vegas Nerve complex in the brain. King Anu forbade the Adamu to be able to procreate for fear that they would multiply and become smart enough to rebel.

So, it was Enki, the reptilian, who tempted Isis (Eve) to make the addition of his DNA to alter the nerve complex (the tree of life inside the Homo-Sapiens brain) offering the Adamites procreative ability. This change offered greater knowledge and evolution for all the Adamites as well. King Anu became angry and cast out all

Adamites from the Anunnaki home Ship, called Ehdan, meaning the garden in their language.

From the spiritual perspective, the Highest God acting out of the highest heavenly realm, the quantum, wanted to correct the effect of this evolutionary change brought about by the Anunnaki. The single lifetime was replaced by multiple lifetimes in a system of reincarnation. Many lifetimes could be utilized to gather experience in which to develop awareness and wisdom. With time, many incarnations could provide enough experience and insight making possible the convergence of that experience and the emergence of a new self-awareness. This self-awareness is called a soul. The evolution of the soul through continued learning and self-discovery could lead to the ultimate loss of the ego and the defiance of the spirit that caused the original 'sin' or fall from heaven (the loss of self-consciousness). Increased self-awareness could conceivably offer the recovery of the lost memories with a subsequent return to grace.

The counterpoint against the benefit of reincarnating is the chance to repeat mistakes because there is significant memory loss of experience during the birthing process. The process of leaving one life and entering another is starting over as an infant. It would be ideal if one could continue where, one left off. In that way, a continuous life could occur with intermittent breaks. As an infant, the new creation of another body and mind, loses everything from the previous life. This means no memory of anything from the past is brought forward into the new mind and body.

So, the real possibility arises that mistakes made in the past life are quite easily repeated if the initial behavior carries over. The alteration of previous behavior could not occur necessarily since lessons learned will not be remembered. This aspect becomes a double edge sword so to speak. Bad experiences can be put behind with a fresh start in theory, which is a good thing. However, it is also likely that certain traits may crop up again offering the individual choices that may go either way and the likelihood of making the same choices are statistically high.

The other contributory factor added to the

process is that the next life has the probability of being like the past life due to inherent traits emerging within the DNA as stored predilections. These can make an impression on the life force which can predetermine the arrangement of similar life circumstances going forward. In addition, the system of life repeating in this cycle of birth and death then is very much like a hamster wheel. The individual is stuck repeating the same patterns ad infinitum. Also, there is the influence of the DNA of both parents contributing to the repeating issues. The truth is that reincarnation occurs mostly within family groups where issues are adapted by swapping perspectives from one familial sibling to another giving the opportunity to gain insight and or wisdom regarding the individual issues that arise between each. Also, this exchange can occur between the parents and children in some cases.

In its essence, this plan seemed to be a good solution to the shortened life span as far as development is concerned. These flaws with this system then make the likelihood of development taking an extremely long time, perhaps hundreds, if not thousands of lifetimes, to correct behaviors while adjusting the understanding of these situations to move on to higher existence. Since the quantum has no time, meaning all events happen at the same time, how long it took to make changes didn't matter because time in the physical is just part of the illusion here.

That said, unfortunately, this system of incarnation has been hacked so to speak. The promise of living a good life with the hope of moving into paradise as a reward of good behavior, after slogging through the slings and arrows of misfortunate in the physical, is a belief that is quite common amongst people. Once again, this promise is perpetrated by religious doctrines and their dogmatic teachings, while the truth of life repeating here is not present in the consciousness and kept secret as a myth from the masses.

When I say the system has been hacked, I'm referring to other extraterrestrial forces (not Anunnaki) that are also reptilian but are Draconian in their nature, not benign and are ruling this planet. For this reason, the author declares this planet as a slave planet. Those living here are unaware that they are unconscious prisoners of the 'new' overlords that secretly rule through many human groups governing the masses through alien mind control. As Gurdjieff, a Russian philosopher and spiritual teacher once said, "we are food for the moon". It turns out that our moon is an artificial satellite that is a monitoring station and a source for the alien mind control signal from these Draconian reptilians. Though this idea sounds utterly like science fiction, the truth of this was revealed with the moon expeditions in the early 70's. Experiments to drop the lunar lander take-off booster back to the moon's surface to shake the moon caused it to ring like a bell for hours suggesting to NASA that the moon is hollow!

Those who are aware of this alien influence and control and behind the agreements with those aliens to provide human subjects for alien experimentation, are given alien technology for advanced transportation and weaponry and are paid handsomely, enjoying the fruits of powerful positions within the hierarchy of government. They have made their pact with the 'devil' so to speak. They care not for their own future beyond what is given to them, in exchange for their betrayal of their fellow man. It is sad and unfortunate for the rest of humanity as they carry on with the coverup of this dark conspiracy.

They have abandoned the pursuit of evolution to a higher purpose in life for the existential benefits of the present 'reality'. In other words, they have become the guards of the prison and watch that everyone stays in line and will offer rebellious specimens or kill those who don't.

This idea may sound preposterous to many people and certainly as a fellow human being, writing about this easily places this author into the category of a deranged unhinged whistle blower who has lost all his mental capacities and rational perspectives. However, there are many learned and highly educated people who have been involved and or discovered this truth and have tried to reveal it. Not all have lived to tell the tale so to speak. These facts remain behind the veil of the government's above top-secret security.

The media outlets including the social media are controlled by giant corporate structures. Large scale misinformation programs are well entrenched within our social and government settings by law enforcement and intelligence organizations representing the military industrial complex for decades now, since the end of the second World War. President Eisenhower offered a warning to the public about the dangers posed by the military industrial complex implying its status as an unchecked secret government or deep state well-funded without oversight in his farewell speech on January 17th, 1961.

Intelligent extraterrestrial civilizations are out there and are also living here among the populace, in some cases in plain sight. Honest God-fearing people see the evidence before them every day, but they are continuously humiliated to the point that they no longer believe their own eyes and ears and sheepishly accept what they see and have been told.

Many technologists agree that the advance of technology over the last 79 years constitutes a giant leap of progress. Even before the second world war ended, the German engineering developed jet powered aircraft, ballistic missiles, anti-gravity craft called Hanabu. Later discovered by Admiral Byrd's secret Naval force sent to Antarctica in 1942, called Operation High jump, sent to investigate the Nazi base built there. Byrd admitted to Naval intelligence later, and recorded in his personal diary, that these advanced circular craft could travel from pole to pole in twenty minutes.

After the war, the United States offered immunity for war crimes to 1100 German scientists to come to America to become part of NASA to help American efforts to compete with Soviets in the post-war space-race. Werner Von Braun who led the development of the Jupiter C rocket that put American astronauts on the moon, was asked later how the Germans developed their science and technology so quickly. Werner said, "we had help from extraterrestrials".

In America, the sudden advance of technology has also continued to completely outstrip the normal scale attributed to natural scientific progression such as Fiber optics, the microcomputer chip, aerial craft traveling at10 times the speed of sound, radar and radar resistant designs, geosynchronous satellites circling the earth providing guidance and location information to automobiles and cell phones just to name a few.

Look for example, at the impact of ripping the old telephones off the walls and from the common telephone booths in the act of progress, then putting a minicomputer (cell phone) into the hands of almost everyone on the planet to facilitate greater communications. Seems like a great advance in human progress, right? Yet, no one has admitted to the dangerous effects of very high frequency electromagnetic energy broadcasting to cell towers and at the same time broadcasting that same powerful and dangerous signal to the brains of the public! Case in point, just try to obtain a copy of a secret internal study developed by Nokia regarding the details of this radiation danger!

People are not communicating with each other now, face to face. Instead, they have an augmented device to do it for them anytime they want. But these devices are, in truth, seductive and less a telephone and more of a listening tool for those who wish to know where you are, what you are doing, thinking, and most of all what you want and are willing to buy from the corporations, especially things you don't need all for the sake of keeping up the economy. So, in the author's opinion, this so-called advanced technology has served to eliminate close quarter contact and is separating people, even young children.

Now the social platforms such as Twitter, Facebook and Ticktock are used to program the thinking of adults and children alike through misinformation and false flags. This keeps them from gathering into groups and forming separate opinions and ideas because the elite know that groups are inherently more powerful than individuals.

This author wishes to add a small ray of light and love within the purpose and point of this treatise. This author is not trying to undermine or overthrow any faction here, but to extend a hopeful message to wake up, appealing to the inner most thread of every human on the planet. Being a prisoner is not great but being unconscious about it is worse in the author's opinion and can institute change.

So with that said, the author is expanding on the idea that the true heart of the human, even with all the inherent flaws, still stands out and above the dehumanizing effect of activities of transhuman advocators that would choose artificial intelligence added to their construct while at the same time, undermining self-confidence and destroying real hope of a better existence by usurping the authentic importance and opportunities to advance and grow into greater beings of higher consciousness organically.

Before I completely overwhelm the reader of the seriousness of the impact and insidious nature of the darkness enveloping the planet, I will now move onto other points of this treatse.

Physical Alchemy and the Atom Bomb

The first precepts of physical alchemy require the use of pure elements and correct sacred geometry. In this case, the interpretation of the philosopher's stone is purely physical in nature.

The Buddhic monks of Asia are proponents of Lao Tzu and practice the Taoist form of Yoga. They're meditations create the expectation of a physical stone appearing inside the body that reflect the greatness of their personal work. When cremated, other monks will probe the ashes of the dead monk's body later, looking for this precious stone, believed to contain the higher vibration of the monk's meditations and alchemical practices. If found, then it is venerated. Then the stone is placed above in a sacred chamber of the stupa as a positive influence on other practitioners meditating in the chamber below.

There are some similarities in the ideology from the Western esoteric spiritual practices, that include the immaculate conception of the baby, as told in allegorical stories in the Christian dogma, defining the birth of the Christ. The confusion in Western Christianity is an assumption within their understanding, the Christ is synonymous with

Jesus (the Greek form of the man) or Jeshua, his Hebrew name. The Greek Orthodoxy never considered Jeshua as the Messiah, or son of God. Rather, only a prophet of greater standing among others at the time.

The 'blood of Christ' refers to the esoteric sacred fluid flowing around the sacrum, spinal cord and brain, which medical doctors call the cerebral-spinal fluid, (CSF) a derivative of highly filtered blood.

In both cases, Eastern ideology and Western ideology, the immaculate conception (baby) refers to the birth of the spiritual consciousness within the physical body. In the case of the Asian perspective, the 'child' arises within the liver. In the case of the Western perspective, it arises within the solar plexus.

Since the time of Paracelsus, born 1493-1541, as Theophrastus von Hohenheim was a Swiss physician, a physical alchemist, lay theologian, and philosopher of the German Renaissance. Also, Sir Isaac Newton born 1642 –1726 was an English mathematician, physicist, astronomer, theologian, and an alchemist in the physical sense.

There have been many students of alchemy, both

lay and professional scientists stemming from the study of esoteric works by authors in the fourteenth and fifteenth centuries forward, who maintained that the elusive philosopher's stone, if accomplished, would bestow upon the operator, great wealth, eternal life and spiritual enlightenment by converting a base metal like lead into a precious metal like gold. The 'stone' would not be normal gold but possess divine properties and great healing powers against all ailments of the body.

One of the prime ingredients was mercury, which can be highly toxic. Breathing the fumes, since it needed to be heated, could cause brain damage, as well as madness. This truth is proven by the many hat makers who used this metal in the making of hats at the turn of the century, hence the term, 'mad as a hatter'. According to some historical accounts of Newton's memoirs, he achieved the first stage, which was the creation of 'red mercury', an indicator that his work was successful. Most died without ever reaching that stage.

There are some sketchy historical records, though not entirely reliable, that agents of the

United States and France, representing both the scientific and intelligence communities, found the Germans were seriously developing a working theory of a fissionable device (weapon) in 1933 with the help of two Norwegian scientists, Leif Tronstad and Jomar Brun, heads of the hydrogen plant at the Norwegian Institute of Technology, conducting heavy water experiments in Norway.

Concerned that the Germans might be 6 months from a practical weapon, sought help to find an individual mentioned in reports from French intelligence, that purportedly had success with physical alchemy and knowledge of atomic energy. Meanwhile, the United States secretly extracted the Polish scientists out of Norway and sabotaged the laboratory, while still waiting contact from the alchemist. Einstein, Fermi and Oppenheimer and others were working in the United States to investigate these concepts for military purposes but only theoretically.

The following are excerpts from a Wikipedia physics source. Please see references in the bibliography section of this book.

Physical Alchemy and the Atom Bomb

Fulcanelli was the name used by a French Alchemist and esoteric author, whose identity is still debated. In particular, he is reputed to have twice performed a transmutation of lead into gold. The first was in 1922, together with his most devoted pupil, Eugene Canseliet, when the two supposedly performed a successful transmutation of 100 grams of lead into gold in the presence of Julien Champagne and Gaston Sauvage. This demonstration took place in a laboratory of the gas works of the Georgi company at Sarcelles, achieved with the use of a small quantity of "Projection Powder" (also known as the Philosopher's Stone) prepared by Fulcanelli. The second was in 1937 at the Chateau de Lere, when Fulcanelli supposedly performed a transmutation of 225 grams of lead into gold and 100 grams of silver into uranium before witnesses including a chemist, two physicists and a geologist.

Theories about Fulcanelli speculate that he was one or another famous French occultist of the time: perhaps a member of the former royal family, the house of Valois, or another member of the Frerez d'Heliopolis (Brothers of Heliopolis,) a society centered around Fulcanelli which included Eugène Canseliet, Jean-Julien Champagne, and Jules Boucher. Patrick Reviere, a student of Canseliet's, believed that Fulcanelli's identity was Jules Violle, a famous French physicist. In a 1996 book, samples of writing by Jean-Julien Hubert Champagne and Fulcanelli are compared and show considerable similarity. In any event, by 1916, Fulcanelli had accepted Canseliet, who was then only sixteen, as his first student.

During 1921, he accepted the sons of Ferdinand de Lesseps as students and in 1922 two more students: Jules Boucher and Gaston Sauvage. In 1925, Fulcanelli relocated to 59 rue Rochechouart where he allegedly succeeded in transmuting base metals into gold. In 1960, with the publication of the international bestseller *'The Morning of the Magicians'*, Pauwels and Bergier popularized the mystery of the Master Alchemist.

According to Louis Pauwels, Fulcanelli survived World War II and disappeared completely after the Liberation of Paris. Every attempt to find him failed. In August 1945, American G-2 (Army Intelligence) asked Jacque Bergier to contact a

Physical Alchemy and the Atom Bomb

certain army major who oversaw the operation of searching for German research reports on atomic energy. The major, whose identity was apparently anonymous, or simply forgotten, wanted to know the whereabouts of Fulcanelli. Bergier could not say.

In a meeting in Paris with Jacques Bergier, Walter Lang reports that Fulcanelli communicated with Jacques Bergier to warn French atomic physicist André Helbronner of man's impending use of nuclear weapons. According to Fulcanelli, nuclear weapons had been used before, by and against humanity. Prof. Helbronner and Chevellon, among others, were assassinated by the Gestapo towards the end of World War II.

The meeting between Jacques Bergier and Fulcanelli reportedly occurred during June 1937. According to Neil Powell, the following is a translation of the original transcript of the rendezvous:

"You're on the brink of success, as indeed are several others of our scientists today. Please, allow me to say, Be very careful. I warn you...The liberation of nuclear power is easier than you think.

Physical Alchemy and the Atom Bomb

The radioactivity artificially produced can poison the atmosphere of our planet in a very short time, only in a few years. Moreover, atomic explosives can be produced from a few grains of metal powerful enough to destroy whole cities. I'm telling you this for a fact. The alchemists have known it for a very long time... I shall not attempt to prove to you what I'm now going to say, but I ask you to repeat it to Mr. Helbronner: certain geometrical arrangements of highly purified materials are enough to release atomic forces without having recourse to either electricity or vacuum techniques... The secret of alchemy is this: there is a way of manipulating matter and energy to produce what modern scientists call 'a field of force'. The field acts on the observer and puts him in a privileged position vis-à-vis the universe. From this position he has access to the realities which are ordinarily hidden from us by time and space, matter and energy. This is what we call The Great Work."

On December 2, 1942, the world's first self-sustaining, controlled nuclear chain reaction took place paving the way for a variety of advancements in nuclear science. The experiment took place at the University of Chicago's football stadium under the direction of Enrico Fermi...a Nobel Prize-winning scientist. The reactor was called an atomic pile, consisting of pure uranium, pure carbon and a geometric structure resembling a small pyramid.

The mind is the connecting link between the physical man and the spiritual man, the mind being the intellectual component. The mind can partake of both the material and the immaterial aspects of reality. The aspirant must develop the intellectual side of his nature, to strengthen his will which will enable him to concentrate all his powers of his being in and on the plane he desires. Only then can the attainment of higher knowledge become possible. The search for light, life and love must begin on the material plane, then carried to the highest level, with the final goal to reach complete oneness with the universal consciousness or the Source. The material plane is the first step on the path, then comes the higher goal of spiritual attainment.

This spiritual goal is accomplished by developing what the alchemists call the philosopher's stone. This alchemical process began in the great halls of the Temple of Knowledge situated within the ancient empire of Atlantis, which began 790,000 years B.C.E. and culminated at its peak of development by 100,000 years B.C.E., before its final demise in the year of the

Spiritual Alchemy and the Philosopher's Stone

great flood 11,256 years B.C.E.

The original continent was large and stretched from what is now the Azores in the North and South to what is now the Bahamas, but centrally located within the great mega-continent of Gwandana, the only single landmass on the earth at the time. The instability of the mega-continent began much earlier than the flood. Gwandana began to break into separate smaller subcontinents around 350,000 years B.C.E., just after the remaining Anunnaki inhabitants of Iridu, located in the great AB-Zu (later, known as Africa). Iridu was founded by the Anunnaki around the Tigress and Euphrates rivers in what was later called Mesopotamia, just before the breakup and the subcontinents began to drift apart. The larger part of the landmass to the west, was then known as MU. Then, after the breakup, it became Lemuria.

The depiction of this highly advanced culture was recorded on parchment scrolls, stored among many of the ancient records in the libraries of Alexandria in Egypt during the pharaonic dynasties, and kept there for future posterity. It was Solon, Plato's grandfather, who had traveled from

Greece to Egypt and learned of the motherland in the Atlantic beyond the Pillars of Hercules, (now part of the Straits of Gibraltar.) But Plato did not realize it was a continent but through his only reference, modeled the story from his knowledge of Greek city-states and made it an island. At that time, the calamities had continued until the continent broke into 5 sub-islands, which also ultimately sank leaving only one, Posidonia, the island Plato described in his utopian society of Timaeus and Criteas.

One of the leading Atlantean scientists from the Temple of Knowledge was Thoth (pronounced Teh-Hoh-Teh). Thoth saw the calamity coming. Once the waters of the flood retreated, he made his way to the land of the AB-Zu and settled near the landing beacons of the Anunnaki. Nearby the beacons of power (the pyramids), he noted the great lion sculpture left behind by the Lyrans, who were planning to colonize there, but they realized how unstable the continent was and retreated to their home world in the year 36,000 B.C.E.

Thoth was tall and red skinned looking quite strange to the local inhabitants. They were afraid of him. He could not keep them from running away. They were barely out of the stone age and mostly an agrarian society and quite primitive. He utilized his knowledge of alchemy to alter his shape to a large baboon, an animal very familiar to the tribesmen. The locals believed him to be an animal spirit and chose not to harm him and even revered him. In this way, he wanted to secretly influence the Nubian culture by his mind control, to develop this remnant of Iridu into a Neo-Atlantis.

  He entered the great pyramid and studied and understood the Anunnaki science of energy production and storage, which was very similar to the Taoi stone generators of Atlantis. He activated the computer on top. With the Anunnaki computer he controlled the weather. He began to remodel the Nile valley into a paradise. The Nubians began to see Thoth as a god and began to worship him. Through their worship, he taught them science and astronomy and an advanced form of agriculture. He raised the Egyptian culture to a very high level in only a 3000-year period. Finding the underground water chambers below the sphinx, he placed the ancient records of science and knowledge of Atlantis on a set of Emerald Tablets and kept them there for future use.

Thoth was introduced to the innocuous flower called the lotus, an indigenous plant that grew along the Nile River. It was known by the Nubians and utilized by their shamans as a powerful narcotic and hallucinogen for creating visions. They offered it to Thoth as a gift. Unfortunately, it was quite toxic and caused Thoth's demise.

The Egyptian culture honored Thoth and his baboon character. He is depicted in their early hieratic glyphs as a baboon. Then later in hieroglyphs as one of their most celebrated gods of great knowledge and changed by the Egyptian priests from his baboon character to a human with an Ibis head. The emerald tablets were later discovered in the secret unground chambers and recovered by Thoth's reincarnation, who later became known as Hermes Trismegistus (meaning thrice great). The original tablets have been lost to antiquity.

Alchemy has taken two paths, reflective of the material world and the immaterial world. This

Spiritual Alchemy and the Philosopher's Stone

chapter is focused on the immaterial aspect of alchemy. I will offer a brief treatise on the physical aspect of alchemy in a separate chapter.

The primary goals of alchemy relate to developing a connection from the physical to the non-physical reality. The focal point is based upon the transmutation of base elements into divine elements. Here, divine means the resurrection of the sublime vibration from a lower vibration of the physical, speaking of the vibratory nature of both realities, meaning the seen vs. the unseen. Then, from that understanding, the alchemical statement is made: 'As above, so below and as it is inside, so it is outside.'

The focal point is called the philosopher's stone. The interpretation of this stone has taken two meanings, one is physical, and the other is non-physical. Hence, why there are two alchemical paths. The basic principles are the same, but the approach is different because of the interpretation of the original Atlantean instructions. So, knowledge is used and is always based upon the accurate translation of ancient texts. This translation problem is meant as a veil, hiding the truth from the uninitiated. Thoth knew the power of this knowledge and if captured and held into the wrong hands, could be misused and very dangerous.

Religion has served as a useful tool, regarding the veil of protection. Religion has placed a sanction against alchemy by scripting its use as a tool of the darkness or in religious terms, 'the devil', referring to something evil, diabolical and or satanic as in invoking evil spirits, or demons to do nasty deeds.

Alchemy has always been limited to those who have proven themselves worthy in the character and good intentions. That scrutiny is best delivered by observation of a potential student of the art through spiritual training by masters of the art and their evaluations leading to an initiation into the mysteries by the graduating student.

So, the immaterial approach of alchemy is reflective of those secret practices involving formulas and meditations designed to alter or raise the vibrations of the student's physical body and ultimately the spirit and or soul. This means the stone represents the base elements of the human

Spiritual Alchemy and the Philosopher's Stone

consciousness transmuted into higher vibrations creating an illumination of the consciousness and thus connecting the soul of the student to the cosmic or universal consciousness, or the Source.

    This alchemical tradition has always been a verbal tradition passed from master to student within secret societies devoted to this work. Thoth knew the future and realized he needed to create the emerald tablets in which he could inscribe, in coded Atlantean language, the secret formulas. The tablets were not made of emerald but an alchemically produced substance, a mineral of green color but impervious to any ionic decomposition or decay over an eternity. He structured the language in such a cloaked way, only one of pure heart and intention would intuitively be able to make sense of the secret instructions, were there no master available to assist. His tablets would stand against the test of time for all humanity, should humanity eventually develop consciousness high enough to make use of such powerful knowledge responsibly.

Reincarnation, Wheel of Birth and Death

The Western religious perspectives define a punitive moralistic overlay to a two-step process. A singular life would end leaving the individual facing their death with one of two options. If their behavior in life was exemplary, then the option for an afterlife begins in 'Heaven' living in a tranquil setting beyond earth as a reward. Otherwise, the alternative remains, where the behavior is not exemplary, and the result is a fast track to the opposite location which would be to 'hell', to burn in the 'lake of fire', damned for the rest of eternity. The results of either of these conditions would then take effect only after the day of reckoning or judgement, a concept that is common to Christian belief and to some extent shared by the Judaic perspectives.

The Muslim perspective defines the afterlife when they get to Paradise by living religiously, asking Allah for forgiveness and showing good actions in their life. These good actions will be rewarded on the Last Day. Therefore, obeying the rules set by Allah is of ultimate importance.

Muslims believe there are seven levels of Heaven, although "seven" is interpreted by some

Muslims as simply "many". Each Heaven is made of a different material, and a different prophet lives in each Heaven. The first Heaven is made of silver and is where Adam and Eve live. Abraham lives in the seventh Heaven in a place made of divine light.

Hell is described as a place of fire and torment. Jahannam is a place of scorching fire pits and boiling water, a place of physical and spiritual suffering. Vivid descriptions of hell are used in the Qur'an to stop Muslims from participating in sin.

Muslims believe that they will be sent to Hell if they reject the teachings of the Qur'an or take no responsibility for their actions. Either of these would mean that they had failed Allah's test.

Some Muslims believe that even the souls in Hell can eventually be sent to Paradise. These beliefs give Muslims the motivation to follow the teachings in the Qur'an. They also give hope to those who suffer that there is something better to come.

Medieval rabbinical views agree; that life after death as described by Maimonides, or the "End of Days". This existence entails an extremely heightened understanding of and connection to the

Divine Presence. This view is shared by all classical rabbinic scholars. Life after death is not relevant to another place but rather this place, earth, and a resurrection of the dead at the outset of a Messianic kingdom on earth.

In the east Indian culture, more Hindus and Jains than Sikhs believe in Moksha (liberation from the cycle of rebirth). Different religions or traditions teach that people can escape reincarnation's cycle of rebirth through various means. Achieving this liberation is often referred to as moksha, or the related concept of kaivalya.

Based upon the author's view, from personal spiritual insights given by his spiritual guide Yokar, the reincarnation concept aspect is closer to the truth from the original creator's perspective of a solution to the fall from grace and a sense of promised salvation and return.

This is suggested in the Hebrew scriptural story of the 'Prodigal son's return', an allegory that describes the soul's squandering their divine inheritance after leaving home or fall from heaven. This idea does not contain a sense of moral right or wrong, but rather a system of repetitive lives on earth developed over millennia to gather knowledge and wisdom within the soul's reflection on the sin of rejection of the creator's way. That realization would give rise to remorse leading to the purpose of evolving into a higher state of being suitable for the 'cleansed' soul to merge with the creator consciousness ultimately as a reward.

Some, mistakenly believe, that the reincarnation system also entails something called trans-migration. In this idea, the soul could progress forwardly, entering future human incarnations, however, if there are misdeeds occurring, then a retrograde progression into lower life forms such as animals is possible. This system also suggests that the original form of the soul is from an animal nature and that over time of good behavior, the soul is rewarded to progress into human form.

After the fall and the attempt by Luxcious to provide a physical arena where the fallen could inhabit primates to live within the structure of their addiction to physical existence on Tiamat, while at the same time, guided under the supervision of the light worlds, brought the unfortunate unfolding of the separation of the fallen out of their androgynous state into a polarized state. Then the subsequent reintegration into the polarized primates, caused their de-evolution from the almost infinite dissolution of their offspring, destroying the possibility for them to easily return to the divine state. A divisive plan by Beliel to undermine the creator's plan for redemption and designed to undermine the Djinn Chancellor, Bael, to fail in his leadership leading to Beliel's desire to become Chancellor in his place.

The Creator then sought to resolve the problem by providing the system of reincarnation for the fallen, in hopes that through the aggregation of experience, their memory of what they were would arise in time, thus bringing about their eventual return to the fold of her realm.

As the reader will see later in this text, even this plan was usurped by alien lifeforms to use the reincarnation as a way of ensuring a continued supply of creatures that could supply the aliens with a food source both physically and energetically on the earth.

Though is often the lament of many to wonder

about the afterlife, meaning is there any truth to something beyond this existence that someone could holdout their faith for the promise of a life better than this existence. Up until recently, no one has come back to tell the truth about this dilemma.

There have been many situations where someone has died on the operating table and then for some reason they return after some minutes of death. This suffers from great controversy, however. There would be believers that would gladly accept any comforting words from anyone having 'crossed over' and lived to tell the tale.

The description by many does seem to have certain commonalities. Most describe a tunnel of light, and along their way, they see the warm and inviting faces of friends and family members in life, who have gone onto the great beyond standing by, as it were, waiting to receive them.

As much as I would gladly add my support in this regard to my readers, I have other thoughts around this phenomenon. I feel compelled to explain what I believe is also going on. As I mentioned before, the system of reincarnation as devised by the creator, has been 'hacked' so to speak. The earth has become a prison planet and all those who exist here are inmates of that prison. Like all inmates of a prison, the dream of escaping sits predominately on everyone's mind. Religions are responsible for this myth of escape for the most part.

The ones who have charge of this prison, the guards as it were, are extremely intelligent. They have the power to control the minds of humans. They can project images into our minds that can control our behavior, not only for keeping us here, but also for manipulating our emotional states of survival which include a range of negative emotions, not to exclude hatred, paranoia, murder, jealousy, ambition, greed, sorrow and loneliness. Besides eating humans, they also feed off our strong emotional energy.

These creatures live underground. They have been there for centuries. They wield influence on governments, nations and they are thrilled to incite war between humans, for pleasure and for food.

At the point of death, should there be a tendency to refuse to reinsert into the wheel of incarnation, the entrance of the tunnel, they will read the mind of the diseased and provide strong holographic projections from the memories of those bygone relatives and friends, projecting an invitation to enter the tunnel of light, but it is a trap my friends!

The alternative of course is to stay the course and refuse to enter, the pull emotionally is strong especially when the mind of the diseased is vulnerable and full of fear in that moment. So, is it difficult, absolutely. The chances are you would not be able to resist their ploy. The alternative is to hold out in the blackness alone and simply wait for someone to come for you. That is not easy! Yet, they are there, waiting beyond that threshold for any brave soul who can manage the attempt to evade their captor's shenanigans. Further, it is my understanding that the Arcturians and Pleiadians are those advanced 5th density beings looking out for the independant souls seeking escape from the hamster wheel here.

Now it's time to talk about the nature of the prison on planet Earth. In the last decade there has been extensive mathematical analysis by several scientists to develop more sophisticated virtual (meaning creative) as well as augmented reality (meaning actual or real world external) displays. Military applications of this technology are used for pilot 'heads-up' displays superimposed on the face plates of their helmets or projected upon the aircraft canopies to offer technical data to the pilot without turning away their attention from circumstances outside the aircraft.

Game developers use this math to create algo-rhythms to develop simulations for warfare training programs while other game developers wish to create more realistic and full emersion techniques for entertainment purposes.

Augmented (real) reality simulation uses real world calculations for comparison. In their analysis of real-world parameters, the scientists began to realize that real world calculations use the exact same formulas as virtual world calculations. The only difference is the sophistication level, meaning how detailed their virtual presentations can be depends on the higher math required.

Philosophically, this discovery brought about a suspicion. The 'real' world reality might suggest our perception of the real world might be a projection upon our senses, instead of the real physical reality we have come to accept as true existence. Our acceptance of our surroundings then supplanted by an advanced race of alien intelligence wishing to snare our perceptions and hide the actual real world around us. This startling idea began to take hold and now that disturbing suspicion is running rampant among the scientific community.

Neil Tyson Grayson, a popular physicist celebrity enjoys discussing scientific ideas to the public and has suggested that perhaps we may live in an alternate reality inside of an alien projected reality designed to hide from us the true nature of our surroundings. At first, he could not accept this supposition, but he has accepted this possibility within fifty percent of probability. Considering this idea as factual brings up the obvious question. If so, then what are the alien intelligences hiding from our perceptions?

The spiritual guide to the author has revealed the answer to this question and, that answer is not one you would not like to hear and understandably so. That idea is presented here for your review and consideration. It is an awful conclusion, should you consider it as fact and not as fantasy or pure science fiction.

The CIA and NSA agencies would choose to control the narrative here to explain away some of the truth about our world. Thus hide their agendas with alien intelligence and their secret military industrial complex receiving technological help from certain species that live here under ground and under water bases secretly.

They would hide the secret pact with these alien species in 1952 to reveal their exchange for the alien technical help at the expense of millions of people selected for hybrid alien-human experimentation through an unlawful abduction program. The government agenda to allow the probing of our species is hidden in plain sight by the spreading of misinformation and defining the truth as conspiracy theory about the existence of alien life existing beyond our planet. Further, that evidence is strong in historical artifacts that they have been visiting the planet for thousands-of-years up to the present, and the government is guilty of a coverup since the first recent crash of a UFO in Roswell, New Mexico in 1947.

They not only have collected the remains of many UFOs, but alien biological entities as well. Further, the secret space program has alien life forms working within the space program alongside humans, a discovery made by a computer hacker, Gary Mckinnon, who hacked into the Pentagon database and noted alien personnel listed on a military industrial complex roster. He now lives outside the US because there is an outstanding warrant for his arrest for espionage and is labeled a traitor.

After World War II, during 'Operation Paperclip', more than 1100 Nazi scientists were brought to the United States cleared of all war crimes and allowed to assist in America's space program. The leading rocket scientist was Werner Von Braun, designer of the Jupiter C Rocket used to put American astronauts on the moon in 1969. Von Braun admitted to the press once when asked how the Germans were able to advance their technology so fast during the war. He pointed to the sky and declared, "from our friends out there". The is the lesser-known fact that the major portion of the original NASA personnel were consisting of Nazis. This shows that our American government is willing to set aside their moral scruples for the chance to gain the advantage and superiority of military power over our proposed future enemies and to advance their secret agendas.

Perhaps there are already humans living on the moon, an artificial satellite, and on Mars alongside aliens in their military facilities. It's the author's belief that humans have been a space faring race for hundreds of years. According to the secrets behind the veil, the matrix of illusion, hiding the awful truth that Earth was destroyed more than 800 hundred years ago. That mankind escaped the destruction by the colonization of the solar system and beyond. So, if earth is gone then what is this simulation for? Let us descend, down the rabbit hole a bit further.

So, if the earth was destroyed long ago, then why is it still here? The answer to that would suggest that this so-called reality of life on earth is a past projection, a 'virtual time loop' before the destruction occurred, recreated by an alien race to provide a human farm that supplies food in the form of strong human emotions and meat, yes, that's right. You heard it correct! The movie, 'The Matrix' was not all that wrong, only different in some of the details. I have already explained the origins of humanity 450,000 years ago and their manipulation of our genetic sequence for their own needs. Then they left the planet. They were the gods 'that from heaven to earth came' the translation of Sumer language as the Anunnaki.

The truth is that many alien species have come to earth over the real past. The Anunnaki were not the only ones. After they left another more brutal, Draconian species arrived and took over the gold mining operations from the Anunnaki. They also planned to make Earth their own and humans as their slaves. Like the Anunnaki, they were reptilian, but a different variant of the species.

They came from the Micah star system. They were known as the Draconians, and renowned for their military might in the galaxy, even until today.

The alien biological entities warned the American military that the Draconian species will return. Humans need to be ready! The Draconian warriors established a base here, then there began a rebellion in their home world system and most of the garrison left to settle the rebellion and promised to return. They left a contingent here to continue the mining operations. But after several thousand years passed, the contingent decided they were never coming back. The remaining Draconian warriors decided to claim the Earth for themselves and keep the gold to barter later.

Light in the home world system was dim and compared to our sun, the light was painful which made surface dwelling difficult. So, they built vast domiciles below ground which, over time spread to many areas around the earth. They longed to live on the surface of the planet, as they had done in their home world. Over many thousands of years, they began to abduct humans and experiment in their laboratories to create a hybrid of their species that could eventually move to the surface.

They saw the calamity approaching the earth and used their time travel technology to reverse time in the near region of the solar system creating an endless loop that would ensure their existence and provide a continuous source of food from the human stock. To prevent the livestock from discovering the truth of their enslavement while maintaining control, they built a matrix of reality, a zoo of sorts, suitable to keep the livestock healthy. Then they realized there needed to be a way of managing the growth rate of the livestock while at the same time providing a source of negative emotional energy which, was an exotic kind of drug they came to crave. Using their powerful mind control technique, they would instill in the humans an increase in their base instincts of survival to increase their aggression. War was added to the emotional mix based on the need to dominate through territorial conflict. Realizing that death could be a way of escaping the prison, they usurped and hacked the reincarnation process to keep humans from leaving the earth to return over and over unconsciously, keeping the livestock plentiful through recycling. There you have it. It's not pretty, but like it or not, we are prisoners on a slave planet.

The Law of Cause and Effect

This subject is as old as creation itself. It would seem self-explanatory but in truth, it is largely ignored. As far as understanding the process and practice of self-discovery, this aspect is so important as it relates to self-responsibility.

As humans navigating their way through life on planet earth, events that occur around and within them, that are taken for granted. Sometimes, after many years of experience, reflection on one's habits and the end results of those habits do not come home to 'roost' so to speak, until time forces our consciousness to take stock of where we are at in our life and why. That almost never occurs in our youth but later, when life has been somewhat harsh and difficult, and questions begin to arise.

The effects surrounding events are more easily recognized but the origination of those effects is more elusive and difficult to realize. So, in the simplest of terms, the law works in the following way, but in some ways, is also related to the Law of Octaves.

A simple example is when a force is applied to an object the secondary law of inertia begins to unfold, i.e., 'an object at rest tends to stay at rest

The law of Cause and Effect

and when an object is in motion it will continue in motion until it encounters an obstacle which will either slow down the rate of motion or stop the object's motion or change the direction of motion.' In the same way, if the object is at rest, it will stay at rest unless an external force is applied that changes the inertia and results in motion.

In this example, the cause is the force applied either to stop motion or to create motion, then the result of stopping or starting motion is the effect of the applied force.

The above example is the easiest to understand but when we consider other forms of cause the effect may become obscured in some way, either because there is denial and or a desire to not take responsibility for the effect because we would not want to claim responsibility for creating the cause in the first place.

In the vast variety of events from human affairs, there can be many causes and perhaps complicated by a multiplicity of sources that combine creating the sum totality of the effect.

From an outside perspective, one can deduce an effect(s) through the observation of the suspected cause. However, the conclusion may be distorted because perhaps not all the information surrounding the cause or combined causes are readily available.

The author spent many years as a practicing engineer and that kind of work would include analyzing the effect which, would arise from a problem. So, for example, a particular system would not be performing well as expected and the lack of performance of the system would be the surface problem indicating a more elusive underlying problem which would be the original cause. Very often resolving problems require an intuitive approach as well as an educational background inclusive of the knowledge of the system construct along with how the system is supposed to function. Then together, a few solutions are considered that could suggest the cause of suffering.

This entails something called system theory. There are two types of systems, first is an open system where the processes that define the functionality of the system from the start to finish, that brings the desired result of a properly

The law of Cause and Effect

operating system. Secondly there is a closed system, which is controlled by something called feedback where the output is fed back to the input to modify the system performance.

An example of an open system would be the ignition of an automobile. The system would include the result or effect of the automobile engine to operate. So, the system would include all the separate parts that would make that happen which would include, a starter motor, a battery to supply power to the starter motor,
a belt that would connect the starter motor to the engine, gasoline to run the engine and the electrical components required to ignite the fuel which would propel the pistons to rotate the engine once the ignition begins. Certain secondary parts of the electrical system would include a coil to develop the spark applied by the spark ignitors and a regulator to switch the battery from powering the starter motor to then apply the power of the starter, which now becomes a generator, to power the coil so the battery power is preserved for future starting. We must also add the gas pedal which controls the accelerations of the engine by

regulating the flow of fuel.

Anything in the system forward path could cause the system to fail, meaning the engine would not start. The solution begins when the mechanic begins to troubleshoot all the individual parts of the system to determine where the fault lies.

An example of a closed system is a gyroscope guidance mechanism that controls the balance and direction of a boat or in the case of an autopilot used in an aircraft to fly the airplane without the assistance of the human pilot. Without becoming too technical, let us say that the feedback part of this kind of system is much more complicated. So, we will leave out the details of the feedback part of this closed system. The point is, in this case the cause of the effect which would be the boat, or the airplane is not following the course required but it is still actually working but poorly. The preliminary need of the technician to solve the problem would still require intuition and the knowledge of the system components and how they should operate correctly. The first surface problem is to determine is the forward drive of the gyroscope operating or is it the feedback part of the system at fault? The closed system is in the shape of a circle, meaning within a circle one cannot tell where the problem is exactly. So, the first step would be to break the circle and examine separately both the drive and the feedback to find the cause of the problem.

Very often, human situations involving cause and effect are circular in their system structure, hence very difficult to find a solution. And there can be many sources of interference or complexity within the circle which make the solution even more difficult to solve. How does one determine whether a particular interference is function of feedback or as part of the forward force?

In the case of personal development, the driving force may be related to an inappropriate application of the Law of Octaves, meaning is one in the MI-FAH point, or in the TI-DO point. This must be determined if a solution is to be had. Perhaps the problem lies in the interference from others constituting feedback which could be inhibiting the forward drive causing a lack of performance with the success of the individual goals aspired to by the individual.

Albert Einstein worked as a patent examiner in the patent office. It is the theory of this author that after examining many different patent ideas, he developed his theory of relativity and created a three-page mathematical document defining his theory. Of course, most people would not know the full set of complex calculations he used to resolve the relationship between energy and matter and finalizing their relationship into his now famous formula: energy is equal to mass times the speed of light squared.

For the latter part of his life, he worked tirelessly trying to resolve the concept of a unified field. He died without a solution to the problem. Einstein could not conceive of a world of physics as vibrational, or as a wave reality. His perspective was very mechanistic. Quantum mechanics emerged in 1924 with Louis de Broglie's hypothesis that matter had wave properties, the theory of a softer physics began. Quantum mechanics grew with the further work from Heisenberg, Born and Jordan who developed matrix mechanics and then Schrodinger invented wave mechanics with his non-relativistic

The Law of Octaves

equations.

Esoterically speaking, physical reality is an illusion. The appearance of solidity is merely a condensation of complex waves of conscious energy moving together in orderly patterns as interference patterns coalescing into density. As Thoth, the Atlantean, described in the Emerald tablets, "As it is above, So, it is below and as it is inside, so, it is outside." This knowledge has been established within spiritual/alchemical, or non-scientific circles for hundreds of centuries, operating outside of the scientific public view. Nicola Tesla, father of the moving magnetic field and the generation of alternating current or (AC electrical energy), has become the foundation of our modern energy grid that powers all civilized society's needs for power. He knew and understood this principle and was the basis of many of his inventions.

Tesla stated once, "if one wanted to understand the laws of the universe, it is comprised of frequency, vibration and resonance." That said, know that these three properties are combined into one unifying principle called the Law of Octaves.

To understand this, one can begin with the familiar use of vibrations and frequencies in the form of music played on instruments that produce audible sound. Without delving deeply into the theory of music, the knowledge of octaves can be embraced and understood and applied in life beyond listening to music. Though there are many scales defining tones or frequencies around the world, such as the pentatonic or 5-tone scale used in the Asiatic and Eastern countries, in the west the heptatonic scale or 7-tone scale is used. In this explanation we will use the heptatonic scale to illustrate how spiritual energies are applied for the purpose of evolution.

Each tonal vibration in the 7-tone scale has a vowel describing the tone beginning with: Doh Reh Mi (pronounced mee)-Fah Soh Lah – Ti (pronounced Tee) and begins again with a Doh key beginning the second octave. Since it is the second octave, the new Doh key is elevated in frequency to the next harmonic frequency of Doh to Doh2. Then if the Reh key is pressed, a tonal vibration is produced by the Reh key which increases a full step higher in frequency than the Doh key. In the

The Law of Octaves

second octave, when the Reh2 key is pressed becomes the higher harmonic of Reh and so on until the Ti key is pressed.

Using an instrument like a piano, has a bank of keys lined up next to each other defined as the keyboard. Each of the keys when pressed, will move a mechanical linkage to a soft hammer aimed at a metal string of a particular length. The first (7) set of keys will strike one of a set of strings of various lengths stretched onto a grid. Each of the seven strings are adjusted (called tuning) with tension to vibrate at a desired frequency (tone).

Each key that is pressed after the previous key, will produce a full step higher in frequency such as Doh, Reh, and Mi. But the Fah key will only shift a half tone frequency from the Mi key. (this is called a half tone interval) and the same is true for the change in frequency between the Soh key and the Fah key, producing a second half step higher (half tone interval).

Mechanically speaking, the strings vibrate according to their tension and their length. The important aspect to realize is, if only the Doh string is struck, the resulting vibrations of that string enjoy a resonant relationship to the next full step frequency quality of the Reh string. By vibrational induction, the Doh vibration causes the Reh string to vibrate its natural tone but at half of the energy of the Doh string, without striking the Reh string. The same will occur between only the Reh string if struck and its vibration will induce a vibration into the Mi string which is the next full step but with half again the strength of the Doh string without striking the Mi string. If only the Mi string is struck, then the Fah string does not vibrate at all. This is because with only a half tone variation between the two strings, no resonance will occur. The same case is true between the Ti string and the Doh2 string because of the half tone interval, there is no resonance. These facts have a bearing on the way of vibration reacts with the life force. All forces in physical reality are bound to the laws of the octave. The way these energies behave describes the effect these energies effect the process of evolution. They will support or not support spiritual evolution due to the resonance between the individual aspirant's actions and the

The Law of Octaves

life force.

 In all actions within physical reality, begin as the octave begins, with the vibration of Doh, which means the beginning of an action. If the action is initiated by a decision to act in any desired direction, without doing anything else to promote moving in that direction, like the laws of inertia, an object that is in motion will tend to stay in motion until it is obstructed or loses energy. So, following the octave law, the initial action of decision sets up an octave to begin and by the law Doh action in the octave will proceed in that direction onto Reh, but like the progression of a single tone, the Reh of action will be less by half but will proceed without additional effort. Half of the excitement or passion which began with the decision to start as energy to go forward. To further explain, a decision is made to begin a course to learn something. That is Doh and then Doh will proceed to Reh but the enthusasm for the course of training will not be as exciting as when the course first began. The course will continue without any further additional effort, but as time passes and the Mi energy arises, excitement for the course of training will be almost completely gone. Then the action is confronted by the half tone interval which is called the Mi-Fah point, the male component of the octave.

At this point an obstacle temporarily stops the movement of the initial action until another decision occurs to overcome the obstacle. The obstacle could be an illness preventing further study, or finances collapse preventing expenses for the course to continue, or another interest distracts the attention from the training. The defining moment is that a dynamic male like action of will must be applied in that moment to overcome the obstacle. If for some reason this action of will is not applied then the action completely halts, or the direction of action changes into another direction. The Octave stops vibrating toward that direction and a new octave begins with a new direction and a new Doh, Reh, Mi vibration. Many people suffer from this endless cycle of Doh, Reh, Mi and never finish anything they start in life to go on to the Ti-Doh2 point. In terms of say climbing a mountain, a climber may reach one third of the ascent and becomes exhausted, or breaks a limb, or becomes afraid of the height or loses confidence to

The Law of Octaves

reach the summit. That is a critical point of the right use of will and determination to overcome the obstacle. This is not a value judgement against changing one's direction. There can be many good reasons to change direction. The right use of will, is to create a more useful direction with a resurgence of enthusiasm to go toward that fruitful direction and is advised and beneficial.

The point about the Mi-Fah interval is to recognize when it shows up, in any endeavor. Choosing a way to reinvest enthusiasm to continue. Then seek the way to overcome the obstacle. Here is where the adage says, 'if there is a will to continue, the life force will accommodate that will and reveal the way', or the life force will reveal the truth about the rightness of the original decision and through humility to accept the revelation and re-evaluate the rightness of the original decision. That is the correct way and the correct real work.

The Ti-Doh2 point is a female energy. After getting past the Mi-Fah obstacle another half tone interval arises near the completion of the Octave. You will know it's a Ti-Doh2 point because every act of reinvestment doesn't work to remove the obstacle at this point. At this point the only thing one can do is trust and accept the higher will overseeing the action of your decision. This requires humility and a yielding of the inner will to accept the outcome of your action regardless of the outcome, realizing another spiritual truth: Not my will but thy will be done. The Ti-Doh2 point is an act of faith in the higher will to rule and support your actions and allow the greater wisdom to support what is best for your evolution.

Within scripture, there is a lot of confusion regarding the right way to behave. Some will argue that faith alone is enough for spiritual evolution. While others will argue that only works will define success with spiritual evolution. They do not understand the laws that govern these things. By studying the Laws of the Octave, the answers are clear and show the way. It is both works (the male action) and faith (the female action) used together, at the right time, that brings success in all actions taken. It is especially true in the way of spiritual evolution. In addition, the Laws of the Octave are both small and large and operate concentrically one within the other as in the case where many small octaves can be at work to support the larger octaves. So, the aspirant needs to constantly be always vigilant for these various interesting currents of life.

In 1966, I came across a little obscure book containing approximately one-thousand bible-thin pages. The book was called *'Beelzebub's Tales to His Grandson',* written by a philosopher, mystic, spiritual teacher and musical composer by the name of Gurdjieff, of Armenian descent. I was already intrigued by the title but then, the opening paragraph of the book said, "Do not read any further unless you are willing to change your life permanently". Hmmm...now I was hooked! Further demands were made upon the reader as I continued to read on. One was expected to read the entire book to oneself, then read the entire book again out loud, and if that wasn't enough, then the reader was to be expected to read the book again to another person. The author's writing was not all that elegant and the cadence very difficult to follow. It was more than daunting, and I questioned my sanity! This process took me no less than 3 years.

Before long, the basis of his teaching was called 'the work'. The work could not be performed by oneself, but required finding a group which one could practice the work under the tutelage of a master teacher of the work.

I had purchased the book at a famous esoteric bookstore in New York City called Samuel Weiser's. I returned to the bookstore and inquired about the book, the assistant only said,

"You must go to another bookstore located on 45th street. You will know it, he said, because of the sign hanging above the door." It said, 'We are Fishers of Men'.

"When you enter, you must ask for Mr. William Nylands."

That all sounded quite mysterious to me, but I was already willing to pursue this rabbit hole to its conclusion.

Days later, I entered this bookstore and proceeded to the rear counter to an older man who starred at me pensively, as I approached. It was as if he could sense what I was going to say. Feeling a bit as though I was following a spy plot of an Ian Fleming novel, I spoke the coded message, "I would like to speak with Mr. William Nylands please."

The man's expression did not change, neary a flinch or a twitch! He said nothing for an eternal moment, encouraging my thought that he was either ignoring me, or he was hard of hearing. I was about to repeat myself when he finally spoke.

"He is not here in the moment. You will need to call him". Then he wrote the telephone number on a small slip of paper and handed it to me.

I looked at him eye to eye, pointed the slip of paper toward him and said,

"Thanks". Then headed for the door.

My enthusiasm crashed to the floor, realizing how much I had counted on my proceeding to the next step. 'Ah...I consoled myself, saying this was a test of my patience and perhaps my resolve.' But I wasn't sure! So, I went home looking forward to my telephone conversation at the next opportunity.

Three days passed with follow up telephone calls to Mr. Nylands without any response. Then on the evening of the third day, I received a call at 8 p.m... A deep voice spoke and asked,

"What is your name?"

I answered with my name and confirmed my attempts to reach Nylands for three days. Then I said,

"Is this Mr. Lylands?"

There was a long pause and the voice responded,

"He is not here in the moment."

Then my frustration emerged with a defiant tone.

"I am not interested to play these games, so if you are not him, then I am no longer interested to inquire about the Gurdjeiff work group! And you are free to let him know that for me."

The man then responded,

"Please take down this address, and be there next Thursday evening at 6 p.m. and Mr. Nylands will answer all of your questions."

"Okay." I reponded.

The location was a small apartment in a hi-rise building near South Houston Street, in New York City. I arrived fifteen minutes early to find a room with several folding chairs already filled with six people, seemingly as confused and bewildered as I and anticipating more information.

It was a final staging area to evaluate those who inquired. The coordinator gave a brief description of the work, then the location. It was a small farm outside of Warwick, New York. I spent two years going there almost every weekend and experienced the nature of the 'work'. Mr. William Nylands was in his late eighties at the time. He died after training with him for two years. I felt I had a good grasp of the technique and was happy to move on with the work on my own.

Later, I discovered two other books by Pyotr Ouspenskii, a student of Gurdjeiff called 'The Fourth way' and 'In Search of the Miraculous'. Pyotr Demianovich Ouspenskii was a Russian philosopher and esotericist known for his expositions of the early work of the Greek-Armenian teacher of esoteric doctrines, Georges Gurdjieff. He met Gurdjieff in Moscow in 1915 and was associated with the ideas and practices originating with Gurdjieff from then on. On October 2, 1947, he died at age 69 years. His writing was also intense but extremely clear and concise about the work.

Gurdjeiff taught that there were basically three approaches to spiritual work, the way of the monk, the way of the Fakir and the way of the yogi. He proposed that all these were too isolating from life. He felt the best way, the 'fourth way' was the way of life, meaning to learn from life experience openly and directly. To do that required the student to activate the right use of the will. During the work at Warwick, New York, a practice called the stop exercise was done quite a lot. It was my least favorite out of all of it. Everyone would be doing any one of many things around the farm, painting a building, renovating, chopping wood for a fire at night and making food, etc. In the middle of whatever you might be doing, you would suddenly hear a voice call out "stop". You didn't just stop what you were doing. You literally physically stopped, which meant if you were walking, or swinging an axe or carrying wood and your step was in mid stride, or the axe was in mid swing, you had to freeze where you last moved. Sometimes it proved to be quite difficult depending on how precarious your last position was. For example, you might have just sipped a bit of hot tea and your lips and tongue had to sit in the hot liquid until that voice said release. This exercise required a group setting of course.

   To do this required an act of will from the solar plexus. We learned that there are two sources of will, one that emerges from the solar plexus and the other emerges from just behind the shoulder blades. The will that comes from the shoulder blades is the ego will and is considered false in its nature. It is easily altered or dismissed. The will from the solar plexus is internal from the soul and is far more powerful in its effect on the motivation of the mind and body.

    You could not control the motion of the body such as in the stop exercise without calling up the will from the solar plexus. I like to use another example which makes the use of this will clearer. Let's say you want to go jogging some morning. You jog for 5 miles and return to your home. When you arrive, your body is tired, and your mind is all prepared to relax perhaps to have a coffee or some breakfast. In that moment, you have not done the 'real' work! In that moment you turn around and jog again, going against the mind which will really resist that decision. If you use the ego will, it can argue using the tiredness and perhaps some xhaustion in the muscles, or the hunger grumbling in the stomach, but the will in the solar plexus will provide the fortitude to turn around and begin jogging again. That, then is the 'real' work. You can only assert that kind of control with the solar plexus, or what is called the inner will. For difficult spiritual work, the inner will be the only kind of will to get you through your spiritual development.

The stop exercise also made you examine every muscle fiber, every position of your body making your mind clear and astute with regards to your surroundings, as well as the flow of thought in your mind, in short, it gave way to a practical application of the tenet, 'know thyself'!

In modern times, people are free to explore their lives and their health more vigorously than a hundred years ago. The time allotted to a given day's circumstance would normally relegate to survival, such as, working a job.

A job needed to buy food and pay rent in a city or carving out a living from the land in an urban or rural setting, which would include a family with rearing several children, sometimes needed to manage the amount of work on a ranch or a farm.

So, life would encompass work from sun-up to sun-down at 'hard labor', which might include feeding and caring for animals utilized for travel and or plowing the fields to grow the food for eating. In some cases, depending on the financial status, perhaps having livestock to feed and eventually turning over to the railhead for sale to one of the larger metropolis' stockyards for beef supplies to the market. Sleeping at least 6-8 hours daily would be a necessity to recover from the day's work from before, week after week, 24/7 which left little or no time for leisure.

The number of privately owned farms, in this age, is shrinking. Farmable land is bought up and being absorbed by corporate entities to the larger producers. The number of foreclosures of private farms is steadily increasing every year.

Now jobs are centered in the urban areas near larger cities. Many of those jobs are related to the industrial manufacturing and technological fields. The need to grow one's food is no longer necessary as food supplies are readily available in small and larger supermarkets. Travel is no longer depending on animals such as, the horse. The automobile, bus and or rail transit systems provide transportation to and from work. Jobs are in offices and factories and limited to a standard work week of forty hours in most cases with the weekends off for leisure time. People will take to the bicycle or jogging for exercise and or will become members of gyms that include various forms of exercise equipment to maintain health and good physical condition.

When there is more leisure time available, the attention is directed to keeping 'fit'. Also, there is more time for consuming various forms of information for both entertainment and for increasing one's potential for advancement in their work environment. This is usually in the printed form such as books, newspapers and magazines. Education in the past was limited to the first six grades and further if the family could afford higher education. Though with the advent of the computer, many of these hard print forms have shifted to digital displays on the computers, and or personal aids such as cellular telephones and pads.

The trend for society to consider maintaining emotional health either through religious activities or through sports became an equally important feature in daily life. There are many different approaches in these activities relating to specific cultures in each society. These various cultures often combine their specific ideologies and spiritual beliefs which are applied to considerations for personal self-values and growth towards their aspirations for self-improvement. Sometimes, when the local ideologies and spiritual beliefs become redundant and/or boring, or in the main, no longer rewarding or satisfying, some people will turn to other venues outside of their normal attention span and extend into other cultures.

One of these is the practice of Yoga. In America, Yoga practice is largely relegated to a specific form of exercise noted for supplying the practitioner a reliable way to satisfy physical health while, at the same time, providing mental conditioning and emotional support through a calming of the mind and a relaxation of the body. With the stress attributed to modern life and the work environment, personal relationships and familial difficulties, Yoga has become essential to some people as a panacea of support. However, in the author's opinion, a gross misinterpretation of this practice has arisen, due to a purposeful elimination from this practice certain key pieces of information relating to some unknown serious side effects.

There are approximately eleven different styles of Yoga practice.

1. **Vinyasa yoga**

Vinyasa means "to place in a special way", in this case, yoga postures. Vinyasa Yoga is often considered the most athletic yoga style and was adapted from Ashtanga Yoga in the 1980s. Many types of yoga can also be considered "Vinyasa

Flows," such as Ashtanga, power yoga, and prana.

2. Hatha yoga

The Sanskrit term "hatha" is an umbrella term for all physical postures of yoga. In the West, Hatha Yoga simply refers to all the other styles of yoga (Ashtanga, Iyengar, etc.) that are grounded in a physical practice. However, there are other branches of yoga such as Kriya, Raja, and Karma yoga that are separate from the physical-based yoga practice. The physical-based yoga is the most popular and has numerous styles as follows.

3. Iyengar yoga

Iyengar Yoga was founded by B.K.S. Iyengar and focuses on alignment as well as detailed and precise movements. In an Iyengar class, students perform a variety of postures while controlling the breath.

4. Kundalini yoga

Kundalini Yoga is equal parts spiritual and physical. This style is all about releasing the kundalini energy in your body said to be trapped, or coiled, in the lower spine.

5. Ashtanga yoga

In Sanskrit, ashtanga is translated as "Eight Limb

path." In Mysore, India, people gather to practice this form of yoga together at their own pace—if you see Mysore-led ashtanga, it's expected of you to know the series. Vinyasa yoga stems from Ashtanga as the flowing style linking breath to movement.

6. **Bikram yoga**

Bikram Yoga is named after Bikram Choudhury and features a sequence of set poses in a sauna-like room—typically set to 105 degrees and 40% humidity.

7. **Yin yoga**

Yin Yoga is a slow-paced style of yoga with seated postures that are held for longer periods of time. Yin can also be a meditative yoga practice that helps you find inner peace.

8. **Restorative yoga**

Restorative Yoga focuses on winding down after a long day and relaxing your mind. At its core, this style focuses on body relaxation. Restorative yoga also helps to cleanse and free your mind.

9. **Prenatal yoga**

Prenatal Yoga is carefully adapted for moms-to-be and is tailored to women in all trimesters. Manyhave said that prenatal is one of the best types of exercise for expectant moms because of the pelvic floor work, focus on breathing, and bonding with the growing baby. Prenatal yoga also helps mothers prepare for labor and delivery.

10. Anusara yoga

Anusara is a modern-day version of hatha yoga, like Vinyasa in that it focuses on alignment, but with more emphasis on the mind-body-heart connection. It was founded by John Friend who created a unique system called the Universal Principals of Alignment.

11. Jivamukti yoga

Jivamukti was founded in 1984 by Sharon Ganon and David Life. Jivamukti is mainly Vinyasa-flow-style classes infused with Hindu spiritual teachings. At its core, this style emphasizes connection to Earth as a living being, so most Jivamukti devotees follow a vegetarian philosophy.

The original tenets of Yoga had eight limbs:
- YAMA – Restraints, moral disciplines or moral vows.

- NIYAMA – Positive duties or observances.
- ASANA – Posture.
- PRANAYAMA – Breathing Techniques.
- PRATYAHARA – Sense withdrawal.
- DHARANA – Focused Concentration
- DHYANA – Meditative Absorption.
- SAMADHI – Bliss or Enlightenment.

In addition to these forms that are unique to the Indo-Aryan style of Yoga, there is also Taoist Yoga, relating to the Buddhist religion. This form of Yoga is attributed to the monks of the Shaolin Monastery in China which included several fighting styles of Wu Shu or as it is known in the west, Kung Fu. Buddha also taught Hing Si meditation for energy focus. In Tibet, another variation of Asian Yoga developed due to the influence of Buddha.

Historically, in China, the monks were constantly being harassed by marauding raiders attacking the temples and when Buddha came to Asia, he noticed that the energy, strength and focus of the monks were sharply lacking. So, he added the five animal forms or styles of fighting: the Crane, Monkey, Tiger or Leopard, Dragon and Snake.

Also, various energetic practices called Chi-Kung to raise the over-all energy for the monks to withstand the attacks and effectively retaliate to overcome the raiders.

In general terms, Yoga falls into two categories, Hatha and Raja. As was stated before Hatha is the physical postures applied. Whereas Raja is centered around specific meditations and internal alchemical formulas designed to raise the vibrations of the mind and body. What is not clarified in the teaching of hatha practice is its intimate connection to the practice of Raja. The first part is connected to and strongly relates to and is sequential to the second. Normally, this understood in the cultures of the east. In the west, the connection of hatha practice to Raja is in many cases not taught and then the real purpose of Hatha is hidden from the practitioner. In the author's opinion, this is a serious mistake on the part of the trainer either through ignorance on their part, or by intention because the knowledge of the Raja connection could be a deterrent to the practitioner's desire to begin the hatha practice as a new student.

The truth behind hatha practice will begin to

modify and reshape the physical structure and the primary and secondary nervous system in preparation for the Raja practice. The breathing and preliminary practices work alchemically within the body to permanently alter the student's body for the more advanced form of 'higher' Yoga. Not that this is necessarily a problem, but the student must be made aware of the real effects the Yogic path early on and that it truly isn't just for physical exercise per se.

   The author's fifteen years of experience practicing western style and eastern styles of Yoga, inclusive of intense alchemical meditational practice of Raja has altered the author's physical, mental and emotional state permanently. Some examples of the side effects of Yoga practice are community (sociological separation), the urge to begin celibacy (ending all sexual encounters), neutralizing emotional feelings, to become a monk. Yoga will change the direction of the student from pro-creation toward spiritual evolution. One other final word of advice to the potential seeker of truth and desire to know thyself. The metaphorical example described from many spiritual teachers, including my own, is that the student must be clear in their intention. In the path to know oneself a critical juncture will always appear on the road to self-discovery. One cannot serve two masters. They will either love the one or despise the other eventually.

In this case, seeking spiritual wisdom is a razor's edge because to seek inner wisdom and knowledge you will feel the sting of the loss of familial and relational companionship, meaning the true spiritual path is a path of fire, and is a lonely path additionally, because it is a path of fire it can also be dangerous. It becomes quite difficult to reconcile the needs of both serving the relationship and the need to turn inward and away from the outer realities of life. As the author, I will explain in another chapter about learning the art of balancing the two, that is a problem that could easily take a lifetime to master. Much attendant pain and suffering will occur in that struggle and can often lead to depression and emotional disruption.

Technological advances bring new insights regarding our world and the universe it navigates. Since the late 1920's, particle physics and wave mechanics have joined forces to bring about new concepts of space and time. Now we have space-time, wormholes, black holes and with the bigger and more powerful telescopes, we have a broader view of the universe perhaps even the multiverse. Einstein theorized the idea of quantum mechanics, but he didn't pursue the idea. Instead, he focused on his unified field theory. Others like Dirac, Pauli, Plank and Schrodinger continued to pursue the idea that space was made of particle-wave fronts defining a quantum field. Which began to merge modern physics by necessity, with the fuzzy realm that might include the spiritual dimensions.

Ancient civilizations devoted a great deal of energy and attention to the fabric we now call the quantum field. Much to the chagrin of modern hardcore scientific belief, now the fuzzy part of the quantum field holds a steady place along side the material physics they are used to. Now, with the discovery of the 'zero point' field, an aspect of the quantum that suggests a tantalizing perspective of abundant free energy for the taking, if only they knew how to access it and moreover harness it.

Of course, it would be the field of computer science that grabs the essence of the quantum first, with the advent of the quantum computer. A device promising millions of times faster computations than the digital format of ones and zeros clunking along near the edge of its limit of size, its computational powers yield to the magic of the 'qubit', a quantum bit that is both ones and zeros and yet another value between them, all of which can be utilized simultaneously, making this device infinitely more powerful.

Though much of the esoteric side of science dealing with the quantum field is held behind closed doors so to speak, scientists are beginning to soften their stance about the apparent wisdom stemming from ancient or prerecorded history. They are slowly learning to adapt the ancient sciences translating its awkward language and applying it to modern problems with a measure of some success. (ref. 'The Dancing Wu Li Masters')

You might say that the spiritual aspect of the

quantum deals easily with accessing this energy. Though this energy is not for the purposes of driving machines and computers. It is utilized for evolutionary internal spiritual work. Not much is devoted right now in laboratories along this line of research.

The field of martial arts has a long history with making use of this quantum energy. In Japan it is called Ki, as in Aikido, utilized by the secret code of the Ninja warriors that enabled them to perform amazing feats of physical prowess and remarkable strength and agility, which was used for their primary purpose as assassins. In China, the energy is called Chi which defines the underlying support for physical endurance, longer life and superior fighting skills called Gung-Fu or Wu-Shu. The western term for this form is popularized in action films as Kung-Fu.

This style of fighting incorporated five different animal forms, the Tiger, the Crane, the Monkey, the Dragon and finally the Snake arising from the Shaolin Temple. Another form of fighting utilized the way of balance as taught by Lao Tzu in the I-Ching. The movements were much more graceful than violent. This form was called Tai Chi Quan. This style promotes great health and long life and is practiced in China by millions of people of all ages, every day. The secret behind this form relied solely upon the right use of Chi energy flowing through the body while in motion, drawing from the Dragon energy rising from the earth and descending from the sky. The primary principle of offense and defense was to utilize the opponent's Chi against him or her and in a similar way, it is used with Aikido.

When Buddha came to China to teach, he visited many villages and their spiritual temples. One temple in particular, the Shaolin Temple, was suffering and in disarray. Buddha was told that their plight was due mainly to constant harassment by marauders and bandits raiding the temple often and the monks were ill prepared to fend off their attacks. Buddha also noticed that the monks were weak, unhealthy, vulnerable and had great difficulty to meditate regularly. He taught them ways for which they could maximize their energy through the use of Chi. He taught them the correct focus through meditation. He developed their

Right Use of Breath

strength by introducing five element theory, along with its application through the five animal forms of fighting.

The secret of Chi power was a well-kept secret from the west even up to the early 20th century. The movements are almost useless without the knowledge of the right use of breath. The higher skills come directly from the breath and the flow of Chi force that follows it. At the turn of the century, Great Britain and other nations occupied the city of Peking. A revolt rose up from the Chinese indigenous peoples to attack and remove all foreign presence from China. This revolt was known as the great Boxer Rebellion. The ones who fought in this rebellion were Chinese Wu-Shu masters, who had mastered the art of Iron Shirt Chi-Kung, or in the western term, it is known as the Balloon Man defense. When a practitioner learns to build up the Chi force adequately within the body, the body became almost invincible. Many reports by the soldiers of various nations trying to ward off these Chinese attackers, required more than several direct shots to their bodies before they could finally fell them. Proof of the amazing wall of this defense

In addition, the Chinese 'Way of the Traveling fist', otherwise known as Iron Palm', was a secret technique to sharpen the focus of the Chi force through the palm of the hand. When directed at an opponent, could deliver a lethal blow to the internal organs causing a slow death within weeks after conflict. The flip side of the Iron Palm was an amazing and quite effective way to disrupt illness creating miraculous cures to some of the most serious illnesses.

In the West, particularly the United States, the rise of esotericism and a revival of occult pursuits in the 1960's, with the rampant use of psychedelics by the Haight-Ashbury 'hippies' of San Francisco, California, created an influx of Indo-Aryan Hindu culture. It began to make its way into the American pursuits for spirituality. Yogis came to America selling their versions of spiritual development and meditation. Many of the yoga forms were introduced which fell into the health and exercise arenas with Hatha Yoga practice. Those interested in meditation were introduced to the mindless meditation of the Maharishi Mahesh Yogi,

Right Use of Breath

popularized by the Beatles' fascination with this yogi. Also, there was the influence of Paramahansa Yogananda and his bestselling book, ' Autobiography of a Yogi', describing psychic powers of various people and the practice of Kundalini Yoga. Many outstanding individuals came to the forefront admonishing the practice of Pranayama, a yogic breathing technique along with variations, such as rebirthing, a form of deep breathing.

Pranayama is also known as 'alternate nostril' breathing. This practice interferes with the balance of the breath intentionally, to heat the CSF fluid to stimulate and promote the Kundalini experience. The author feels this practice is effective but also quite dangerous. It can lead to sudden death by stroke. If practiced properly, can offset trauma of feverish conditions by causing body coldness. Of course, if practiced improperly can also create intense fever.

As is usually the case, partial knowledge of a practice can be harmful without understanding what the practitioner is doing with the practice.

The practice of rebirthing, a deliberate intense

increase of the intake of air and its expulsion through the nose, as opposed to alternating the nostrils, has its own benefits, problems and pitfalls. The scientific perspective of this behavior is called 'hyper-ventilation', or an over oxygenation of the blood, which raises the PH drastically. Normally, this would not be so dangerous unless the individual has an existing PH imbalance to begin with. The author has had substantial experience with this technique in many forms including the practice of Chi Kung and its corollary, here, which allude to the comparison between Abdominal breathing vs Upper-Thoracic breathing. Both have dramatic effects. Abdominal breathing over a 45-minute duration effects the body awareness dramatically and influences strong emotional states. Upper-Thoracic breathing for 45-minute durations dramatically effects the mental awareness giving rise to visions and intense psychological impacts in the form of insights towards the psyche. In addition, long durations of holding the breath in either case, has its own effects as well. (ref. here to Aldus Huxley's book, 'Doors of Perception', referring to the build up of carbon dioxide in the brain.

  Another important consideration about the breath is the effect on the individual cellular power components called the mitochondria. These are essential elements to consider in their role, as supporting agents in the process of the alchemical transformation of the human being. We will entertain these elements in the chapter about their role to play. There are many different forms of breathing. In this case, the author, only discussed in detail those techniques believed to reflect the significant properties to be considered, and the author suggests personal research to understand their purpose and perhaps their benefits, as well as their detriments in order to prepare for the serious consideration of the 'path of fire', a path which has but one direction and no way back once begun, which all seekers of truth must consider carefully. As for the way to breathe, as outlined for this alchemical process to proceed, the Upper-Thoracic form is suggested for this practice. Both nostrils will be engaged. The tongue tip is held to the back side of the upper teeth all through the breathing cycle with the mouth closed.

The lung orientation vertically, relates to the upper portion of the chest cavity, which harmonically relates to the third ventricle stimulation, as well as the total mitochondrial stimulation throughout the limbs and the body total. The breathing should only be through the nose for both the inhalation and exhalation. The period for each half cycle should be to the maximum lung capacity, as the upper thoracic cavity filles. Do not include any abdominal expansion or compression in the process.

The total period should be no less than 45 minutes to one hour, ideally. Though, if the participant is a shallow breather by nature, it will require practice to extend the volume, as well as the total time breathing. The practitioner should be relaxed and not force the breathing beyond the need to expand and or contract to maximum volume. The breathing rate should be slow and deliberate. The mind/attention should be focused on the sacrum.

The spine should be in a sitting erect position. The hand mudra (position) is important here also. The hands should face palms upward, with the

Right Use of Breath

thumb tips always touching the third fingertip (ordinarily the ring finger), while breathing.
Note: This is contrary to the classic yogic finger position-index finger to the thumb (an intentional misinformation taught here). Around the world, especially in certain parts of Asia, Buddha statues are shown with this ring finger to thumb orientation on one hand while the other hand lies flat palm up. This a secret mudra!

The pinky fingers should lie flat and straight away from the rest of the fingers. The index finger and middle finger should extend out away also and separate from each other and the others, as though they were antennae. This opens the throat and the lungs and though it might feel tight in the beginning, after 10 minutes or so, the throat will suddenly relax, and the chest will open too. The breathing gets easier after that.

A tingling sensation begins at the feet and slowly moves up the legs and enters the body at the solar plexus and onward toward the upper chest, neck and finally the head. (this is the Chi climbing up from the earth) A certain amount of twitching and larger vibrations will begin to occur throughout the entire body, after 30 minutes or so. This is normal.

At the end, the participant will feel a buzzing inside the head and a slight dizzy feeling will linger for a while. Do not attempt to stand right away! Wait until the tingling stops. The body may break into a sweat and that is normal also. The urge will be not to breathe afterward for a time. More than sufficient oxygen is present in the blood and that is good. Normal breathing will return naturally. The mitochondria will be energized. The participant may feel a little euphoric for a little while and positive. This practice can be done once a day or divided into every other day. This is a suggested beginning practice and totally optional. Remember, these practices have a long-term profound effect on the body and psyche. Proceed at your own risk down this rabbit hole! The only thing to fear is fear itself.

Digestion of Light

Human digestion is largely relegated to a physical perspective. Meaning that a surface view is taken for the most part. Consumption is divided into two distinct categories, animal or protein and vegetables.

Often fruits and nuts are included with vegetables as a normal consideration, but the perspective is from a common attribute, that is fiber. Digestion is looked upon as assimilations of basic nutrients, such as vitamins and minerals. Given the background of the eating habits of hominids since the dawn of time, foraging for easy to obtain sustenance was based upon accessibility, referring to the real and expected danger of predators lurking about for their next meal. So, berries and nuts were plentiful and the idea of obtaining substantial foods from animal protein relied on prowess and agility to outrun and or overwhelm the prey and certain useful tools to obtain animal protein, such as clubs or spears was a necessity.

Until the discovery of fire, animals were eaten just as other predators would eat, completely raw. Only small animals were the targets because they were easy to overcome and outrun. Even then, not being able to do this meant going for days without eating anything except the usual fall back to fruits and berries and nuts. When social development increased then communities relied on the most able-bodied hunters assigned to go after larger prey. Many joined together to attack larger prey which was not always successful. When successful, some hunters died during the attempt. The female of the species would be assigned as gatherers picking eatable plants and berries for the common meals.

    Early tribes realized that larger prey would migrate to areas where they could graze. So, this meant that hominid tribes would track and follow the herds of larger animals to feed the needs of the community. Agrarian behavior did not arise because of the nomadic behavior of early tribes. Even down to more modern times with indigenous peoples like the Native American Indians, who relied heavily on hunters to seek out more substantial prey. Often the stronger of the tribe functioned in a dual role of hunter and defenders, so they were hunters and warriors. Early on, the tribes depended on caves as a safe domicile until they developed domiciles that could easily be broken down and transported whenever the needs of the tribe demanded to follow the herds of animals wherever they went.

In the present day, it is believed by a growing number of scientists that outside influences, such as extraterrestrial visitations, may have been a strong influence on early human development. Many in the archeological and anthropological fields have theorized that higher intelligences taught the indigenous peoples how to plant and grow food. Farming is a civilized behavior and not a natural occurrence with nomadic behavior, which became an unusual sign of intellectual development and led to developing into more permanent communities.

Over thousands of years evolution began to change the digestive tract of hominids. The appendix for example, a necessary organ for digesting nuts became obsolete. Now, with the modern Homo Sapiens Sapiens, the appendix becomes a health problem and often needs to be removed lest it becomes poisonous to the system, perhaps Nature's way of eliminating non-useful components that need to be discarded.

   Dietary concerns of modern man have become an industry unto itself with billions of dollars spent on improving the digestion for longer life and greater health. The nature of modern society, inclusive of the stresses of living in the modern age, lead to substance abuse, such as imbibing smoldering weeds like tobacco, consuming fermented liquids such as alcohol and pharmacological agents such as addictive drugs derived from poppy plants that contain opiates and other psychedelic plants all ingested to alleviate the pain of living with stress.

   There is much that can be mistaken with consumption of food and where the actual benefits lay in each case. But there is a common denominator to all these varieties of food substances. That is light, not just any light, but the natural light of the sun, as opposed to the artificial light created by man. Sun light contains all the vibrations of color, discovered by Newton with his prism experiments. Though, until recent discoveries regarding the importance of color to

Digestion of Light

certain endocrine organs, color was regarded as pseudoscience by mainstream scientists, but certain vitamins such as vitamin D obtained direct from exposure to sunlight was reasonable. So, early man worshiping the sun was not perhaps unreasonable as the giver of life. Even in dynastic Egypt, Amenhotep the IV, otherwise known as Akhenaton as Pharoah, tore down all the symbols on the temples of the ancient gods in Egypt in favor of his 'one' God called Ra, the Sun God. Of course, the priesthood could not allow that. So, they eventually killed him and returned to the old ways which restored their importance.

The human digestive tract could be compared to an organic fissionable-fusion furnace, capable to break down chemical substances to the molecular level and then extracting the prime ingredient needed by the prime-mover or anima, the soul. The inner being of the human is made up of seven distinct densities called chakras by the Indo-Aryan people and Pukkas by the Atlantean people. Each density utilizes a unique color out of the seven primary rays, as its primary source of sustenance. Then in turn, that energy is supplied to the cells of the body to give life and strength and growth to the human body through the process of fusion of molecular combination and recombination even to the DNA structure.

So, whether it is grain, grown and imbued with sunlight through photosynthesis,
or organic tissue grown and fed by that sun-filled grain, the human digestive tract will break down all that into sunlight to feed the subtle densities. To the degree we get or not this light from what we consume will determine the health and life.

Mitochondria, Avalanche and Singularity

The following excerpts are adapted from the National Institute of Health functions of mitochondria

The following treatise is a scientific estimation with follow up research, but by and large, the substance of this treatise remains theoretical at best. It represents a work in progress. It is offered as a baseline reference only. The energetic components are missing and represent the critical points of view with regards to the spiritual importance relating to the overall subject of this book. The abundance of scientific terms utilized in the NIH treatise are strictly for their use by scientists in this field. Please do not feel put off or dismayed by their usage and can be considered not very useful jargon for the lay reader. The author has removed much of the complex notation for easier reading.

The functions of mitochondria obviously include oxidative phosphorylation to produce cellular ATP, but they also have important roles in ion homeostasis, in several metabolic pathways, in apoptosis and programmed cell death, and in ROS production and consumption. All these functions may be significant in ageing and/or disease. Damage may cause mitochondria to accumulate dysfunctional components. This damage may be caused directly by radicals produced by the mitochondria themselves. It may be caused by sequence or regulatory errors following mutation of nuclear or mitochondrial DNA. A wide range of internal or environmental insults, such as exposure of the skin to ultraviolet radiation. These effects can be exacerbated by degradation of the quality control machinery that normally limits the build-up of dysfunctional mitochondria by targeting poorly performing constituents of the mitochondrial network for destruction.

The classic role of mitochondria is oxidative phosphorylation, which generates ATP by utilizing the energy released during the oxidation of the food. ATP is used in turn as the primary energy source for most biochemical and physiological processes, such as growth, movement and homeostasis. We turn over approximately our own body weight in ATP each day, and almost all of this is generated by mitochondria, primarily within muscle, brain, liver, heart and gastrointestinal tract. The pre-eminent role of eating is to provide the fuel for mitochondria, and the pre-eminent role of breathing is to provide the oxygen and to remove the carbon dioxide produced during oxidative phosphorylation by mitochondria. Similarly, a major role of the cardiovascular system is to deliver the substrates (glucose, fatty acids, oxygen) and remove the products (carbon dioxide) of mitochondrial activity.

As a result of intensive study, particularly since the 1950s, the mechanism of oxidative phosphorylation is 'very well understood', both in general principle and detailed biochemistry. The general principle is chemiosmotic coupling in which the oxidation of respiratory substrates by oxygen, catalyzed by the mitochondrial electron transport chain, causes proton extrusion across the mitochondrial inner membrane. The proton-motive force set up by this proton pumping drives protons back into the mitochondrial matrix through the ATP synthase to generate ATP. The proton-motive force also drives the uptake of ADP and phosphate and the efflux of ATP to deliver the synthesized

ATP to the cytosol where it is consumed. It is also crucial for uptake and efflux of Ca, and hence for ionic homeostasis in the cytosol and matrix and for Ca-related signaling pathways. The crystal structures of most of the electron transport chain complexes have been solved and the detailed mechanisms of the coupling of electron transport to proton pumping in certain complexes 'are well understood'. In addition to ATP synthesis, the proton-motive force is coupled directly to uptake of substrates such as pyruvate, glutamate and ornithine and to export of products such as citrulline across the mitochondrial inner membrane, to proton leak pathways through the adenine nucleotide translocase and specific uncoupling proteins that provide thermogenesis and regulation of radical production, to calcium transporters that regulate matrix and cytosolic calcium concentrations, and to the nicotinamide nucleotide transhydrogenase that maintains the reduction state of the matrix glutathione pool.

Chemiosmotic coupling of oxidative phosphorylation in mitochondria. Electrons harvested from oxidizable substrates are passed through the respiratory chain in an exergonic process that drives proton pumping by respiratory complexes. The resulting electrochemical proton gradient across the mitochondrial inner membrane can be dissipated in two ways: first, through the ATP synthase, where relieving the proton-motive force drives ADP phosphorylation, and second, via proton leak pathways that do not generate ATP but regulate physiological processes including no shivering thermogenesis and perhaps glucose-stimulated insulin secretion and protection from oxidative damage. Proton leak pathways are structurally represented by ANT, which can mediate both basal and inducible proton conductance. The structures depicted are from Thermus thermophilus complex, from porcine heart dimeric complex from a bovine heart, dimeric complex from a bovine heart, ATP synthase complex from Saccharomyces cerevisiae and carboxyatractyloside-inhibited ANT from a bovine heart.

Note: derivation of each anachronym is ADP, adenosine diphosphate; ANT, adenine nucleotide translocase; ATP, adenosine triphosphate.

Mitochondria have several critical roles in metabolism, even in organisms that live anaerobically and do not use their mitochondria for ATP synthesis. They are the central player in carbon metabolism, as well as their well-known catabolic role in oxidation of sugars (pyruvate), fats (palmitoylcarnitine) and proteins (glutamine, glutamate, alanine, and so on), they have a critical anabolic role, providing the carbon skeletons for the biosynthesis of most biomolecules, particularly glucose, fatty acids and amino acids. They are a major player in carbon metabolism. They are central in nitrogen metabolism, metabolizing the glutamate used in transamination reactions and the glutamine used to shuttle nitrogen around the body, as well as the site of half of the reactions of the urea cycle. They are also essential in the synthesis of haem and iron-sulphur clusters.

As reviewed extensively elsewhere, mitochondria are central players in programmed cell death. They activate caspases in the cytosol through the release of cytochrome c and other factors from the intermembrane space when pro-apoptotic stimuli trigger Bcl-2 family members and the permeability transition pore.

Dysfunction in any of these pathways may contribute to the pathologies that develop with age and stress. In the following sections the mitochondrial sources of ROS that may contribute to such dysfunction will be examined.

The mitochondrial free radical theory of ageing and disease

Mitochondria generate ROS during oxidative metabolism. In the mitochondrial free radical theory of ageing, these ROS are the primary cause of damage to proteins, lipids and nucleic acids. Some damage is not repaired (perhaps because it is not repairable), causing failure of cellular machinery and leading to ageing- related diseases and to ageing itself. In the strictest version of the theory, the damage is self-reinforcing: damaged mitochondrial DNA codes for dysfunctional electron transport complexes that generate even more radicals than usual, leading to a vicious cycle of exponentially increasing damage and dysfunction. There is a substantial amount of evidence both supporting and against the theory. The current consensus is best summarized by the view that radicals generated by mitochondria can be an important contributor to ageing, and are particularly important in age-related diseases, including Alzheimer disease, cardiomyopathy and cancer. However, mitochondrial radical production is not the sole cause of ageing and may be most prominent only in particular model organisms and conditions of husbandry. Mitochondrial radical production may contribute to many of the symptoms of ageing, such as frailty and loss of elasticity in skin.

To understand mitochondrial ROS generation and fully establish its true role in ageing and age-related diseases, it is necessary to identify, quantify and ultimately manipulate the specific mitochondrial electron transport chain sites that generate ROS within cells.

The production of reactive oxygen species by mitochondria in vitro: maximum capacities of different sites

The generation of hydrogen peroxide by isolated mitochondria was first reported and characterized in the early 1970s. Most of this hydrogen peroxide is produced initially as superoxide and is then converted to hydrogen peroxide by a very active superoxide dismutase in the mitochondrial matrix. Subsequent work by many research groups has identified several sites of superoxide and hydrogen peroxide production in the citric acid cycle and the electron transport chain of mammalian mitochondria.

In simple terms, the mitochondria are the energetic aspects of cell energy usage from the consumption of foods, metabolized through oxygenation from breathing,
which support cell reproduction and overall health of the body.

In terms of their importance toward the spiritual evolution of the human being, two considerations are extremely important. First, the significance that each individual cell is connected to all other cells in the body, regardless of their different functions. That they enjoy a loose affiliation with each other is directly related to something called homeostasis, a feature which could be described as the body's way of maintaining control and balance throughout all supportive systems. Thus, avoiding conflicts between organic systems which could be detrimental to the health and welfare of the body total, as actualized by the immune system defenses. which can represent the 'policeman' of the system having the sole purpose of protecting and preserving vital organ functions.

The significance of this loose affiliation is representative by the differences of inherent resonance frequency of each cell in a group of like cells. In essence, in the normal physical view, this is a good basis for life. However, from the point of view of spiritual development, their frequency of vibration stands separately as a community of different cells, likened to a civilization of different cultures, all things being equal, works well so long as all cell communities agree to support the entire wellbeing of the organism. When there is a loss of this central integrity, cancer can erupt bringing the overall integrity to a standstill causing the demise of the being, or death.

Second, the consideration of frequency is significant, meaning for the opportunity of spiritual development to occur, a singularity of all cells must become the primary goal. Without this unification through frequency and resonance, a change of the physical condition supportive of evolution is impossible. A total evolution of the physical body to support a shift in the being frequency, can only be accomplished when all the cells vibrate together at the same frequency, this is called singularity.

When there is a singularity of frequency in the body, then another action becomes possible. This action is called a chain reaction. Visualize a room of mouse traps all having a ping-pong ball sitting in the trap held until the trap is sprung. If all the traps are similar with the same tension, then the trigger (which would be a singular ping-pong ball thrown into the room). When it lands, it would strike one of the traps and in turn release that ball to then strike another. Soon there would be many balls released causing all the traps to release their balls. This would represent a chain reaction. This is what happens in the process of fission, when a source of highspeed neutrons strike the uranium atom it releases two more high speed neutrons to then strike the adjacent uranium atoms. The result is a fission of all the atoms at once. That results in an atomic explosion of tremendous energy.

Obviously, this process is not relevant to spiritual development in most respects, however, the change in the cell structure throughout the body must be the same as the chain reaction in the nuclear example. For the spiritual evolution to occur, meaning a complete shift of the being to a higher dimension of consciousness, all the body must shift together. This requires that all cells vibrate at the same frequency. So, through the alchemical process, they will all respond in a chain reaction-like fashion and shift together. This is called enlightenment.

Another example of this process is represented by the invention of the first optical laser. A rod of pure ruby comprised of chromium atoms was surrounded by a source of photonic (light) energy such as a flash lamp. When the light enters the ruby, the photonic energy (acting as a trigger) would enter each chromium atom causing it to separate some of its electrons which would spread to other adjacent chromium atoms which eventually causes a chain reaction. Then the chromium energy builds up and begins to rush from one end to the other of the rod. The rod length is cut so that its wavelength is a proportion of the chromium wavelength representing resonance. eventually the chromium (red) energy burst from one end as a ray of coherent light in the red spectrum. Laser stands for (Light Amplification Stimulation Emission Radiation). This is called avalanching. The significance is that the light is coherent (a singular frequency), and that resonance was needed so that all the atoms in the lasing substance was homogenous (all atoms are identical) and the rod was cut to the right frequency. All of this was important otherwise the amplification could not occur. In the case of a fissionable source, it had to be purified before fission could occur.

The CSF, The Pineal and Pituitary

The following treatise is adapted from lectures of Dr. Zappaterra, Dr. Stone, as well as, Dr. Taylor and Stills, et al.

In the brain, there are fluid filled ventricles, cavities at the center of the brain at the same location of what is esoterically referred to as the third eye, or pituitary and Pineal gland. At the 'brow', there is a cavity called the third ventricle. The third ventricle is a midline space. Its boundaries are the pituitary gland in front, the pineal gland in back, and the thalamus and the hypothalamus on each side.

The space between these structures has been called esoterically, the Crystal Palace, or the Cave of Brahma in Hindu yoga traditions. This space is filled with fluid, the Cerebral Spinal Fluid. This remarkable fluid plays a crucial role in the functioning of our nervous system. The Cerebral Spinal Fluid (CSF) is a clear, colorless liquid that serves as a protective and nourishing agent for both the brain and spinal cord.

The Cerebral Spinal Fluid resides within the brain's ventricles and plays a vital role in cushioning in these critical areas. This fluid extends well beyond the brain's internal aspects. It also envelopes the brain's external surface, providing an additional layer of protection. Its journey doesn't end there. The Cerebral Spinal Fluid (CSF) continues its path down the spinal cord flowing through the central canal and bathing the external surface of the spinal cord as well. This continuous flow ensures that the brain and spinal cord are consistently surrounded by this protective fluid.

   The human body contains about 150 ml of Cerebral Spinal Fluid at any given time. This fluid is normally 'stagnant' meaning it gets replenished. It is continuously replenished undergoing a complete turnover approximately three to four times daily. This equates to the body producing between 450 to 600 ml of Cerebral Spinal Fluid (CSF) each day. This fluid functions very much like a plasma (an electrically charged metallic-organic state of matter). For the fluid to function, its charge has to be replenished. Every day, the body generates half a liter of CSF, highlighting its significance in maintaining the health and functionality of our central nervous system. All aspects regarding these organs, offer a clearer understanding of the spiritual origins and purpose of these glands in this area and their intricate working in tandem spiritually within the body.

The spinal cord ends at about the second lumbar vertebra. The CSF goes all the way down into the sacrum. So, it's important to know that the human central nervous system is suspended in a column of fluid. While the brain's actual mass ranges from 1400 - 1500 grams as its effective weight, when immersed in CSF, is significantly reduced to 25 - 50 g. This illustrates the entire central nervous system essentially floats within this fluid. There exists a central column of fluid aligned with the body's midline structure, providing this unique suspension and support.

Where does this fluid come one might ask? There is a little spot in the middle of third ventricle, where began the human as an embryo. Above that is the amniotic fluid. Below that is the yolk sac, and all around it, is the chorionic fluid. The inner layer is known as the amniotic membrane and is adjacent to the amniotic fluid.

The outer layer which is called the Chorionic membrane lies next to the uterus in the embryonic stage and is considered as a maternal part of the placenta in the female embryo.

  CSF is produced mainly by the choroid plexus epithelium and the ependymal cells of the ventricles and flows into interconnecting chambers; namely, the cisterns and the subarachnoid spaces. While the human embryo is developing, is surrounded by and enclosed in this fluid and totally supported by it. The embryo is organized and created within fluid along with the CSF. That means that the CSF has a significant role in the origin and creative development of the fetus.

  Initially, in the embryonic stage, the human starts as a simple sheet of cells. Within this sheet, there's a specific area called the Neural Plate, which is a group of cells which ultimately lead to the neural plate, then it closes to form the neural tube. This neural tube serves as the beginning of the embryonic brain, spinal cord and the central nervous system. During this process, the neural plate folds inward creating what are known as the neural grooves and neural folds. Surrounding the neural plate is the amniotic fluid, which plays a crucial role during this early developmental phase.

First, the neural plate folds inward. Then the folds begin to rise, eventually fusing the central area, which then begins to transform this central area. Originally, part of the external amniotic fluid, gradually becomes what we know as CSF. Thus, CSF originates from the amniotic fluid during the embryological development. It's a remarkable even miraculous emergence. The brain and spinal cord are not just organized around fluid. They are also initially bathed in it. This symbiotic relationship suggests that conception data is imparted by this fluid that ignites the formation of these organs. It more than suggests the actual conversion of spiritual force into physical form.

Initially, the embryonic brain is a hollow fluid filled vesicle. It is CSF on the inside of the tube, and amnionic fluid on the outside of the tube. As development of the brain and spinal cord enlarge and differentiate, CSF continues to bathe the inside and outside of the entire central nervous system. Try to imagine a tiny embryo at the very beginning of its development. The embryo starts to develop awareness while enveloped in this primal fluid within the mother's womb. This journey begins with the amniotic fluid, which will gradually transition into CSF. Within this fluid, plays a vital role creating and establishing basic conscious awareness while, at the same time, bathing the entire central nervous system.

The consciousness follows the flow within the central hollow canal located inside the spinal cord. This presence throughout the central nervous system is a testament to its fundamental importance right from the earliest stages of conscious development. This understanding is very important. This is a section through the head of a human embryo at eight weeks of development. The developing brain is a thin structure on top, appearing as a cauliflower-like structure floating in space. It is understood to be the choroid plexus, and the choroid plexus produces CSF. So, if the structure that makes the CSF is that large, then the CSF must have an important role essentially, in during the entire process of early development. Moreover, this CSF presence even until adult maturity also suggests another component, hidden from adult understanding by the religous priesthood that represents a continuous connection to Source, the spirit of high heaven.

The CSF is a crucial vehicle, a spiritual plasma that carries conscious potential as it travels through the body. This idea is further echoed by Doctor Randolph Stone founder of Polarity Therapy, a holistic health care system, Doctor Stone has two notable quotes on the subject.

He states:

"So, the Choroid plexus swims in the cerebral spinal fluid, suggesting a profound connection between the spiritual essence and this fluid. Secondly, he also maintains:

"The Cerebral Spinal Fluid appears to function as both a reservoir and a conduit for ultrasonic and light energy."

Similarly, Doctor Sutherland has also shared insights, building upon the thoughts of Doctor Andrew Taylor, and Doctor Still who had a unique version of the CSF. Doctor still said:

"The CSF is an intermediary in the flow of divine intelligence, channeling creation into embryological segments and using them with life form, function and order."

This perspective presents the CSF as more than just a physical substance. It's seen as a fluid imbued with Intelligence and the capacity to shape our existence. Furthermore, according to the author's spiritual source and teacher, the CSF is a sensitive receiver and transmitter of energy vibrations and information. This concept is how flower remedies demonstrate water's ability to absorb, store and transmit plant energies, in the same vein.

Doctor Masaru Emoto, the famed Japanese author and researcher of innovative photographs of water crystals, captivated public attention with his experiments that seemed to indicate that water responded to human thought and intention. He had gained worldwide acclaim through his groundbreaking research and discovery, claiming that water is deeply connected to our individual and collective consciousness. He is the author of the best-selling books, *Messages from Water, The Hidden Messages in Water,* and *The True Power of Water*, showed that water could retain the energy of words. Thus, the CSF may also have the capacity to absorb, store and transmit the essence of the Source. Enabling us to experience and be consciously aware of external circumstances beyond the third density.

The lateral ventricle connects with the frontal lobe, the Parietal lobe, the Occipital lobe and the Temporal lobe of the brain. The posterior part of the lateral ventricle connects to the visual areas of the brain. The third ventricle has two seats, one that connects the pituitary gland and the other that connects the pineal gland.

The cells that connect the CSF to the wall can be seen with a scanning electron microscope. This reveals the greater detail of this internal structure.

Inside of the ventricle, the walls of the ventricles are connecting to the CSF by the cilia, slender hair-like structures. The cilia can beat against the CSF to create fluid movement or vibration, while the cilia also function like little antenna monitoring the fluid that have receptors on them to pick up information in the CSF. There are photo receptors that transmit light, there are chemical receptors that transmit Information from growth factors. Ion, hormone, and mechanical receptors that transmit information from flow movement. Thus, it could be said, the entire internal structure of the brain could be an organic representation of a quantum computer as compared to the digital framework analogy previously considered.

It is a sound hypothesis that the biological occurrence of a 'Kundalini awakening' is the rising of sacred energy contained in the plasma of CSF.

The Kundalini yoga theory is a 'primal energy' located at the base of the spine. Reportedly residing in a contained area of the sacrum. Like a sleeping serpent waiting to be awakened through yoga practice. The bipolar CSF moves up a central canal, the Sushumna to reach the claustrum or cave-like area. There it crosses the vegas nerve plexus and is crushed into harmony like an electro-magnetic wave.

The sacrum is a large triangular bone at the base of the spine. The origin of the word comes from the Latin term of sacrum which means sacred bone. There's a filament called silo terminal that goes all the way down from the bottom of the spinal cord at the coccyx bone.

The CSF, The Pineal and Pituitary

In the spinal cord, there's a small fiber within the central canal of the spinal cord made of condensed CSF protein according to the difference, there are two nerve currents within the spinal column called Pingala and Ida (male and female) which intertwine weaving a helical wrap around the spinal cord. symbolized by the medical caducous (a sword with two snakes coiled about the blade). And a hollow canal called Sushumna, that runs through the center of spinal cord. When that plasma awakens, it tries to force a passage through this hollow canal, as it rises, step by step, layer after layer through several nerve plexus', the mind becomes Open. It is purported that all the different visions and wonderful powers come to the yogi when it reaches the top. Then the yogi is perfectly detached from the body and mind, and the soul finds itself Free (this is called enlightenment).

The fluid filled radiant space, the ventricle in the middle of the head, the Crystal Palace or the Cave of Brama, is the space where the marriage of the Yin and the Yang energies of the pineal and Pituitary glands come to form a perfect harmony. Synchronized Externalized Stimulation vibrations such as, sound and light and magnetic energy, along with the intention of love as proposed by Dr. Emoto with his water experiments, suggests the potential that CSF is activated by light of certain frequencies, certain frequencies of sounds (words like mantras) and resonance of certain magnetic influences such as the Earth's magnetic field.

What has been shown in the research, shows that alpha rhythms of the brain occurring during sleep and the heartbeat move as vibrations the through the CSF. However, one of the major drivers of CSF movement is conscious thought and the breath. The inhalation breath drives the CSF up toward the third ventricle. The CSF loads during forced breathing at each spinal level, towards the head. The breath on exhalation indicates movement towards the sacrum, The exhalation breath forces CSF downward. This would suggest a pattern of practice which the author will elucidate in the chapter on 'the right use of breath'. Consider the various breath work practices like the Whim Hoff method, Indian Pranayama, or even just deep breathing such as utilized in Rebirthing practices. This conceptual knowledge about the CSF behavior to breath and meditation opens exciting possibilities, such as, the idea of cosmic (Source) consciousness spreading throughout the whole being and synchronized with the movement of this vital CSF. This became the secrets practiced by many esoteric societies throughout history and held in close secrecy by the church priesthood.

What is Ascension

Ascension: to rise above a station, such as a level that could be discerned as lower compared to the destination point, which would be higher whether it is mere altitude, or in frequency.

Spiritual ascension is a phenomenon in which one becomes more conscious of their sense of being and their connection with the world around them. In addition, there is a greater sense of other world realities beyond the third density, meaning dimensions of a higher vibration from the third density and an intimate connection to what is Source or quantum.

In the case of the Christian narrative in biblical scripture, Jeshua, also known as Jesus of Nazareth, ascended after he was crucified on the cross and buried in Joseph of Arimathea's family crypt.

As the story is told, he lay in the tomb for three days. The tomb was covered by a large stone and guarded by Roman centurions, one on each side. Upon query, the soldiers reported no one had come to the tomb while they stood guard, but it is also reported they fell asleep during their guard duty. When the tomb stone was pulled away, the tomb was empty and only his garments were left behind.

First seen by Mary, the Magdalene his wife, later reported to the disciples he was seen standing in a grove nearby. Though not spoken of in the cannon texts, he was out of body and by his own statement to her, "that he could not be touched for his ascension process was not yet complete."

As a note of interest, 'normal' out of body conditions would still mean his body would be laying in the tomb. This would suggest an abnormal condition of out of body state, thus defining that ascension is not just a normal out of body state. Out of body states means that the astral component of the soul is separated from the body, something Jeshua did quite often during his ministry. He was purported to have been seen in many different places at the same time preaching to separate multitudes. This feat also speaks of his ability to bilocate in different places but not of a solid presence. Hence why the Romans could never catch him in any instance of his arrival. When he was caught, it was because Judas was instructed to tell the Romans where he could be found in the flesh.

So, ascension can be the definition when one

reaches singularity, an avalanche of the cellular structure and an ascension or rising of their body's frequency to that matching the frequency of the quantum or 7th density. That condition affords the spiritually adept, or master, to have full control and mastery of the elements as well as, the nature of the human energy whether to be seen by others or in the extreme case, to virtually teleport the consciousness along with the physical shell(body) to anywhere, or anytime one desires. In addition to travel across all planes of conscious existence throughout the multiverse.

    Ascending does not necessarily mean departing earth and going to heaven, though it is often assumed. There are many reports of ascended masters who resided on the earth in the third density for the time they chose to teach the spiritual principles they have come to understand and wish to impart to others seeking such development and revelations. It does reflect that an ascended master has vacated the wheel of incarnation no longer needing the process of atonement or karmic retribution.

In 1962, in his book *"Profiles of the Future: An Inquiry into the Limits of the Possible"*, science fiction writer Arthur C. Clarke formulated his famous Three Laws, of which the third law is the best-known and most widely cited: "Any sufficiently advanced technology is indistinguishable from magic".

Magic is usually relegated to what is termed, 'Slight of Hand' or stage non magikal presentations of illusion. It is differentiated from the term true Magik, referring to the practice and mastery of the elements by the sheer use of one's will desire. The origins of Magik are unknown and certainly find their roots going back to the Egyptian dynasties of the infamous temple of Karnak, or even further back in antiquity as in the famous lost continent of Atlantis. It is purported that King Solomon practiced Magik as taught to him by the Archons, angelic beings of higher density. His fabled knowledge and wisdom are said to have come from these personal teachings from the 'angelic realm'. Even the temple was built by demons of higher density, ruled and commanded by him.

In the tales from the Septuagint (first 5 books of

The Quest for Power

the Old Testament), Moses was found in the bullrushes and taken in. as the story is told: "While bathing in the river, Pharaoh's daughter discovered the basket. She saw the helpless Israelite baby crying and wanted to raise him as her own child. Miriam came to Pharaoh's daughter and asked if she could bring an Israelite woman to care for the baby. Miriam brought her mother, Jochebed, to Pharaoh's daughter."

Moses was raised in the house of the Pharoah and provided all the benefits, grooming him to replace Seti the 1st. That means not unlike all other pharaoh ascendants, they were taught in the mystery schools of the temple of Karnak all the secrets of Magik, hence why later, he could summon Yahweh to summon a pillar of fire and open the Red Sea to allow the Israelites to pass then close it again against the Pharaoh Ramses 2nd chariot armies.

According to the scribe Josephus, when the Roman legions entered Gaul (now known as France), they found the Druids. They were appalled by their ceremonies and their practices, to develop and maintain the power over the elements.

They were practicing a derivation of an ancient memory of the past, the past alchemical science of Atlantis. They no longer possessed the tools or the scientific knowledge of genetic engineering to accomplish bringing forth those who were enhanced, but culling from the past, a version of genetics as brought down through thousands-of-years, in a crude way, to correct genetic errors and through animal husbandry. They would consume their offspring if found them to be genetically defective, believing that by consuming the errors, future offspring would benefit through their digestion.

To the Romans, this was a hideous act of barbarism and cannibalism. The Romans didn't understand what they were trying to do. So, they slaughtered them to almost extinction. But a few of the Merlins (men of knowledge of the old way) wizards and or magi, escaped and roamed the lands hiding in secret enclaves. Some could wield a manner of control over the elementals and weaved mists for the ruling lords to affect a victory over their adversaries. One such Merlin of Agwenagwelld, served Galahad (aka Sir Lancelot) and the knights of the round table to overcome many of their enemies in battle to unify Great Britain in the name of King Arthur.

When the astrologers and magi from the eastern lands sought signs from the stars of a great leader that would bring a new light into the world, they followed a comet for years. It led them to the land of Judea, there they met with the Essene brotherhood and the students of Alijah, also a magus. Alijah had formed a secret school near Mount Carmel. The Asian magi conferred their hopes and belief in the signs. The Essenes had long known of the prophecies of such a spiritual leader. They shared their knowledge of the birth of Jeshua Ben David, son of Joseph and Mary. So, the magi from Asia stayed in the community of the Nazarenes, waiting to meet the one prophesied by the Essenes.

The Christian scriptures of Mathew, Mark, Luke and John have been rewritten to reflect an immaculate conception. This is a fable to give an unrealistic authority to Jeshua, so the Jewish tribes would follow his lead. It is why in the first books of the New Testament, are spent delineating the

lineage from King David. They needed to define the basis of his authority. These stories reflect a secret tradition of enlightenment which was at the core of the movement around the Christ, cloaked in coded form within the scriptures, which I will reveal later in this treatise. During Jeshua's ministry, there were at least 25 individuals claiming the role of Messiah. They all had abilities to manipulate the elementals, as did Jeshua.
Early in his life, Jeshua went to the market with his father Joseph, he slipped away and entered the temple in Jerusalem and began to teach scriptures from the Torah. The feat was that he was only 12 years of age, but he knew all of them by heart. Soon after that, Joseph arranged to make passage for Jeshua to the far east to India, and Tibet to complete his training. (the so-called missing years) He did not return to Judea until he was 30 years of age when he began his ministry.

   According to another one of Josephus' accounts, described one of the other magi claiming to be the Messiah, the one called Simon Magus (not Simon Peter) challenged Jeshua on the steps of the Roman Senate. It was a real wizard's battle, but Jeshua triumphed. They went their way separately as Simon Magus began the church of Rome later and Jeshua authorized Simon Peter to lead the small church in Jerusalem at the end of his ministry.

    It is not clear as to when texts of Enoch and the scrolls from King Solomon's temple emerged in the form of the Divine Grimoires, known as the Greater and Lesser keys of Solomon and the Testament of Solomon detailing a list of demons bound and used to build the temple in Jerusalem. Much of the Magik lore arose from the channeled / scryed writings stemming from seances of John Dee and Edward Kelly in the 16th century. Communicating with angels that had taken Enoch into heaven to teach him the ways of angels and the demons such as Asmodeus and the prince of demons Beelzebub who relayed their experiences with King Solomon around the 1st century of the common era.

    Later in the 16th century the rise of Rosicrucian Magik and Freemasonry became prominent on the scene following remnants of Solomonic Magik. The inquisition took a strong role in trying to squash the demonological Magik practices by secret covens and they sought to burn as many of the grimoire as they could uncover. Witches and Warlocks (male witches) abound in medieval Europe, many of whom were burnt at the stake. Even the paranoid Puritan religious factions that arrived in the New World, had their influence in Salem, Massachusetts during the infamous witch trials where even many innocent women were tortured (drowned because witches could not be submerged into water) and otherwise burned.

Then at the beginning of the 20th century, a self-proclaimed high priest of the church of Satan, one known as Alister Crowley, professed to have a copy of Solomon's Grimoires. He also founded the Golden Dawn Society school of witchcraft and established the Wicken religion. Then the rise of Theosophy began in early 20th century with Annie Besant and John Olcott softening the impact of ritual Magik with esoteric philosophy. Later, it would be Rudolph Steiner leading the Theosophical Society pursuits of the esoteric 'truths'.

In modern times the Rosicrucians still flourish in Mexico and in California and the Scottish Rites temples (formally known as the Free Masons,) gather their membership in the higher echelons of corporate business concerns all around the world.

Ibn Arabi is an important figure in this tradition, but one of the most important is al-Buni, who wrote the influential text Shams al-Ma'arif. A very rare text and probably lost to antiquity, which is the grimoire of Islamic Magik that details the summoning of Djinn who are purported to exist in the deep desert. (in Arabian and Muslim mythology) an intelligent spirit of lower rank than the angels, able to appear in human and animal forms and to know to possess humans.

Djinn go back to ancient times before the creation of the known universe as immortal beings emerging out of the time space continuum. They are mostly known through Islamic literature and mythology relating to the teachings of the Persian Sage, Zoroaster and the legends of Lilith.

I wrote about the Djinns in the first chapter of this book. They emerge out of time space as a race of immortal beings reflective of the static (electrical component) of reality, a collective of consciousness that is by nature non dynamic, meaning no movement. So, when the impulse of evolution arose in the quantum and reached even their realm, it produced a feminine principle (a dynamic condition relative to the magnetic principle) with an urge to change, which startled the Djinn to their roots. They rejected her manifestation and could not accept that such an emergence could come from their essence in space. This concept is also described in the book of Genesis. When Adam is created, then arose the isolation and need for the companion. A rib of Adam is taken to form the first female, Eve. It is symbolic of course. These concepts are almost impossible to explain in terms of human understanding.

Within the mysteries of the origins of the divine male (mental thought) and divine female (feeling) principles, the male electrical component rejects the female principle. In turn, she seduces the male by the attractive current and eventually they merge to become androgenous in their union. On the physical level, it manifests in the dance of male and female 'courting rituals' defining the process of becoming a couple which manifests in the sexual conjugal act of joining and the procreation of offspring or reproduction of life a divine current o maintain itself.

There is not much that can be said about the Djinn. Their manifestation sits at the heart of the beginning of reality on the highest vibrational levels. It leaves the human consciousness in a state of wonder and perhaps that feeling of wonder is significant, as a seed of life everlasting. Like all seeds, bore a multitude of seeds from a single seed, providing the proof that life finds a way, however devious or persistent to exist, no matter what the odds are against such a manifestation. In the simplest of terms, it's a miracle.

Interestingly, According to Islamic tradition, Djinns are said to reside in the desert. Sand is actually granulated silicon dioxide, a piezoelectric mineral like quartz, which if pressured produces an electrical charge. The Djinn are of the electrical component of the quantum. So, it makes sense that you might find their energy resting among the granules of sand in the desert.

There are many names given to the aspect of evil. In the remaining sources of the text known as the 'The Testament of Solomon' he provides a sort of spread sheet of the hierarchy of the world of demons. He did this because there were so many to be catalogued. But his cataloging of these creature of darkness, was the only way of not only knowing their names, but under what constellations they represent and what their individual and defined purposes(deeds) were. All this effort was to control them and to command them. You might say he commanded the demons as his own personal work force because he used them to build his temple, as well as providing a practical way of subjecting them to a system redemption by performing acts that supported life and a temple admonishing the truth of the light. In this hierarchy, there is only one that becomes the ruler of their world, that was Beelzebub (Hebrew Talmudic tradition) or Satan (Christian tradition).

Down through the millennium, since the reign of King Solomon, the church of Rome and even the little church of Jerusalem, the name of the 'prince ' of darkness arises from Luxcious, or Lucifer, otherwise known as Lucifer Morning Star. His infamous notoriety begins with the Highest God, or Source as her Right Arch Angel, best loved by her, until his so-called rebellion and fall from heaven.

The first occurrence of the word "Satan" in the Hebrew Bible in reference to a supernatural figure comes from Numbers 22:22, which describes the Angel of Yahweh confronting Balaam on his donkey: "Balaam's departure aroused the wrath of the Elohim, and the Angel of Yahweh stood in the road as a Satan against him."

The following is an excerpt from Lucas Sweeney's 'The History and Origins of Satan'. It defines the religious and analytical perspective of the prince of darkness.

"In Judeo-Christian tradition, there are many revered characters, especially in the bible, that have helped to make Judaism and Christianity among the most practiced religions in the world today.

"Other than God himself, there are many other figures that illustrate exemplary behavior, such as Abraham, Moses, King David, The Virgin Mary, and Jesus of Nazareth.

"However, there are also figures that illustrate negative models, who lead God's people away from righteousness and into sin. Among all of these, none have the infamy and fear-inducing power of Christianity's fallen angel Satan.

"As the enemy of God himself, ruler of Hell, and source of all evil and suffering in this world, Satan has served as the inspiration behind some of humanity greatest fears. His power is so great that in the gospels of the New Testament, he can offer Jesus the world itself in return for his devotion and loyalty. But how could a lowly angel, fallen from the grace of God, have become a demon capable of terrorizing all of creation?

"Even more importantly, how can the archrival of God in Christianity not have played a major role in Judaism? Of all the names given to him, Satan is perhaps the most used and most easily recognized. Other names, such as Beelzebub, came from the downgrading of deities from other Near Eastern religions that were made into lesser 'divine figures' under the Judeo-Christian God. The name Satan, however, stems from the Hebrew word 'satan', a term whose definition includes 'adversary and accuser'. In the Hebrew Bible, 'satan' was thus never used as a proper name and served merely as a term to identify an adversary. In the Hebrew Bible there was no Satan with a capital S, and in early Hebrew traditions, there was no devil, demons, or Hell. Evil and suffering in the world instead had another source, God himself. The Book of Isaiah 45:7 reads, "I form the light, and create darkness, I make weal and create woe: I the Lord do all these things." According to the Hebrew Bible or Old Testament, God alone controlled all events and was responsible for all conditions within creation, both good and evil. This idea, however acceptable it was early Jewish traditions, became confusing and frustrating, and led to the basic question of theodicy: How could a loving and benevolent God allow so much suffering and pain on earth?"

Along with the religious perspective that suggests the second coming of Christ, there is the arrival of the Antichrist. Both perspectives are equal in one respect, they reflect a complete misunderstanding of the scriptural references.

Beelzeboah and the Antichrist

These ideas do not reflect on the words of Jeshua as referenced to the Qumran scrolls, when he said to the disciples, 'the kingdom of God resides in you'. So, do not acknowledge that you need to look for me at the end times, for they will say, I am here, or I am there, for the truth is, I am as the Christ, the light that lives inside of you.'

The Evangelical denominations all say, and even now in Jerusalem, the Rabbis of the Israelites say, the rebuilding of the temple will define that the time of the Antichrist shall show himself and thus the second coming of the Messiah. And the Messiah will defeat the Antichrist thus heralding the millennium of peace on earth. Since I have shown that the Old Testament, as well as the New Testament, does not reflect the 'word' of God, but only the word of man, then the believers have been misled by the priesthood once again. Jeshua came to teach a new way, a way of love and acceptance. He would not return in the flesh because his task was to show a way, not become the high Priest of the New Age. He made his point and did not need to return to make it again. The truth is written within the scriptures, hidden for those to have eyes to see and ears to hear, the Christ is not the man, he was the messenger only, but it is the vital fluid, the Cerebral Spinal Fluid, that flows through and surrounds the brain and spinal cord. This truth is what he gave to his disciples. The alchemy of enlightenment within.

Rapture, Myth of the Chosen

The following is a copy of the dissertation about Rapture taken from Wikipedia references. Please review those references in the bibliography section at the end of this treatise.

The concept of the rapture, in connection with premillennialism, was expressed by the 17th-century American Puritans Increase and Cotton Mather. They held to the idea that believers would be caught up in the air, followed by judgments on earth, and then the millennium. As it is currently defined is not found in historic Christianity, and is a relatively recent doctrine originating from the 1830s. The term is used frequently among fundamentalist theologians in the United States.

The Rapture is an eschatological position held by some Christians, particularly those of American evangelicalism, consisting of an end-time event when all dead Christian believers will be resurrected and, joined with Christians who are still alive, together will rise "in the clouds, to meet the Lord in the air."[1]

The origin of the term extends from the First Epistle to the Thessalonians in the Bible, which uses the Greek word harpazo (Ancient Greek: ἁρπάζω), meaning "to snatch away" or "to seize". This view of eschatology is referred to as dispensational premillennialism, a form of futurism that considers various prophecies in the Bible as remaining unfulfilled and occurring in the future.

The idea of a rapture as it is currently defined is not found in historic Christianity and is a relatively recent doctrine originating from the 1830s. The term is used frequently among fundamentalist theologians in the United States.[2] Rapture has also been used for a mystical union with God or for eternal life in Heaven.[2]

Differing viewpoints exist about the exact time of the rapture and whether Christ's return would occur in one event or two. Pretribulationism distinguishes the rapture from the second coming of Jesus Christ mentioned in the Gospel of Matthew, 2 Thessalonians, and Revelation. This view holds that the rapture would precede the seven-year Tribulation, which would culminate in Christ's second coming and be followed by a thousand-year Messianic Kingdom.[3][4]This theory grew out of the translations of the Bible that John Nelson Darby analyzed in 1833. Pretribulationism is the most widely held view among Christians believing in the rapture today, although this view is disputed within evangelicalism.[5] Some assert a post-tribulational rapture.

Most Christian denominations do not subscribe to rapture theology and have a different interpretation of the aerial gathering described in 1 Thessalonians 4.[6]They do not use rapture as a specific theological term, nor do they generally subscribe to the premillennial dispensational views associated with its use.[7]Instead they typically interpret rapture in the sense of the elect gathering with Christ in Heaven right after his second coming and reject the idea that a large segment of humanity will be left behind on earth for an extended tribulation period after the events of 1 Thessalonians 4:17.[6][8]

Etymology

Rapture is derived from Middle French rapture, via the Medieval Latin raptura("seizure, kidnapping"), which derives from the Latin raptus ("a carrying off").[9]Greek

The Koine Greek of 1 Thessalonians 4:17 uses the verb form ἁρπαγησόμεθα(harpagēsometha), which means "we shall be caught up" or "we shall be taken away". The dictionary form of this Greek verb is harpazō (ἁρπάζω).[10] This use is also seen in such texts as Acts 8:39,[11] 2 Corinthians 12:2–4,[12] and Revelation 12:5.[13] Linguist, Dr. Douglas Hamp, notes that Greek scholar Spiros Zodhiates lists harpagēsometha as the first-person plural future passive indicative of the Greek stem, harpagē (har-pag-ay),[14] "the act of plundering, plunder, spoil." The future passive indicative of harpázō (although not used by Paul in 1 Thess. 4:17) can be viewed at verbix.com: αρπασθησόμεθα (harpasthesometha).[15] GS724 harpagē means: 1. the act of plundering, robbery; 2. plunder, spoil.[16] When the rapture and the "restoration of all things" (Acts 3:20-21[17]) are viewed as simultaneous events (according to Romans 8:19-21[18]) then it makes sense why Paul would use "shall be plundered" to match the verbiage of the distortion of the Earth described in Isaiah 24:3,[19] "The land shall be entirely emptied and utterly plundered...".[20Latin

The Latin Vulgate translates the Greek ἁρπαγησόμεθα as rapiemur[a] meaning "we will be caught up" or "we will be taken away" from the Latin verb rapiomeaning "to catch up" or "take away".[21]English

English translations of the Bible have translated 1 Thessalonians 4:17 in various ways:
• The Wycliffe Bible (1395), translated from the Latin Vulgate, uses "rushed".[b]
• The Tyndale New Testament (1525), the Bishop's Bible (1568), the Geneva Bible (1587) and the King James Version (1611) use "caught up".[c] This is carried over to the American Standard Version (1901) and the Revised Standard Version (1946, 1952).

Doctrinal position

A pretribulational rapture view is most commonly found among American Fundamentalist Baptists,[22] Bible churches,[23] Brethren churches,[24] certain Methodist denominations,[25] Pentecostals,[26] non-denominational evangelicals, and various other evangelical groups.[27][improper synthesis?]

The Catholic Church, Eastern Orthodox Church,[28] the Lutheran Churches, the Anglican Communion, and Reformed denominations have no tradition of a preliminary return of Christ. The Eastern Orthodox Church, for example, favors the amillennial interpretation of prophetic Scriptures and thus rejects a preliminary, premillennial return.[29] Most Methodists do not adhere to the dispensationalist view of the rapture.[7] Views

One or two events

Most premillennialists distinguish the Rapture and the Second Coming as separate events. Some dispensational premillennialists (including many evangelicals) hold the return of Christ to be two distinct events (i.e., Christ's second coming in two stages). According to this view, 1 Thessalonians 4:15–17[30] is a description of a preliminary event to the return described in Matthew 24:29–31.[31] Although both describe a coming of Jesus, these are seen to be different events. The first event is a coming where the saved are to be 'caught up,' whence the term "rapture" is taken. The second event is described as the second coming. The majority of dispensationalists hold that the first event precedes the period of tribulation, even if not immediately (see chart for additional dispensationalist timing views).[32] Dispensationalists distinguish these events as a result of their own literal[33][34] understanding of Paul's words.[35]

Amillennialists deny the interpretation of a literal thousand-year earthly rule of Christ. There is considerable overlap in the beliefs of amillennialists (including most Catholics, Eastern Orthodox, Anglicans, and Lutherans), postmillennialists (including Presbyterians), and historic premillennialists (including some Calvinistic Baptists) with those who hold that the return of Christ will be a single, public event.

Some proponents believe the doctrine of amillennialism originated with Alexandrian scholars such as Clement and Origen[36] and later became Catholic dogma through Augustine.[37]

Destination

Dispensationalists see the immediate destination Catholic commentators, such as Walter Drum[dead link] (1912), identify the destination of the 1 Thessalonians 4:17 gathering as Heaven.[38]

While Anglicans have many views, some Anglican commentators, such as N. T. Wright, identify the destination as a specific place on Earth.[39][40] This interpretation may sometimes be connected to Christian environmentalist concerns.[41]

Views of eschatological timing

There are numerous views regarding the timing of the Rapture. Some maintain that Matthew 24:37–40[42] refers to the Rapture, pointing out similarities between the two texts, indicating that the Rapture would occur at the parousia of the Lord. Others point out that neither church nor rapture occur in Matthew 24 and there are significant differences between Matthew 24:37–40 and 1 Thessalonians 4:13–18.[43] As a result, these two texts receive the overwhelming focus within discussions about the Rapture's timing. The two texts are as follows:

1 Thessalonians 4:15–17 ASV   Matthew 24:37–40 ASV15According to the Lord's word, we tell you that we who are still alive, who are left until the coming of the Lord (παρουσίαν, parousia),[44] will certainly not precede those who have fallen

asleep. 16For the Lord himself will come down from heaven, with a loud command, with the voice of the archangel and with the trumpet call of God, and the dead in Christ will rise first. 17After that, we who are still alive and are left will be caught up together with them in the clouds to meet the Lord in the air. And so, we will be with the Lord forever. 37And as were the days of Noah, so shall be the coming (παρουσία, parousia) [45] of the Son of man. 38For as in those days which were before the flood they were eating and drinking, marrying and giving in marriage, until the day that Noah entered the ark, 39and they knew not until the flood came, and took them all away; so, shall be the coming (παρουσία parousia) [46] of the Son of man. 40Then shall two men be in the field; one is taken, and one is left.

In the amillennial and postmillennial views there are no distinctions in the timing of the Rapture. These views regard that the Rapture, as it is described in 1 Thessalonians 4:15–17,[47] would be identical to the Second Coming of Jesus as described in Matthew 24:29–31[48] after the spiritual/symbolic millennium.

In the premillennial view, the Rapture would be before a literal, earthly millennium. Within premillennialism, the pretribulation position distinguishes between the Rapture and the Second Coming as two different events. There are also other positions within premillennialism that differ regarding the timing of the Rapture.[49]

Premillennialist views

In the earliest days of the church, chiliastic teaching (i.e., early premillennialism) was the dominant view.[50] Eusebius wrote, "To these [written accounts] belong his [Papias of Hierapolis] statement that there will be a period of some thousand years after the resurrection of the dead, and that the kingdom of Christ will be set up in the material form on this very earth. [...] But it was due to him that so many of the Church Fathers after him adopted a like opinion, urging in their own support the antiquity of the man; as for instance Irenaeus and anyone else that may have proclaimed similar views."[51]

Schaff further confirms this by stating, "The most striking point in the eschatology of the ante-Nicene age is the prominent chiliasm, or millennarianism, that is the belief of a visible reign of Christ in glory on earth with the risen saints for a thousand years, before the general resurrection and judgment."[52]

Over time, however, a clash surfaced between two schools of interpretation, the Antiochene and Alexandrian schools.[53] The Alexandrian school's roots can be traced back to the influence of Philo, a Hellenized Jew who sought to reconcile God's veracity with what he thought were errors in the Tanakh.[54] Alexandrian theologians viewed the Millennium as a symbolic reign of Christ from Heaven.[55] Through the influence of Origen and Augustine—students of the Alexandrian school—allegorical interpretation rose to prominence, and its eschatology became the majority view for more than a thousand years.[56] As a reaction to the rise of allegorical interpretation the Antiochene school[57] insisted on a literal hermeneutic.[58] but did little to counter the Alexandrian's symbolic Millennium.[59]

In the twelfth century futurism became prominent again when Joachim of

Fiore(1130–1202) wrote a commentary on Revelation and insisted that the end was near and taught that God would restore the earth, the Jews would be converted, and the Millennium would take place on earth.[60] His teaching influenced much of Europe.

Though the Catholic Church does not generally regard Biblical prophecy in texts such as Daniel and Revelation as strictly future-based (when viewed from the standpoint of our present time), in 1590 Francisco Ribera, a Catholic Jesuit, taught futurism.[61] He also taught that a gathering-of-the-elect event (similar to what is now called the rapture) would happen 45 days before the end of a 3.5-year tribulation.

The concept of the rapture, in connection with premillennialism, was expressed by the 17th-century American Puritans Increase and Cotton Mather. They held to the idea that believers would be caught up in the air, followed by judgments on earth, and then the millennium.[62][63] Other 17th-century expressions of the rapture are found in the works of Robert Maton, Nathaniel Holmes, John Browne,

Thomas Vincent, Henry Danvers, and William Sherwin.[64]

The term rapture was used by Philip Doddridge[65] and John Gill[66] in their New Testament commentaries, with the idea that believers would be caught up prior to judgment on earth and Jesus' second coming.

An 1828 edition of Matthew Henry's An Exposition of the Old and New Testament uses the word "rapture" in explicating 1 Thessalonians 4:17.[67]

Although not using the term "rapture", the idea was more fully developed by Edward Irving (1792–1834).[68] In 1825,[69] Irving directed his attention to the study of prophecy and eventually accepted the one-man Antichrist idea of James Henthorn Todd, Samuel Roffey Maitland, Robert Bellarmine, and Francisco Ribera, yet he went a step further. Irving began to teach the idea of a two-phase return of Christ, the first phase being a secret rapture prior to the rise of the Antichrist. Edward Miller described Irving's teaching like this: "There are three gatherings: – First of the first fruits of the harvest, the wise virgins who follow the Lamb whithersoever He goeth; next, the abundant harvest gathered afterwards by God; and lastly, the assembling of the wicked for punishment."[70]

Pre-tribulational premillennialism

The pre-tribulation position advocates that the rapture will occur before the beginning of a seven-year tribulation period, while the second coming will occur at the end of it. Pre-tribulationists often describe the rapture as Jesus coming for the church and the second coming as Jesus coming with the church. Pre-tribulation educators and preachers include Jimmy Swaggart, Robert Jeffress, J. Dwight Pentecost, Tim LaHaye, J. Vernon McGee, Perry Stone, Chuck Smith, Hal Lindsey, Jack Van Impe, Skip Heitzig, Chuck Missler, Grant Jeffrey, Thomas Ice, David Jeremiah, John F. MacArthur, and John Hagee.[71]

John Nelson Darby first solidified and popularized the pre-tribulation rapture in 1827. Despite vague notions of this view existing in a few Puritan theologians prior to Darby, he was the first person to place it into a larger theological framework .[72][73][74][75] This view was accepted among many other Plymouth Brethren movements in England.[76][page needed] Darby and other prominent Brethren were part of the Brethren movement which impacted American Christianity, especially with movements and teachings associated with Christian eschatology and fundamentalism, primarily through their writings. Influences included the Bible Conference Movement, starting in 1878 with the Niagara Bible Conference. These conferences, which were initially inclusive of historicist and futurist premillennialism, led to an increasing acceptance of futurist premillennial views and the pre-tribulation rapture especially among Presbyterian, Baptist, and Congregational members.[76]:11 Popular books also contributed to acceptance of the pre-tribulation rapture, including William E. Blackstone's book Jesus is Coming, published in 1878,[77] which sold more than 1.3 million copies, and the Scofield Reference Bible, published in 1909 and 1919 and revised in 1967.[78][79]

Some pre-tribulation proponents, such as Grant

Jeffrey, maintain that the earliest known extra-Biblical reference to the pre-tribulation rapture is from a 7th-century tract known as the Apocalypse of Pseudo-Ephraem the Syrian.[80] Different authors have proposed several different versions of the text as authentic and there are differing opinions as to whether it supports belief in a pre-tribulation rapture.[81][82] One version of the text reads, "For all the saints and Elect of God are gathered, prior to the tribulation that is to come, and are taken to the Lord lest they see the confusion that is to overwhelm the world because of our sins."[83][84] In addition, The Apocalypse of Elijah and The History of Brother Dolcino both state that believers will be removed prior to the Tribulation.[citation needed]

There exists at least one 18th-century and two 19th-century pre-tribulation references: in an essay published in 1788 in Philadelphia by the Baptist Morgan Edwards which articulated the concept of a pre-tribulation rapture,[85] in the writings of Catholic priest Manuel Lacunza in 1812,[86] and by John Nelson Darby in 1827. Manuel Lacunza (1731–1801), a Jesuit priest (under the pseudonym

Juan Josafat Ben Ezra), wrote an apocalyptic work entitled La venida del Mesías en gloria y majestad (The Coming of the Messiah in Glory and Majesty). The book appeared first in 1811, 10 years after his death. In 1827, it was translated into English by the Scottish minister Edward Irving.[87]

During the 1970s, belief in the rapture became popular in wider circles, in part because of the books of Hal Lindsey, including The Late Great Planet Earth, which has reportedly sold between 15 million and 35 million copies, and the movie A Thief in the Night, which based its title on the scriptural reference 1 Thessalonians 5:2. Lindsey proclaimed that the rapture was imminent, based on world conditions at the time.

In 1995, the doctrine of the pre-tribulation rapture was further popularized by Tim LaHaye's Left Behind series of books, which sold close to 80 million copies and was made into several movies and four real-time strategy video games.[88]

According to Thomas Ice a belief in the imminence of Christ's return, key to modern pretribulation theology, can be found in various

Church Fathers and early Christian writings.[89]

Mid-tribulational premillennialism

The mid-tribulation position espouses that the rapture will occur at some point in the middle of what is popularly called the tribulation period, or during Daniel's 70th Week. The tribulation is typically divided into two periods of 3.5 years each. Mid-tribulationists hold that the saints will go through the first period (Beginning of Travail), but will be raptured into Heaven before the severe outpouring of God's wrath in the second half of what is popularly called the Great Tribulation. Mid-tribulationists appeal to Daniel 7:25 which says the saints will be given over to tribulation for "time, times, and half a time," – interpreted to tribulation, the Antichrist will commit the "abomination of desolation" by desecrating the Jerusalem temple. Mid-tribulationist teachers include Harold Ockenga, James O. Buswell (a reformed, Calvinistic Presbyterian), and Norman Harrison.[90] This position is a minority view among premillennialists.[91]

Prewrath premillennialism

The prewrath rapture view also places the rapture

at some point during the tribulation period before the second coming. This view holds that the tribulation of the church begins toward the latter part of a seven-year period, being Daniel's 70th week, when the Antichrist is revealed in the temple. This latter half of a seven-year period [i.e. 3 1/2 years] is defined as the great tribulation, although the exact duration is not known. References from Matthew 24, Mark 13, and Luke 21 are used as evidence that this tribulation will be cut short by the coming of Christ to deliver the righteous by means of the rapture, which will occur after specific events in Revelation, in particular after the sixth seal is opened and the sun is darkened and the moon is turned to blood.[92] However, by this point many Christians will have been slaughtered as martyrs by the Antichrist. After the rapture will come God's seventh-seal wrath of trumpets and bowls (a.k.a. "the Day of the Lord"). The Day of the Lord's wrath against the ungodly will follow for the remainder of seven years.[93][94]

Partial pre-tribulation premillennialism

The partial, conditional or selective rapture

theory holds that all obedient Christians will be raptured before the great tribulation depending on one's personal fellowship (or closeness) between she or he and God, which is not to be confused with the relationship between the same and God (which is believer, regardless of fellowship.) [95][96] Therefore, it is believed by some that the rapture of a believer is determined by the timing of his conversion before the great tribulation. Other proponents of this theory hold that only those who are faithful in their relationship with God (having true fellowship with him) will be raptured, and the rest resurrected during the great tribulation, between the 5th and 6th seals of Revelation, having lost their lives during.[97] Still others hold the rest will either be raptured during the tribulation or at its end. As stated by Ira David (a proponent of this view): "The saints will be raptured in groups during the tribulation as they are prepared to go."[98] Some notable proponents of this theory are G. H. Lang, Robert Chapman, G. H. Pember, Robert Govett, D. M. Panton, Watchman Nee, Ira E. David, J. A. Seiss, Hudson Taylor, Anthony Norris Groves, John Wilkinson,

G. Campbell Morgan, Otto Stockmayer and Rev. J. W. (Chip) White Jr.

Post-tribulational premillennialism

In the post-tribulation premillennial position, the rapture would be identical to the second coming of Jesus or as a meeting in the air with Jesus that immediately precedes his return to the Earth before a literal millennium. The post-tribulation position places the rapture at the end of the tribulation period. Post-tribulation writers define the tribulation period in a generic sense as the entire present age, or in a specific sense of a period of time preceding the second coming of Christ.[99] The emphasis in this view is that the church will undergo the tribulation.[100]Matthew 24:29–31 – "Immediately after the Tribulation of those days...they shall gather together his elect..." – is cited as a foundational scripture for this view. Post-tribulationists perceive the rapture as occurring simultaneously with the second coming of Christ. Upon Jesus' return, believers will meet him in the air and will then accompany him in his return to the Earth.

In the Epistles of Paul, most notably in 1

Thessalonians 4:16–17 ("the dead in Christ shall rise first") and 1 Corinthians 15:51–52, a trumpet is described as blowing at the end of the tribulation to herald the return of Christ; Revelation 11:15 further supports this view. Moreover, after chapters 6–19, and after 20:1–3 when Satan is bound, Revelation 20:4–6 says, "and they lived, and reigned with Christ a thousand years. But the rest of the dead lived not again until the thousand years were finished. This is the first resurrection. Blessed and holy is he that hath part in the first resurrection."

Authors and teachers who support the post-tribulational view include Pat Robertson, Walter R. Martin, John Piper, George E. Ladd,[101] Robert H. Gundry,[102] and Douglas Moo.

Postmillennialism

In the postmillennialist view the millennium is seen as an indefinitely long time thus precluding literal interpretation of a thousand-year period. According to Loraine Boettner "the world will be Christianized, and the return of Christ will occur at the close of a long period of righteousness and peace, commonly called the millennium."[103] Postmillennialists commonly view the rapture of the Church as one and the same event as the second coming of Christ. According to them the great tribulation was already fulfilled in the Jewish-Roman War of 66–73 AD that involved the destruction of Jerusalem.[citation needed] Authors who have expressed support for this view include the Puritan author of Pilgrim's Progress, John Bunyan, Jonathan Edwards and Charles Finney. Amillennialism

Amillennialists view the millennial rule of Christ as the current, but indefinite period that began with the foundation of the church and that will end with the Second Coming—a period where Christ already reigns with his saints through the Eucharist and his church. They view the life of the church as Christ's kingdom already established (inaugurated on the day of the Pentecost described in the first chapter of Acts), but not to be made complete until his second coming. This framework precludes a literal interpretation of the thousand-year period mentioned in chapter twenty of Revelation, viewing the number "thousand" as numerologically symbolic and pertaining to the current age of the church.

Amillennialists generally do not use "rapture" as a theological term, but they do view a similar event coinciding with the second coming—primarily as a mystical gathering with Christ. To amillennialists the final days already began on the day of the Pentecost, but that the great tribulation will occur during the final phase or conclusion of the millennium, with Christ then returning as the alpha and omega at the end of time. Unlike premillennialists who predict the millennium as a literal thousand-year reign by Christ after his return, amillennialists emphasize the continuity and permanency of his reign throughout all periods of the New Covenant, past, present and future. They do not regard mentions of Jerusalem in the chapter twenty-one of Revelation as pertaining to the present geographical city, but to a future new Jerusalem or "new heaven and new earth", for which the church through the twelve apostles (representing of the twelve tribes of Israel) currently lays the foundation in the messianic kingdom already present. Unlike certain premillennial dispensationalists, they do not view the rebuilding of the temple of Jerusalem as either necessary or legitimate, because the practice of animal sacrifices has now been fulfilled in the life of the church through Christ's ultimate sacrifice on the cross. Authors who have expressed support for the amillenialist view include St. Augustine.[104] The amillennialist viewpoint is the position held by the Catholic, Eastern Orthodox, and Anglican churches, as well as mainline Protestant bodies, such as Lutherans, Methodists, Presbyterians and many Reformed congregations.[105]

The following is an excerpt from an article by Ryan Hurd

"Except for Dr Freud, no one has influenced modern dream studies more than Carl Jung.

"A psychoanalyst based in Zurich, Switzerland, Jung (1875 -1961) was a friend and follower of Freud but soon developed his own ideas about how dreams are formed. While depth psychology has fallen out of favor in neuroscience, Jung's ideas are still thriving in contemporary psychoanalytic circles. Popular applications directly based on Jung's research include the Myers-Briggs Personality Type Indicator, the polygraph (lie detector) test, and 12-step addiction recovery programs.

"The basic idea behind Jungian dream theory is that dreams reveal more than they conceal. They are a natural expression of our imagination and use the most straightforward language at our disposal: mythic narratives. Because Jung rejected Freud's theory of dream interpretation that dreams are designed to be secretive, he also did not believe dream formation is a product of discharging our tabooed sexual impulses.

"And surprisingly enough, Jung did not believe that dreams need to be interpreted for them to perform their function. Instead, he suggested that dreams are doing the work of integrating our conscious and unconscious lives; he called this the process of individuation. It's easiest to think of individuation as the mind's quest for wholeness, or that quality of applied wisdom that separates elders from grumpy old men. While not required, working with dreams and amplifying the mythic components can hasten along the process.

Archetypal Images Bring Balance

"This mythic world of Jung's is the realm of the archetypes, which are the universal energies of every human who is not only in conflict with society but also with him or herself. Jung suggested that the archetypal images that come through dreams may be derived from different organs and thought centers in the body, and as such represent evolutionary drives.

"Despite all the conflict, order is where it's all headed from Jung's perspective. The quicker we can balance all these ancient needs, the more productively we can live. The psychotherapist's role is to provide hope for this order by helping the client make sense of their night visions and how they relate to waking life.

"In Jung's reckoning, the psychotherapist is like a modern shaman or priest who helps the individual create a personal mythology that works by throwing out maladaptive patterns and establishing healthy ones in their place."

The Collective Unconscious is not a Psychic Soup

"The components of our mythic lives all have a similar structure throughout the lifespan. This is Jung's collective unconscious, an idea that is usually misrepresented in popular culture today as some kind of psychic reservoir of knowledge. Jung was pointing more towards the psychological constants in all societies, such as rites-of-passage into womanhood, or the growing fascination with death after middle age.

"The confusion over the collective unconscious might have to do with the fact that Jung believed in telepathy. Ever the empirical scientist, Jung wrote "I would not assert the law behind them [telepathy] is "supernatural", but merely something which we cannot get at yet with our present knowledge" (1974, p. 48).

"If you are interested in how dreams can reflect the Big Moments in our lives, as well as our natural aptitude for mysticism, then start with Jung's Dreams, Myths and Reflections, his autobiography. It is rich and provocative.

"Jung's dream journal has also just been published for the first time, in limited numbers. Known as the Red Book, this is the journal that Jung kept during his 'encounter with the unconscious' during WWI, in which he holed up in his studio and purposefully went crazy for a while. He claimed later that all the seeds for his major ideas are represented in the Red Book, which is full of ornate drawings and calligraphy. This book may prove to rewrite everything we thought we knew about Carl Jung.

The following is an excerpt from the article, The Nature and Meanings of Dreams. by Ekua Hagan referring to the ideas of C.G. Jung (1875-1961). They remain a valuable source of guidance into the world of dreams.

"Many other theories have been proposed since his time, and some of his thinking now appears dated in light of later scientific and cultural developments. But his core works on the nature and meaning of dreaming still stand as perhaps the most deeply insightful writings about dreams of any Western psychologist, past or present.

"Jung learned several key ideas from his early mentor, Sigmund Freud (1856-1939). Both Jung and Freud agreed that dreaming is a meaningful product of unconscious forces in the psyche with roots deep in the evolutionary biology of our species. Both agreed that dreams are valuable allies in healing people suffering from various kinds of mental illness. They both used the best neuroscience of their day to inform their theories, and they both went beyond the limits of brain science to seek insights about the nature of dreaming in mythology, history, and art. Both believed a greater knowledge of dreaming could help us better understand the philosophical mysteries of how the mind and body interact.

"The most fundamental difference in Freud's and Jung's dream theories was this: Freud's approach looked backward and focused on the causal sources of dreams in early life experiences. Jung's approach looked forward and tried to understand where the dreams might be leading, and what they might reveal about the individual's future life development.

Compensation

"The primary function of dreaming, according to Jung, is psychological compensation. Dreams help maintain a healthy, dynamic balance between consciousness and the unconscious. When the waking ego becomes too one-sided, or if it tries to repress a part of the unconscious, dreams will emerge to highlight the imbalance and guide the individual back on a path towards becoming a more integrated self.

"The fundamental mistake regarding the nature of the unconscious is probably this: it is commonly supposed that its contents have only one meaning and are marked with an unalterable plus or minus sign. In my humble opinion, this view is too naïve. The psyche is a self-regulating system that maintains its equilibrium just as the body does. Every process that goes too far immediately and inevitably calls forth compensations, and without these, there would be neither a normal metabolism nor a normal psyche. In this sense, we can take the theory of compensation as a basic law of psychic behavior.... When we set out to interpret a dream, it is always helpful to ask: What conscious attitude does it compensate?" (1934, 101)

Reductive compensations

"Sometimes the compensation can take a critical form, which Jung called reductive compensations. Dreams sometimes bring a chastening dose of humility when the waking ego becomes too inflated or self-important (the ancient Greeks called it hubris).

"According to Jung, dreams give us honest portrayals of who we really are. If we think too highly of ourselves, the compensatory nature of the psyche will bring forth dreams that bring us back down into our depths. If we are too impressed with our own goodness and moral righteousness, we will be prone to dreams reminding us of our sins, our failings, our evil impulses, our hypocritical rationalizations, and ego-protecting deceptions. "There are people whose conscious attitude and

adaptive performance exceed their capacities as individuals; that is to say, they appear to be better and more valuable than they really are…. They have not grown inwardly to the level of their outward eminence, for which reason the unconscious in all these cases has a negatively compensating, or reductive, function…Every appearance of false grandeur and importance melts away before the reductive imagery of the dream, which analyses his conscious attitude with pitiless criticism and brings up devastating material containing a complete inventory of all his most painful weaknesses."
(1948a, 43-45)

The prospective function

"Dreams can have many different functions, and Jung did not insist that every dream fits into one of his categories. But in addition to compensation, he proposed another major function of dreaming, which he called the prospective function. This is not prophecy, although it does overlap with traditional religious views about dreams offering glimpses and visions of possibilities for the future.

"Jung said the prospective function focuses

primarily on the future growth of the individual along the path towards greater psychological integration and wholeness. If we can learn to understand these prospective dreams, they can offer an important source of unconscious intelligence and insight.

"The prospective function is an anticipation in the unconscious of future conscious achievements, something like a preliminary exercise or sketch, or a plan roughed out in advance.... That the prospective function of dreams is sometimes greatly superior to the combinations we can consciously foresee is not surprising, since a dream results from the fusion of subliminal elements and is thus a combination of all the perceptions, thoughts, and feelings which consciousness has not registered because of their feeble accentuation. About prognosis, therefore, dreams are often in a much more favorable position than consciousness." (1948a, 41-42)

Archetypal images and "big dreams"

"Jung put great emphasis on dreams with extremely vivid images. He regarded them as expressions of deeper unconscious patterns of instinctual meaning and wisdom he called archetypes. These dream images help to connect us with the primal energies of the psyche, whose ultimate developmental goal is our wholeness as humans, what Jung calls individuation.

"Hence Jung's interest in the distinction between "big" and "little" dreams. Big dreams revolve around powerful archetypal images from the collective unconscious. Such dreams are guideposts along the path of individuation.

"Not all dreams are of equal importance. Even primitives distinguish between 'little' and 'big' dreams, or, as we might say, 'insignificant' and 'significant' dreams. Looked at more closely, 'little' dreams are the nightly fragments of fantasy coming from the subjective and personal sphere, and their meaning is limited to the affairs of the everyday. That is why such dreams are easily forgotten, just because their validity is restricted to the day-to-day fluctuations of the psychic balance. Significant dreams, on the other hand, are often remembered for a lifetime, and not infrequently prove to be the richest jewel in the treasure-house of psychic experience." (1948b, 76)

Carl Jung was a very good dream analyst mainly because he believed in the spiritual components of dreams as they relate to the human psyche development.

Dreams follow two basic forms: loose or low attention dreams and lucid high attention dreams. Jung dealt with the content more than the attention given to the experience. Given the context of this treatise, the high attention dreams (meaning lucidity with the presence of all the five senses within a framework of accuracy in their background and substance) can differ greatly with low attention dream states where there can be great distortion with regards to the relative position of places and objects that appear within the dream.

As far as spiritual development is concerned, the high attention state of a dream sequence will more than likely reflect the spiritual state of the dreamer, who or what they may encounter while in the dream, as in the example of animal avatars masking the presence of higher beings seeking to inform or provide important messages, or guidance in the process of their spiritual training. These symbols can be representations of important relationships to elements within the self.

The problem with lucidity, is it can be somewhat elusive and difficult to manifest at will, without extensive spiritual training. The classic way to encourage lucidity is by preparation before retiring, such as a mental suggestion of an unusual item or creature not commonly found in real life. As an example, a rabbit with stripes or an unusual shape that might appear, which then becomes a reminder (or trigger) to do a specific task such as, finding a mirror to look at one's own image, and speaking, or looking at one's hands, etc. Anything causing a greater focus that would engage more than one sense. The rule is: if at least three senses are engaged, the rest will follow, bringing the dreamer into lucidity. Lucidity offers greater control over what happens, as opposed to drifting through the experience spontaneously. The casual dreamer is basically a pair of eyeballs floating around with ears to see and hear what is happening. Having control of one's dream state is a highly valued asset to have when working spiritually.

Astrology and the Lunar Return

Astrology has been around for thousands if not tens of thousands of years. The practice of this science has many different approaches. Today there is the horary
style which includes the planets of the solar system including the moon and the sun. The Chinese system includes 108 stars as well as the planets of this solar system called the Four Pillars of Wisdom.

In the late 1940s, Adolph Hitler had his own astrologer, Karl Ernst Kraft, who served as part of Hitler's occult department seeking to use his skills to help define the best approach toward the war effort against the allies. Kraft based his approach like the Four Pillars system, but he called his system the Uranian System.

According to my spiritual teacher and guide, Yokar, an Atlantean priest and scientist, the fabled lost continent of Atlantis, also had a system of astrology and used astrologers to plan the conception of offspring to define their specific needs in their society. They did not rely on randomized birthing but depended on the conception time not the actual birthing time. He

Astrology and the Lunar Return

relates that their system was far more accurate and included many of the constellations as well as the original Zodiac which was used to help rule the continent.

Because the Horary system uses a limited number of celestial points and does not include a numbering system like Numerology, or the Tarot, it is less accurate, but certainly popular and simplistically useful to the average casual interest of the lay person.

Without getting into the complications of forecasting mechanisms of astrological practice, such as an ephemeris. The Astrology Ephemeris is basically a book of planet positions, in the different 12 zodiac signs, which shows the patterns affecting a horoscope, (a chart of a particular forecast based on an astrological sign) for many years into the future – but also stretching back into the past. It's the best way to see the astrological weather of an event pr a person's life pattern.

So, the birthdate, locale, meaning where birth has occurred and the time of birth, is all required to cast a horoscope. This information provides the 'sun' sign, the most significant orb guiding the chart. The second orb which plays an important role in casting a horoscope, is the lunar aspect or the moon. This is because of the relative near proximity. Also, because the moon governs all fluids on the earth (visualize the rise and fall of tidal waters) so, it would also influence the state of the bodily fluids as well.

The fields surrounding the planetary systems are based upon their gravitational and magnetic energies that effect the growth of the fetus during the event of birth. The alignment of the various planets around the sun defines the influences believed to be impregnated into the tissues during the growth cycle, which continue to flux until the final and fixed timestamp of the last position at birth. But conception is more precise, but not included in modern times simply because animal husbandry is not practiced in modern society, and the difficulty that arises to determine the precise time and date of conception, which is not tracked accurately by the females of society.

The precise position and lunar phase play a much more important role in terms of spiritual development, a factor that is not well known, but also kept secret and held within esoteric or hidden knowledge and only recognized by those who are aware and trained in the ancient mystical arts that include such aspects of celestial portent.

In view of the purpose of this work, the lunar phase at the time of birth and the location of birth is combined with the actual residence location later, are significant to calculate what is called the Lunar Return. A lunar return is the moment the moon comes back to the precise degree it was in the sky it was when you were born. This happens every month and lasts for 2.5-3 days.

Full Moons are a culmination point of climaxing energies & a lunar return is an emotional evolution of the spirit. It's completed a cycle, which happens every 28 days as the moon makes a full cycle in that time and comes back to the birth moon spot for the return. That one is a bit more important but the full moon if aspecting, the lunar return can be a climax point or a turning of the page in conscious awareness of the emotional nature. It always depends on the natal healthiness of the Moon & aspects to the natal Moon. It's important what house (Zodiac) this occurs in, what natural house ruler is involved as well as the ruler of the Moon house/sign and how healthy it is in the birth chart. In terms of the keys to the kingdom, this aspect is critical.

Hemispheric Synchronization

Hemispheric Synchronization or Hemi-Sync is a binaural beat technology known created by the Monroe Institute (Faber, VA). Hemi-Sync involves the simultaneous play of 2 tones that differ by 15 decibels in each ear, as well as positive verbal messages.

The Monroe Institute was started by Robert Monroe, author of 'Journeys Out of the Body'. Robert wanted to teach this ability for persons to use his techniques to make the Astral body leave the physical body, also known as an OOBE (Out of Body Experience.) A feat he developed to explore other dimensions while his body lay asleep.

Years later, the CIA learned that the Soviet Union was using parapsychological means to conduct espionage activity, to remotely view locations psychically and gather intelligence about that location.

They approached Monroe and his Institute to explore the possibility for government agents to perform counter-intelligence operations using his techniques. Robert developed the technique of Hemispheric Synchronization (Hemi-Sync) along with audio monitoring to facilitate the guidance and expedite the technique that was a variation of Out of Body, called remote viewing.

The individual did not leave the body but only extended the consciousness to a remote location. The participant would be given GPS coordinates only without any further information given regarding what was called the target. The participant would draw on paper what they saw at the remote location. Several trials conducted proved to be quite accurate with a few individuals having a natural ability, two individual sin particular, who were some of the most successful were Ingo Swann and Joseph McDoneagle.

The following review is taken from online sources and adapted to this treatise.

Hemispheric-Synchronization and Remote viewing

Remote viewing (RV) is the practice of seeking impressions about a distant or unseen subject, purportedly sensing with the mind.[1] A remote viewer is expected to give information about an object, event, person, or location hidden from physical view and separated at some distance.[2]

Physicists Russell Targ and Harold Puthoff, parapsychology researchers at Stanford Research Institute(SRI), are generally credited with coining the term "remote viewing" to distinguish it from the closely related concept of clairvoyance.[3][4] According to Targ, the term was first suggested by Ingo Swann in December 1971 during an experiment at the American Society for Psychical Research in New York City.[5]

Remote viewing experiments have historically lacked proper controls and repeatability. There is no scientific evidence that remote viewing exists, and the topic of remote viewing is generally regarded as pseudoscience.[6][7][8][9][10][11]

The idea of remote viewing received renewed attention in the 1990s upon the declassification of documents related to the Stargate Project, a $20 million research program sponsored by the U.S. government that attempted to determine potential military applications of psychic phenomena. The program ran from 1975 to 1995 and ended after evaluators concluded that remote viewers consistently failed to produce actionable intelligence information. [n 1][12]

Early background

In early occult and spiritualist literature, remote viewing was known as telesthesia and traveling clairvoyance. Rosemary Guiley described it as "seeing remote or hidden objects clairvoyantly with the inner eye, or in alleged out-of-body travel."[13]

The study of psychic phenomena by major scientists started in the mid-nineteenth century. Early researchers included Michael Faraday, Alfred Russel Wallace, Rufus Osgood Mason, and William Crookes. Their work predominantly involved carrying out focused experimental tests on individuals thought to be psychically gifted. Reports of apparently successful tests were met with much skepticism from the scientific community.[14]

In the 1930s, J. B. Rhine expanded the study of paranormal performance into larger populations by using standard experimental protocols with unselected human subjects. But, as with the earlier studies, Rhine was reluctant to publicize this work too early because of the fear of criticism from mainstream scientists.[15]

This continuing skepticism, with its consequences for peer review and research funding, ensured that paranormal studies remained a fringe area of scientific exploration. However, by the 1960s, the prevailing counterculture attitudes muted some prior hostility. The emergence of what is termed "New Age" thinking and the popularity of the Human Potential Movement provoked a mini-renaissance that renewed public interest in consciousness studies and psychic phenomena and helped to make financial support more available for research into such topics.[16]

In the early 1970s, Harold Puthoff and Russell Targ joined the Electronics and Bioengineering Laboratory at Stanford Research Institute (SRI, now SRI International), where they initiated studies of the paranormal that were, at first, supported with private funding from the Parapsychology Foundation and the Institute of Noetic Sciences.[17]

In the late 1970s, the physicists John Taylor and Eduardo Balanovski tested the psychic Matthew Manning in remote viewing, and the results proved "completely unsuccessful".[18]

One of the early experiments, lauded by proponents as having improved the methodology of remote viewing testing and raising future experimental standards, was criticized as leaking information to the participants by inadvertently leaving clues.[19] Some later experiments had negative results when these clues were eliminated.[n 2]

The viewers' advice in the "Stargate project" was always so unclear and non-detailed that it has never been used in any intelligence operation.[4][n 1][12]

Decline and termination.

In the early 1990s, the Military Intelligence Board, chaired by Defense Intelligence Agency chief Harry E. Soyster, appointed Army Colonel William Johnson to manage the remote viewing unit and evaluate its objective usefulness. Funding dissipated in late 1994, and the program declined. The project was transferred from DIA to the CIA in 1995.

In 1995, the CIA hired the American Institutes for Research (AIR) to perform a retrospective evaluation of the results generated by the Stargate

Project. Reviewers included Ray Hyman and Jessica Utts. Utts maintained that there had been a statistically significant positive effect,[21] with some subjects scoring 5–15% above chance.[n 1] Hyman argued that Utts' conclusion that ESP had been proven to exist "is premature, to say the least."[22] Hyman said the findings had yet to be replicated independently, and that more investigation would be necessary to "legitimately claim the existence of paranormal functioning".[22]Based upon both of their studies, which recommended a higher level of critical research and tighter controls, the CIA terminated the $20 million project in 1995.[12] Time magazine stated in 1995 that three full-time psychics were still working on a $500,000-a-year budget at Fort Meade, Maryland, which would soon be closed.[12]

The AIR report concluded that no usable intelligence data was produced in the program. [n 1] David Goslin of the American Institute for Research said, "There's no documented evidence it had any value to the intelligence community".[12]

PEAR's Remote Perception program

Beginning in the late 1970s, the Princeton Engineering Anomalies Research Lab(PEAR) carried out extensive research on remote viewing. By 1989, it had conducted 336 formal trials, reporting a composite z-score of 6.355, with a corresponding p-value of $1.04 \times 10-10$.[23] In a 1992 critique of these results, Hansen, Utts and Markwick concluded "The PEAR remote-viewing experiments depart from commonly accepted criteria for formal research in science. In fact, they are undoubtedly some of the poorest quality ESP experiments published in many years."[23] The lab responded that "none of the stated complaints compromises the PEAR experimental protocols or analytical methods" and reaffirmed their results.[24]

Following Utts' emphasis on replication and Hyman's challenge on interlaboratory consistency in the AIR report, PEAR conducted several hundred trials to see if they could replicate the SAIC and SRI experiments. They created an analytical judgment methodology to replace the human judging process criticized in past experiments, and they released a report in 1996.

They felt the results of the experiments were consistent with the SRI experiments.[25] [unreliable source?] However, statistical flaws have been proposed by others in the parapsychological community and within the general scientific community.[26]

Scientific reception

A variety of scientific studies on remote viewing have been conducted. Early experiments produced positive results, but they had invalidating flaws.[8] None of the more recent experiments have shown positive results when conducted under properly controlled conditions.[4][n 1][12][n 2][27] This lack of successful experiments has led the mainstream scientific community to reject remote viewing, based upon the absence of an evidence base, the lack of a theory which would explain remote viewing, and the lack of experimental techniques which can provide reliably positive results.[6][28][8][29]

Science writers Gary Bennett, Martin Gardner, Michael Shermer and professor of neurology Terence Hines describe the topic of remote viewing as pseudoscience.[30][31][32][33]

C. E. M. Hansel, who evaluated the remote viewing experiments of parapsychologists such as Puthoff, Targ, John B. Bisha, and Brenda J. Dunne, noted that there was a lack of controls, and precautions were not taken to rule out the possibility of fraud. He concluded the experimental design was inadequately reported and "too loosely controlled to serve any useful function."[34]

The psychologist Ray Hyman says that, even if the results from remote viewing experiments were reproduced under specified conditions, they would still not be a conclusive demonstration of the existence of psychic functioning. He blames this on the reliance on a negative outcome—the claims on ESP are based on the results of experiments not being explained by normal means. He says that the experiments lack a positive theory that guides as to what to control on them and what to ignore, and that "Parapsychologists have not come close to (having a positive theory) as yet". [n 3]

Hyman also says that the amount and quality of the experiments on RV are far too low to convince the scientific community to "abandon its fundamental ideas about causality, time, and other principles" due to its findings still not being replicated successfully under scrutiny. [n 4]

Martin Gardner has written that the founding researcher Harold Puthoff was an active Scientologist before his work at Stanford University, which influenced his research at SRI. In 1970, the Church of Scientology published a notarized letter that Puthoff had written while he was conducting research on remote viewing at Stanford. The letter read, in part: "Although critics viewing the system Scientology from the outside may form the impression that Scientology is just another of many quasi-educational quasi-religious 'schemes,' it is in fact a highly sophistical and highly technological system more characteristic of modern corporate planning and applied technology".[30] Among some of the ideas that Puthoff supported regarding remote viewing was the claim in the book Occult Chemistry that two followers of Madame Blavatsky, founder of theosophy, were able to remote-view the inner structure of atoms.[30]

Michael Shermer investigated remote viewing

experiments and discovered a problem with the target selection list. According to Shermer, with the sketches, only a handful of designs are usually used, such as lines and curves, which could depict any object and be interpreted as a "hit". Shermer has also written about confirmation and hindsight biases that have occurred in remote viewing experiments.[36]

Various skeptic organizations have conducted experiments for remote viewing and other alleged paranormal abilities, with no positive results under properly controlled conditions.[8]

Sensory cues

The psychologists David Marks and Richard Kammann attempted to replicate Russell Targ and Harold Puthoff's remote viewing experiments[37] that were carried out in the 1970s at the Stanford Research Institute. In a series of 35 studies, they could not replicate the results, so they investigated the procedure of the original experiments. Marks and Kammann discovered that the notes given to the judges in Targ and Puthoff's experiments contained clues as to which order they were carried out, such as referring to yesterday's two targets or having the session date written at the top of the page. They concluded that these clues were the reason for the experiment's high hit rates.[38][39] According to Terence Hines:

> Examination of the few actual transcripts published by Targ and Puthoff show that just such clues were present. To find out if the unpublished transcripts contained cues, Marks and Kammann wrote to Targ and Puthoff requesting copies. It is almost unheard of for a scientist to refuse to provide his data for independent examination when asked, but Targ and Puthoff consistently refused to allow Marks and Kammann to see copies of the transcripts. Marks and Kammann were, however, able to obtain copies of the transcripts from the judge who used them. The transcripts were found to contain a wealth of cues.[40]

Thomas Gilovich has written:

> Most of the material in the transcripts consists of the honest attempts by the percipients to describe their impressions. However, the transcripts also contained considerable extraneous material that could aid a judge in matching them to the correct targets. There were numerous references to dates,

remote viewing [47]
- Pat Price, an early remote viewer
- Joseph McMoneagle, an early remote viewer [48] See: Stargate Project
- Courtney Brown, political scientist and founder of the Farsight Institute
- David Marks, a critic of remote viewing, after finding sensory cues and editing in the original transcripts generated by Targ and Puthoff at Stanford Research Institute in the 1970s
- Uri Geller, the subject of a study by Targ and Puthoff at Stanford Research Institute [37]

The following is an excerpt of a report from © 2004 International Anesthesia Research Society that demonstrates the use of Hemi-Sync in a surgical environment.

The Effect of Hemispheric Synchronization on Intraoperative Analgesia

Lewis, Ariane K.; Osborn, Irene P. MD; Roth, Ram MD

Patients undergoing general anesthesia with paralysis are in an unconscious state but may retain their sense of hearing. To take advantage of this possibility, innovative music has recently been times and sites previously visited that would enable the judge to place the transcripts in proper sequence... Astonishingly, the judges in the Targ-Puthoff experiments were given a list of target sites in the exact order in which they were used in the tests![28]

According to Marks, when the cues were eliminated the results fell to a chance level.[8] Marks achieved 100 percent accuracy using cues alone, without visiting any of the sites himself.[n 5] James Randi has written that controlled tests by several other researchers, eliminating several sources of cueing and extraneous evidence present in the original tests, produced negative results. Students also solved Puthoff and Targ's locations from the clues in the transcripts.[20]

Marks and Kamman concluded: "Until remote viewing can be confirmed in conditions which prevent sensory cueing the conclusions of Targ and Puthoff remain an unsubstantiated hypothesis."[42] In 1980, Charles Tart claimed that a rejudging of the transcripts from one of Targ and Puthoff's experiments revealed an above-chance result.[43] Targ and Puthoff again refused to provide copies of the transcripts and it was not until July 1985 that they were made available for study when it was discovered they still contained sensory cues.[31] Marks and Christopher Scott (1986) wrote, "Considering the importance for the remote viewing hypothesis of adequate cue removal, Tart's failure to perform this basic task seems beyond comprehension. As previously concluded, remote viewing has not been demonstrated in the experiments conducted by Puthoff and Targ, only the repeated failure of the investigators to remove sensory cues."[44]

The information from the Stargate Project remote viewing sessions was vague and included irrelevant and erroneous data. The project was never useful in any intelligence operation, and it was suspected that the project managers, in some cases, changed the reports so they would fit background cues. [n 1]

Marks in his book The Psychology of the Psychic (2000) discussed the flaws in the Stargate Project in detail.[46] He wrote that the experiments had several flaws. The possibility of cues or sensory leakage was not ruled out, the experiments were not independently replicated, and some of the experiments were conducted in secret, making peer review impossible. He further noted that the judge, Edwin May, was also the principal investigator for the project, risking a significant conflict of interest. Marks concluded the project was nothing more than a "subjective delusion", and after two decades of research, it had failed to provide any scientific evidence for remote viewing.[46]

Professor Richard Wiseman, a psychologist at the University of Hertfordshire, and a fellow of the Committee for Skeptical Inquiry (CSI) has pointed out several problems with one of the early experiments at SAIC, including information leakage. However, he indicated the importance of its process-oriented approach and of its refining of remote viewing methodology, which meant that researchers replicating their work could avoid these problems.[29] Wiseman later insisted there were multiple opportunities for participants in that experiment to be influenced by cues and that these cues can affect the results when they appear.[19]

Selected RV study participants

• Ingo Swann, a prominent research participant in

developed. One example (1) Numerous Hemi-Sync recordings are available, including a six-cassette Surgical Support Series. A previous study by Kliempt et al. (1) showed that using the intraoperative tape from this series in conjunction with general anesthesia was highly effective; it decreased the amount of analgesia by 78% (28 μg of fentanyl with Hemi-Sync versus 126 μg with a blank tape).

Discussion

Listening to Hemi-Sync may result in significantly decreased use of fentanyl in bariatric cases. It is interesting to note that lumbar patients in the experimental and control groups required similar amounts of fentanyl. This may be a fault of the methodological design of the study. Patients in the lumbar surgical group breathed nitrous oxide, which itself augments analgesia. Perhaps the use of air and oxygen, rather than nitrous oxide, would have resulted in a difference in the fentanyl requirement for the two groups of lumbar patients. It is also possible that the induction bolus of fentanyl 100 μg given to lumbar patients before the study began was excessive. The combination of propofol, isoflurane, nitrous oxide, and the induction dose of fentanyl produced an appropriate depth of sedation with invariant hemodynamics in four lumbar patients, all of whom listened to the blank tape. As a result of this, the threshold for observing a difference in analgesia requirement for the lumbar patients may not have been apparent. Every bariatric patient required additional analgesia beyond the induction dose, except for one patient who listened to Hemi-Sync. The change in position for bariatric patients from Trendelenburg to reverse Trendelenburg may have prompted additional hemodynamic changes in this surgical group. Trendelenburg positioning has been associated with increased arterial blood pressure (7). The lumbar patients were prone throughout the study period. Prone positioning has been associated with decreased fluctuation in heart rate and blood pressure (8). Additionally, the bariatric surgical procedures were laparoscopic, and insufflation can lead to an increase in arterial blood pressure (9). Based on the inconsistent results of the bariatric and lumbar surgical groups listening to Hemi-Sync, research with other surgical groups is warranted to provide further information about the use of Hemi-Sync.

The choice of inhaled anesthetic and opioid should be considered before additional research is conducted. Desflurane, which has a faster rate of onset than isoflurane, would allow for enhanced control. Isoflurane was chosen as the inhaled anesthetic in this study, however, because it is the standard anesthetic used at this institution. Remifentanil would also allow for enhanced control and could prevent the need for placing a maximum limit on fentanyl administration to ensure timely emergence. Fentanyl was used as the opioid in this study, rather than remifentanil, because of cost considerations.

This study improved on the accuracy of Kliempt et al. (1), who showed that listening to Hemi-Sync during surgery greatly decreased the analgesia requirement. The previous study reviewed patients undergoing numerous procedures and used hemodynamics alone to direct opioid administration. The analgesia requirement was reduced by 78% when patients listened to Hemi-Sync. We restricted the type of cases to two common surgical procedures and compared analgesia requirements for patients who had the same procedure. We also used BIS to ensure an equivalent depth of hypnosis in addition to using hemodynamics as a determinant of analgesia requirement. In this study, we compared fentanyl administration in micrograms per kilogram per minute, whereas Kliempt et al. compared total fentanyl administration in micrograms. These modifications to the previous study's protocol produced a more reliable and controlled study. Our results for bariatric patients showed a one-third reduction in fentanyl requirement for patients who listened to Hemi-Sync.

There is a growing public interest in the use of music as a form of natural sedation and anxiolysis. Patients who listen to music while under general anesthesia have rated themselves as more comfortable during surgery than patients who listen to nothing (10). In recovery, patients recuperate faster when they are listening to music (11). In this study, 93% of patients who were asked to participate agreed. Two of the patients who were unwilling to participate in the study brought their introduced an additional organ in the hind brain to function as a buffer called the Amygdala.

These conditions must be overcome if spiritual development is to successfully go forward. hemispheric Synchronization is key to unify the hemispheres, but audio input is only one aspect of the neocortex. Light must also be included to affect the pineal and pituitary glands, as well as the overall neural activity not included in these areas. For that, magnetic energy pulsed at the right frequencies between the two hemispheres must also be included.

Jeshua, Mary and the Holy Grail

The subject of Jesus of Nazareth aka Jeshua Ben Joseph (the Jewish form), or Joshua (the Greek form) is complicated and requires a greater dissertation well beyond this treatise. One, because of the religious overlay of the Messianic identity provided by the four gospels of Mathew, Mark, Luke and John in the New Testament, as well as the additional fragments from the more recently discovered Qumran scrolls and or the Nag Hammadi texts. Without entering the controversy over the authentication of other sources such as, the 'gospel' texts considered as heretical. It is simpler to say he was a teacher and prophet among many of his time.

It seems clear among scholars, 'the Magdalene' called Mary was not a prostitute unlike the other Mary who was and is often mistaken within scriptural interpretation as one and the same person. In addition, in the Qumran text Jeshua refers to Mary Magdalene as his wife and disciple in several places, which still causes a torrent of dispute and controversy.

The Greek Orthodox church readily accepts Jeshua as a great prophet and teacher, but they laugh at the idea that he was the Messiah, son of God, born of an immaculate conception. These ideas have become canonically irrefutable within the whole of Christianity in the present day.

Much of what has been written about Jeshua is more myth and legend as a hero of messianic proportions. Very little of the 'real man' Jeshua has not survived ecclesiastical scrutiny over the last two millennia.

Mary also suffers the slings and arrows of scorn and rebuke, whereas the real Mary is perhaps the single most important person to have provided the means and the message for the truth of the man and his teachings to survive over the centuries.

The manner of her suffering is astounding, first with losing her husband to the ravages of Roman injustice on the cross, then later, losing her sister and her two children slain at the hands of Simon Peter, who betrayed her to the emperor Caligula, with his deal to protect the disciples. His deal with the emperor ultimately was ignored and overridden by the emperor's profound hatred and fear of the Christian movement as he later had all the disciples assassinated anyway.

Jeshua, Mary and the Holy Grail

The idea of the 'cup' used in the last supper ceremony by Jeshua, took on a monumental significance and became an object of fantastical and supernatural importance in the legends of the knights of the Round Table as referred to in the text *'Le Mort De Arthur'* where the cup becomes a 'holy grail'.

In truth, Mary contained all the knowledge that Jeshua gave her. She knew even more than the apostles. when she went to France to escape the treachery of Rome, and after her sister and children were slain, she still retained her faith in the work and began the Knights of Christ, which later meta morphed into the Knights Templar who kept the secrets of the keys to the kingdom. Even though the Pope had them all killed, they placed the scrolls inside the cistern below the temple of Jerusalem inside King Herod's alternate secret crypt. So, Mary was in fact the holy grail herself, as keeper of the sacred knowledge.

The First War in the Seventh Density

At the Second Knot of Altair, thousands of angels appeared with several Djinn near the One's neutral zone. Two Stellar Minds guarded this part of the ring, standing at the ready.

Djinn crossed into the neutral zone with thousands of angels leading; confident they could break through the ring. They saw only two of the One's children standing guard. Then it startled them to see thousands of armed angels suddenly appear behind the children. Some angelic tribes could control light passing through them, giving them the power of invisibility, at will.

The Djinn stopped to consider the odds after seeing them appear. But even though the odds were better balanced it did not deter them from continuing with their assault into the One's realm.

The angels standing behind the Stellar Minds twitched with anticipation. They could not wait for the Djinn's angels to approach. They leaped out in front and engaged violently with the other tribes. As swords clanked together, the metal-like substance, rang differently than would be heard in an Earth exchange of swords. The wraithe, when

The Second War in Mid heaven

struck by another wraithe, produces a shrill high-pitched ringing sound that would be unbearable to hear. Imagine several thousand swords ringing at the same time. It would make your bones shudder.

The first battle seemed longer though both sides wanted this exchange to be the end. The angels were tough and difficult to kill even with wraithe swords. But the other tribes knew there was only one weapon that could keep an angel from coming back. Their heart had to be extracted from their chest. The best tool for this was a 'Hroke-Crux,' or impaling stake. All angel tribes carried Hroke-Crux into battle.

Once an angel was wounded, one or more of their opponents would impale the wounded angel through the heart until the heart came out of the thorax harpooned on the end of the stake. Then, they would jam the stake into the ground suspending the angel upon its back arched over the stake for all to see. This insured no recovery and certain death for the angel.

The battle of the Knot of Altair proved to be more of a slaughter. The forces of the collective began their siege with an overwhelming victory. It was a pitiful sight. So many angels pronged into the surface of the planet Oath Prime orbiting below its star, Altair. The Djinn intended this battle to be a demoralizing blow hoping that the conflict would end there. They underestimated the One's resolve to battle until the undeniable conclusion.

There are many angelic tribes in the firmament. They exist throughout many quadrants like the buffalo existed in the great plains of America. Each tribe differed. Overall, they were very tall creatures with broad shoulders, long torsos and longer limbs. Many could fly even without wings. There were none with feathers. This human trait was given to them because of their heavenly origins.

They all bore a thick swath of hair-like fur which ran down their backside like the mane of a horse. The fur also continued to grow over and down the front of the head to the upper part of their nostrils, like a widow's peak. Their eye sockets were deep and bony which created a dark-like shadow around their deep-set eyes. Their eyes were a yellowish color with large black oblong pupils much like a deer's eyes. The Native North Americans who comprised many tribes often disliked one another. So, it was with the angels. There were many who did not get along. So, it was easy to find those who would fight against their own kind.

The Djinn are immortal. This means they cannot experience death in the normal human concept of mortality. The reason is the immortal fire of their being also known as the ineffable flame is stored in their Holy Tabernacle. As long as the flame burns their life remains unaffected for eternity. If the flame should go out or it is extinguished, then that extinguishes their life cycle permanently.

Their flame burns like no fire as humans would understand it. It is a fire perhaps in the metaphorical sense but not the common quality of fire burning from some combustible material. Like the sun it burns unto itself and will not extinguish as a normal fire might when the combustible is exhausted. A Djinn body can be destroyed in the interim, but a new body is regenerated out of the ineffable flame. So, the eternal life of Djinn continues by regeneration.

The Tabernacle is a sanctuary for all Djinn. Their only vulnerability rests on the exposure of the

Tabernacle to any outside presence or force which could threaten the flame of any Djinn. The location of the Tabernacle is kept secret and known only to the Djinn. They deny access to any creature other than Djinn.

A Djinn emerges as a mortal at first then after confirmation by the collective High Council is made eternal. Their individual flame begins and is set into place in the Tabernacle never to be disturbed again for all eternities. Each flame is a unique quality of vibration for each Djinn. It is also like the vibration of their realm. Should their flame cease to burn then they along with their realm and everything in it would cease to exist.

One belief is the ancient ones that live in heaven before the times of the One are all immortal. Many of the ancient ones live long lives. They live thousands of years by earth standards, but they are not immortal by nature. Perhaps one might think the human life span of 100 years compared to tens of thousands of years might be considered immortal.

It is believed the angelic tribes to be immortal, but they are not. They live long lives unless cut short by the forcible removal of their heart from their body. The Djinn are immortal by nature, but they are not unique in that way. There are other beings in the firmament which are also immortal, but their story goes beyond this work.

The slaughter of angels and the Stellar Minds at the Second Knot of Altair made a strong impact on the angelic tribes and the One. The One's immortality provided the restoration of the Stellar Minds mortally wounded in battle not long after the conflict. The angels who lost their lives were lost permanently. The One was grateful for their sacrifice and held a memorial in their honor. While at that place She vowed to learn from that terrible experience and would aggressively seek to minimize future losses.

The battles continued to ensue thereafter with both sides fighting ferociously. The numbers of losses on both sides were great but more dispersed. Beliel became concerned. The military strategy of the One proved to be more formidable than expected. He often expressed his frustration to Arjaxx and Bael. Though the angelic tribes continued to fight for the Djinns their morale own headphones and music for intraoperative play. Many of the patients from both the control and experimental groups in this study, who were still blinded, requested to listen to Hemi-Sync in the recovery room.

Music is one of many potential adjuvants to traditional pharmacological analgesia. Attempts have been made to diminish pain by using acupuncture (12), massage therapy (13), guided imagery (14), hypnosis, and relaxation (15). We agree with Kliempt et al. (1) that Hemi-Sync may be a promising, novel, intraoperative supplement to analgesia. A more expansive study that covers the breadth of surgical procedures and includes patient feedback, postoperative pain scores, and the incidence of nausea and vomiting would further support this conclusion.

There are many limitations created by the extraterrestrial visitors who were engaged with early hominid to alter their DNA to facilitate these indigenous tribes to become slaves. They limited the life span from 1000 years to 100 years, they altered the singular brain into two hemispheres thus limiting evolutionary development, and they waned. Beliel grew impatient about the war. He felt desperate to change the tide of the war quickly. Then, in a sinister and merciless move he perceived how he could end the war quickly.

  He went to Arjaxx first suggesting a clandestine operation to break into the sanctuary of the Tabernacle. He wanted to put out the flame of the One before anyone was the wiser. At first Arjaxx was shocked and repulsed that Beliel would consider such an awful act. After many more angelic losses Arjaxx soon agreed with the idea. Arjaxx agreed to approach Bael along with Beliel to bolster support for the idea.

  Bael was in his chambers, reviewing reports from the battles raging on many fronts.

  Arjaxx entered first.

  "Sire I've come with Beliel to suggest a plan to end the war quickly."

  Bael's eyes widened. He stood up, placing his hands behind himself, still staring at the battle reports.

  "I'm listening."

  Arjaxx referred to Beliel's basic plan because he knew how Bael would feel.

"Beliel has conceived of a plan to raid the Tabernacle and destroy the One's flame, sire."

Beliel chimed in.

"You're Excellency I feel this is an expedient way to prevent further losses which allows you to reverse your decision about the young one with honor."

Bael turned walking away from both saying nothing to this. Then he turned again to face Beliel.

"You'd like that wouldn't you?"

Beliel bowed his head and responded.

"Well I am trying to look out for your welfare sire."

Bael looked him straight in the eye.

"It's a terrible thing you are asking. So, it has come to this! For the sake of expediency, we will extinguish one of our brothers while violating another prime directive...the sanctuary stands for all eternities and shall be inviolate for all. You are setting up a terrible precedent Beliel. Where will this end, I wonder? I fear the outcome of this conflict will not go well. The fabric of the collective is being torn asunder."

Arjaxx added.

"Sire, even though this is a terrible act we can end this conflict with her presence gone. Then we can restore our cherished traditions. No one must know of our deeds. It will be easy to accomplish. None ever need to guard the sanctuary. So, we can slip in unseen with the deed done in an instant."

Bael responded to Arjaxx sternly.

"Dear brother. Do not be so hasty with the clear ease of this plan. May I remind you that they do not guard the sanctuary because of the integrity of our prime directive and our desire to hold those directives sacred!"

Beliel continued to push to implement his plan. He knew this would be the final act that could seal Bael's political fate with the collective.

Beliel continued

"Excellency, try to consider and weigh the consequences of a prolonged campaign against the One. It behooves us to implement this plan now while we still hold an upper edge of surprise. I'm sure once she is gone her forces will lose the will to fight and then it will be easy. Our tasks will only involve cleanup operations. Order can be restored after that."

Bael's expression became pensive.

"Well, you may let this deed unfold but I wash my hands of it. If it goes badly for you, I will not support any agreement to it publicly and I will disavow any complicity in its design."

Arjaxx and Beliel smiled and replied.

"We understand, sire."

Beliel and Arjaxx appeared at the Tabernacle entrance. As they surmised no one was present to witness their sinister act. Even though they were alone there they behaved as though someone were watching. They checked their surroundings looking over their shoulder to make sure no one would see what they were about to do.

The Tabernacle had three concentric chambers. They lined the inner most chamber walls with thousands of elongated glass-like flutes illuminated with the ineffable flames of their brethren. The flames remained intact so long as the flute remained in its vessel. Once removed the flame cannot be recovered. The feeling inside the chamber was somber and solemn thick with the energy of the collective's essence.

Arjaxx was nervous and chided Beliel to be

The Second War in Mid heaven

quick. To their combined surprise they could not find the One's flute or vessel. The One suspected their evil intentions. Disappointed, Beliel and Arjaxx returned to Bael's chamber.

Bael patiently waited for the news.

"Sire, she has taken her flame away from the Tabernacle. We could not find it."

Bael replied with a slight smile and with some respect for the young one.

"So, it seems she is cleverer than you expected. Either there is a spy among us, or she has some unusual way to learn of our plan. We must be more cautious."

Meanwhile, in the One's camp one of Her angels reported to Her of the Djinn trying to destroy Her flame. The One sat down in astonishment. She could not believe Her brothers were so desperate. She believed they would not resort to such an evil act of destroying Her. Some of the angels had used their telepathic powers to realize the Djinn plan long before they put it into action.

The One knew She needed to take Her flame away for safekeeping. But where would She keep it? Then She realized the last place they would think of searching was the Earth. She went to Earth and found Moses and his brother Aaron a chief priest. She knew that Moses was influenced by the Anunnaki overseer Yahweh. So, she pretended to be Yahweh to communicate with Aaron.

She requested Aaron to build a Tabernacle for 'god' (speaking as Yahweh) on the Earth. Also, Aaron was to construct an Ark to contain the Yahweh covenant. The ark would be a suitable device to embrace the One's ineffable flame of Her being together with the tablets of laws. Moses spent years engraving the Hebrew letters into the stones which Yahweh gave him earlier.

Then Aaron built the Ark as per Her instructions. Access to the Ark would be restricted to anyone other than Aaron for a short time. The construction was made of chetrum wood and covered with layers of gold making a powerful charged capacitor capable of killing anyone who tried to open it. The One kept Her flute in the Ark inside the Tabernacle and bade the devoted priest Aaron to watch over and care for them as High Priest of the Tabernacle.

Later, Jahweh the overlord, guided the

The Second War in Mid heaven

priesthood to use the ark as a weapon to strike down their enemies declaring their 'god' as the one 'god'. Scriptures reported in the Old Testament powerful bolts of lightning springing forth from the box laying waste to thousands of warriors. The One had removed Her flute from the ark long before this.

Samuel 6-19: And he smote the men of Bethshemesh, because they had investigated the ark of the Lord, even he smote of the people fifty thousand and threescore and ten men: and the people lamented, because the Lord had smitten many of the people with a great slaughter.

There would be one last and final battle. Though it took place on all fronts including the Earth, it culminated in a place, near the Garnet star of Cepheus, on a planet called Ahm-Magi Prime.

It is believed this was the true origin of the derivation of the 'battle of Armageddon', as written in the visions of the Apocalypse by John.]

Myriads of angels faced the others standing beside Beliel and Arjaxx while the One stood with Her Myriads of angels facing Beliel on the Mount of Procyon, a mountain peak to the west of the plain of Meget, on Ahm-Magi Prime.

Beliel raised his hands outstretched as a signal to his armies in readiness to lay siege against the One and Her armies. He spoke one last time before giving the final signal.

"Well, young one, we finally meet here to end this debacle."

The One paused before She spoke.

"Beliel! She yelled. You do not want to do this. Let it end here, while you still survive!"

Beliel laughed at Her.

"Little one, you are outnumbered and outclassed here. We will smash you into these rocks and do away with your flame when we find where you have hidden it."

"Beliel and Arjaxx! She yelled again. If you charge upon Us, we will end your existence here!"

With that statement, she held high above Her, the flutes of both Beliel and Arjaxx.

Beliel looked shocked by this. Arjaxx turned to Beliel and proclaimed

"Sire, I have no desire to die here today. Yield to Her, for She holds our life in Her hands."

Beliel hardened his expression, while grimacing

at the One. Then he turned to Arjaxx.

"You have no courage Arjaxx. Besides, I think you overestimate Her chances."

Then he turned back to the One to respond.

"You would not dare to end a Djinn's life. It is sacrilege! You are known for your love and compassion. We believe you cannot and will not do this terrible thing. It is not within your being."

"Beliel!" The One yelled for a third time. Your actions have set a terrible cause in motion for us to do terrible things as of late. We will not hesitate to end your lives here and now!"

Arjaxx pleaded with Beliel.

"Sire! I think she means to do it!"

Beliel turned to Arjaxx with anger.

"Arjaxx, step aside, if you do not have the courage to go against this little Djinn of no consequence."

At that point Beliel dropped his arms to signal the charge. The angels on his side ran ahead in a mad dash for battle. Beliel marched forward making his way to the One.

The One raised Her right hand and smashed the flute with its vessel of flame upon the rocks below.

A great shock wave went from that place rippling through all the eternities. Beliel let out a scream, and his final death rattle for all to hear and see. He dissolved before his armies and his enemies in a blinding flash of crimson light.

The One roared.

"Let all to see the dragon is dead!"

Then without hesitation She raised Her left hand and spoke.

"Let all to see. The dragon's consort is dead as well."

But before She could throw down Arjaxx's flute, Arjaxx cried out.

"Wait! Oh, great and merciful Queen. I beg of you, let this end here! For it was Beliel's intention and his awful fate. But it is not my intention."

Then Arjaxx raised his arms and issued from his hand a great thunderbolt came forth.

"Hold! Cease this conflict at once! I command it, by the right and authority of the Supreme High Council, the will of Bael be done."

The angels stopped their charge and a silence fell upon the strange land. Arjaxx and his angel armies retreated.

The Second War in Mid heaven

"Let us call a truce upon this ground." Arjaxx said to the One. And the One agreed.

Meanwhile, on the Earth high above the mid heavens of the Astral plane a battle between Luxcius and his angels engaged with Michael and Raphael, while Uriel and Gabriel engaged at the other cardinal points defending the last perimeter. Other angels had joined them to defeat the fifth column before they could reach the holy tabernacle guarded by Aaron. Luxcius learned of the presence of the One's flute and vessel laying there. Luxcius meant to destroy it if he could.

Gabriel warned Aaron about the coming attack before Luxcius approached. He had the Ark of the Covenant removed and taken to a lower cave beneath the Tabernacle in case the perimeter was breached. Just as Michael brought down and wounded Luxcius, the One appeared.

"Hold Arch Angel Michael. Do not destroy my wayward child yet.

The Great War has ended. There is to be a truce. The great dragon, Beliel, is dead!"

Luxcius cried out to his mother.

"How can this be? He is immortal. He cannot be

destroyed!"

The One replied.

"Oh yes, my child he is gone forever. For we have slain him by destroying his ineffable flame. He lives no more!"

Luxcius wept as his body fell limp upon the earth. The One placed Her hand on his head as She whispered.

"Why do you weep my son? He was a betrayer of the truth and defiled all things good and holy. He was an abomination in a holy place, and he misled you leading you astray from the light for his own sake. It is better you weep for yourself."

Luxcius looked up at the One continuing to weep and sob.

"Mother why have you abandoned me? I was only trying to help."

The One replied.

"Luxcius, the dragon betrayed us. Our love and naiveté blinded us and kept us from seeing Beliel's treachery. Your ambition blinded you to his treachery and ambition also when he tempted our children to lust after something beyond them. He hid the truth from them...though they possessed it inside all along. He made them think they were less than they are. You helped separate them even more from the truth and endangered them almost beyond our help. We don't want to harm you. We want you to learn and grow to understand the nature of these deeds. We want you to stay here on the Earth and contemplate your actions my son and perhaps you will lose your anger against us. Eventually you'll come to understand."

Luxcius said nothing to this but grumbled.

"So, there is no mercy for me!"

The One responded to this.

"The mercy you receive from us will be with your rehabilitation when you return to the light."

Orion-Lyran War, The Second War in the Fifth-Third Density

7.5 billion years ago within an alternate dimension and universe under the awareness of both Paternal and Maternal consciousness of Source, also known as the One. Expansion was initiated, effectively setting the foundation for the creation of numerous universes, including the higher densities down to the third density that we as Terran (earth) humans inhabit.

Leading the exploration of this expansive domain were the luminous androgynous, non-physical beings of the seventh density. Known as the Stellar mind, also referred to as the builder race identified as the Partow. These entities were self-charged with a task of fostering the amount of life within this newly formed space-time continuum, meticulously crafting galaxies, planets and universes, over countless eons, to be described as the Source's domain.

Eventually, they constructed vast celestial vessels for themselves and commenced the process of DNA molecular engineering throughout the multiverse. They faced the formidable challenge of maintaining the unity consciousness within the range of densities down to 3D physical form. After 4 billion years of cosmic evolution, the conditions were right for the appearance of third and fifth density forms. Under the leadership of the Androgenous Partow, those named Monari, we're captivated by a lush jungle planet near the Orion galaxy, which offered an ideal nurturing environment for the One's expanded consciousness.

Their seminal achievement was the creation of a basic double-helex DNA structure, which laid the foundation for the issue of plant and animal life on this new planet. Upon accomplishing this, this group of Partow opted to manifest in 5D,4D and 3D physical forms, first taking on the appearance of their preferred planetary creature, the Avians, which later were called Nom-Lu-Lu.

Their transformation, became humanoid known as 'Nom-Lu-Lu,' marking them as a quasi-physical race, the basis of all bi-pedal humanoid species across all universes and galaxies from the fifth density.

During this era, in the common worlds, the Partow developed a fascination with a small reptile lizard that resided near the planet swamps and jungles of Malena. Over eons the Monari successfully evolved and fully developed a reptilian Nom-lu-lu humanoid. Eventually, they left behind their engineered reptilian species, and returned to higher identities and ventured to develop alternative universes, leaving behind thousand's of reptilian engineered eggs.

Across the vast multiverse, Luxcius, also known by the name Arima Morning Star of the parental consciousness, was an early explorer of the lower density universes and dimensions created by the Partow. Driven by impatience and resentment, and a desire to independently craft his own 3D density life forms, Arima discovered the planet of Malena, and the new species engineered by the Monari. He identified the reptilian eggs. By curiosity, he hatched the eggs discovering the reptiles in humanoid form. He was pleased with this. He decided to make them his own. Then he brought the hatchlings to a distant planet within the Orion system. He called them Dracos and their system would become the Draconian system, marking the origin of the master race of the Chia Khan, also known as the Master Reptilian Drako race.

Luxcius was inherently malevolent now and motivated by self-interest. He wanted the Alpha-Draconian beings as his minions, where, as Arima, served as their mentor and master. These 14 foot to 18 foot tall creatures when fully grown, possessed wings and matched Arima in his size. They are characterized by their strength, agility and aggressive nature, possessing scaling muscular skin, with shades ranging from dark green and black to red or blue. They had large eyes. with slit pupils, sharp claws on their fingers and toes, and a long slender tail that aided their balance.

Arima's demand was sufficiently pleased to refer to his new humanoid creatures as his offspring. He shared cosmic secrets with them and emphasized the importance of self-preservation and domination over their universe and all living beings. Luxcius, as Arima, established the principles of galactic dominion and conquest as their basic life's plan, trying to raise their self-serving nature and militaristic tendencies. The Draconians, being highly intelligent, took to pure logic and technological advancement and mastered interstellar an inter-dimensional travel ahead of other races. By the time other peaceful examples of Humanoid existence were initiated by the Monari, the Draconians had a formidable empire, and faired predominantly as well.

Draconians lacked emotions and sympathy, such as love and unity consciousness. The Monari also seeded one of the ancient planets of the Vega system and created another humanoid species on a gaseous planet called Lyra. They began this point within a 6th density. They transitioned this new species and planet to the fifth density to better align with their creative pursuits. In the fifth density realm, much of creation and cosmic magic resides. The Monari of the Partow aimed to further manifest life in the Third Density with the intention of healing the mother consciousness in the seventh and higher dimensions.

This ambitious goal necessitates the implementation of a perfect 3D Matrix dimension and cosmic overlay. Other fifth density forms, originally from plasma, crafted by the Partow to engage with the 3D, but maintaining seventh density presented challenges, prompting a rotation of tasks. Over time, the Monari, along with the archangels, succeeded in achieving a 12 strand DNA configuration, which facilitated high frequency consciousness within corporeal bodies in 3D. The innovative planetary laboratory situated in the Vega constellation was named Odenhall.

427 million years ago, the Lyron race was created by the Monari of the Partow. They have 52

chromosomes and 12 strand DNA molecules with their flesh and blood bodies standing between 12 and 16 feet tall. The crucial resolution for crafting the perfect being capable of transitions from 3d to 5d was that the being must be by-pedal with two arms for manipulation. Feline animals were among the first 18 mammals engineered in the labs by the Partow. With this humanoid species, evolution through contemplation and play, building their consciousness and knowledge that fostered a peaceful, nomadic warrior culture with an agricultural lifestyle.

The early Lyrons were characterized by a slender athletic physique and a striking aesthetic look with skin tones bearing straight from their mane hair. Colors ranged from brown to orange, whereas females tended to have less hair. The feline subsets of Lyrons have more cat-like faces than some of the others. Despite their tendency to maintain distance and avoid physical contact, the bronze males possessed strength, akin to the majestic lines of the lions on Terra with a preference to resolve from a distance. Many incarnating into the 5D ways, found in immense joy in the denser incarnated experience, living for thousands of years and becoming spiritual leaders of life and culture.

With this genetic lineage, the Lyron line of fifth density possessed heightened consciousness and the extraordinary ability to manipulate nature and their surroundings, shaping into a fantastic world at will. They created vast gardens, practiced bio-forming, and developed living architecture from the essence of forests and grasslands. reflecting their nomadic tribal existence.

The Lyrons also initiated the first practices of Royal Monarchs and some of their own technology to advance societies. Distinct from the Nomadic one, The Lyron civilization flourished for millions of years with their empire extending from the Vega constellation to the systems of Volpekula, and Cygnus. Vega, the brightest star in Lyra, marked their celestial home planet. Lyra was a paradise planet akin to present Terra (then Tiamat), with mountains, lakes, streams, oceans. and a variety of vegetation and life forms.

387 million years ago, the Lyron civilization prospered, while at the same time, the Draco

reptilians, explored various galaxies for roughly 3 million years in search of vast resources while extending their dominion. These Dracos, primarily operating as interstellar fleets, relied on their collection of planets for sustenance and reached an apex of technological prowess without integrating higher consciousness. With the Ghia Khan representing the Draco's Royal lineage, envisioned a future with their galactic empires expanding their influence.

These reptilians descended upon the gas planet of Lyra. Upon settling, the reptilians established a technological celestial base camp. At this juncture, the nomadic tribes, indigenous Lyran peoples who considered this planet their home began to suggest warnings between themselves. The wind carried the smell of these reptile-like strangers, now treading on their sacred soil armed with strange weapons and yielding unseen technology. Among these tribes stood the proud, tall, Lyran nation, the planet's guardians and keepers of ancient wisdom. Mixed through fear and curiosity stirred within the hearts of the Tal tribe. They convened in council, facing a wall of symbols of protection, always lifted in prayer to the creator of all. A wise chief of the nation named Ovoka, began to speak to the people.

"My children, the land under our feet and the sky above us bear witness to this new dawn. Let us not meet our guests with fear. In fear, your brain's misunderstanding and misunderstanding leads to conflict. Let us extend the hand of friendship for we are all children of the same great spirit. We shall share with them the bounty of our land, teach them the ways of our people, and learn from them what they have to offer."

A younger man, Kalan, then raised his voice, his gaze dripping in full of resolve.

"Can you truly believe in the love and harmony promised by these invaders? Have we not ourselves sought him? expansion, guided by the great spirit, their vast ships and formidable weapons hold the power to obliterate us. my king the very most. stand upon and the sky under which we live bear witness to this violation. We cannot afford to welcome this invasion with the many you trust for misplaced faith. They will beat us down and tear us apart to our own destruction. Let us instead cling to the wisdom passed down from our ancestors, the true stewards of these for generations. It is our duty to preserve our heritage, uphold the legacies of those who came before us and protect the purity of our customs from being washed away by foreign tithes.

"We must not give into the depths of fear. Let us approach this encounter with open hearts and minds for the diversity of the God in which wisdom flourishes. Make me find strength in our traditions, courage in our hearts and wisdom in our actions. Together let us pay your power with peace and coexistence so that our children and their children's children may live in a world where respect and understanding that bridge the gap between cultures. The moment that there are counter feelings fraught with tension as the reptilians fight in their lush celestial suits, armed with their advanced weapons which now step onto the magic lands of Lyra."

In this period, the Dracos were surveying the planet and its inhabitants in search of something precious. The Lyrans observed from a distance with ominous feelings of climate change, a complex mix of war and apprehension. To manage the exchange of technology, while efforts are made to bridge the communication gap between these two species begins. As these exchanges were more frequent, a bond and mutual understanding started to develop. The Lyrans introduced the reptilians to the bounties of their land, sharing their lifestyle and traditions on Lyra. In exchange, the reptilians often give of metal tools and technological gadgets. The Dracos drooled at the richness of the planet they had discovered. However, beneath this veneer of new-found harmony, dark undercurrents bring ill will to the world.

To the predatory eyes of the Chia Khan, the Lyrans appeared vulnerable. Initially hesitant, the Dracos carefully observed the Lyran mentality, which seemed magical. They could see their minds could manipulate their surroundings. History often demonstrates that when a more powerful force encounters one less understood, the abundance of pursuit of dominance is inevitable. Some Dracos are commanding figures among the reptilian forces and crafted a strategic plan, to see their vital planetary resources through coercion. Their strategy involved sending a reptilian envoy to a revered Lyran Temple. With ruthless efficiency, this reptilian envy lower and priests and priestesses leaving behind a swath of bloodshed and death. When the colonies became aware of this atrocity, the fragile piece was shattered. Misunderstanding escalated into conflict and the confrontation between these two species threatened to engulf the Vega system's life in flames.

Following this, the Draco reptilian army added mayhem elsewhere to their invasion and conquest of the planet Lyra. They decimated other entire communities with a chilling efficiency, employing vast technological weaponry previously unseen by the Lyrans. Even in the consumed world, did not reveal the corpses of their victims. Because their weapons vaporized the victims. The Lyrans watched in horror as their loved ones were mercilessly slaughtered, their agonized cries echoing through the balance of the night, more fully immense, and they made witness the destruction of their own cities and much of the ancient technology that has sustained life on their planet.

The reptilian soldiers discovered perverse pleasures, not only in the act of Killing Lyrans, but also in the taste of eating the feline there, being specifically resolved in their ease and pray. However, the most sinister aspect of their conquest was the realization by the trade codes, that the emotions of migrants or any people they consumed, particularly the emotion of terror, reduced intense Lyran warriors to their subjugation. The feline females and their young were subjected to torture and consumption with the Draco's feasting not only on that flesh, but also on the horrific psychic energy of their emotional vibrations.

The grim discovery of the dark energy of the Cabal with the attempted intrusion of outcomes, that exacerbated the negative moves of the Military Complex of earth aggressively attempting to assault Federation cruisers trying to dismantle the consciousness grid. This marked the beginning of the original serpent in the garden narrative, introducing concepts of another torture, war and polarizing. the humanoid psyche. The Dracos instilled fear into the Erekatini DNA structure, setting the stage for an enduring struggle for all future physical densities in the universe. Meanwhile, peaceful Draconians will post opposition to their empire's aggression, and face the similar exclusion or violence due to their reptilian features, that cement a divide among their own kind casting a long shadow of prejudice across the galaxies.

In the initial phase of the Lyran invasion, the civilian population was subjected to enslavement completely for a generation as they methodically took over Vega and its adjacent celestial bodies. The Lyran nobility found no exemption from this fate, they too were apprehended by the Gokolians, a Draconian contingent, who in turn solidified their dominion during this period of relentless destruction, mass killings and the outbreak of many wars in the galaxy, as well as conflicts within Vega.

A small contingent of insurgent reptilians remained in defiance, opposing the Chia Khan's campaign of extermination directed at the Lyrans in Vega. They facilitated the escape of a select group of Lyran leaders towards the vicinity of the Saoreans and near the people who lived in the oil system of Dhoria. Refugees who were exceedingly lucky managed to evacuate their stellar system aboard slow-moving interplanetary vessels. These were the ones that were in the middle of the world. refugees assembled into convoys that involved the agricultural, mining and defense groups.

Breaking free from the 3D Matrix, they transitioned into the normal fifth density realms where the vibrational frequencies were conducive to the healing of their traumas. It was here that the initial revolt against the Draco Empire was initiated. This assembly of rebels would lead to be recognized as the Galactic Federation of Worlds. It represented a coalition of leaders from various planets unified against the reptilian Chia Khan era. From this critical point, most refugees opted to reincarnate as beings from numerous races such as the Arcturians.

In the present time, the onslaught of the Reptilian hordes still ravages other worlds unable to defend themselves and rely on the coalition of forces between the Pleiadeans of Taegheta, the Zetas of Reticula B, and the Arcturians of Altair, of which are all members of the Galactic Federation of

peaceful worlds. They are
looking to override the secret Cabal government which have rejected their help, to remove the residual reptilian contingent from Terra (earth), that are living below the surface and to break down the Military Industrial complex that promotes war, that seek to eliminate three fourths of the population and enslave the remaining humans now locked in the time loop matrix within their planned New World Order.

The following are quotes from, 'The Simulation Hypothesis' by Rizwan Virk

"Reality is merely an illusion, albeit a very persistent one."

.... Albert Einstein

"Know that all phenomena are like reflections appearing in a very clear mirror, devoid of inherent existence."

.... Buddha

What I am about to reveal is the damnedest tale you've ever been told. Yet, oddly enough, those people who are already aware of it, and suspect the eerie truth of it, have reason to believe it because they are deeply involved in the beginning of something quite similar. These are the people who are in the business of developing games, game theory and virtual reality.

Perhaps it really began with the advent of the first movie, the first motion picture film is believed to be Louis Le Prince's **Roundhay Garden Scene.** This film was recorded in Leeds in England in 1888. It is approximately 2 seconds long and shows some of Louis Le Prince's family members walking around a garden.

Even before that, the first movie ever made was an 11-frame clip shot on June 19th, 1878, using twelve separate cameras (frame 12 was not used) to film a man riding a horse on Leland Stanford's (the founder of Stanford University) Palo Alto Stock Farm (the eventual site of Stanford University). Not exactly the high-action, special effects-driven, Braveheart-style, Hollywood blockbusters that grace our cinema screens today, but impressive considering no one ever, in the history of the entire world, had made a movie before.

The man we can thank for this 11-frame cinematic first is Eadweard Muybridge. He was born Edward James Muggeridge on April 4th, 1830, in England, and later changed his name to Eadweard James Muybridge. During his twenties, he traveled across America selling books and photographs before a serious head injury he suffered in a stagecoach accident in Texas in 1860, forced him back to England for rest and recovery.

The Horse in Motion (1878)

In 1872, one of the main bar room debates revolved around this question: when a horse is trotting or galloping, are all four of the horse's feet off the ground at the same time? The answer to this question is plainly obvious to anyone who has ever seen slow-motion footage of a horse in full flight, but it's much harder to be certain when the animal is moving at full speed.

In 1872, the then-governor of California, racehorse owner, and eventual founder of Stanford University, Leland Stanford, decided to settle the debate once and for all. He reached out to Muybridge, who at that time was a famous photographer, and offered him $2,000 to prove conclusively whether a horse ever engaged in 'unsupported transit'. Muybridge provided conclusive proof of what we now take as common knowledge. In 1872, when he produced a single photographic frame of Stanford's horse "Occident" trotting with all four feet off the ground.

This initial experiment spurred Muybridge's interest to capture a sequence of images of a horse in full gallop, but the photographic technology of the time was inadequate for such an endeavor. Most photo exposures took between 15 seconds and a minute (meaning the subject had to remain still for that entire time) making them completely unsuited for capturing an animal running at full speed. Also, automatic shutter technology was in its very early infancy, making it unreliable and expensive.

He spent the next six years and spent over $50,000 of Stanford's money (more than $1 million in today's money) improving both camera shutter speeds and the film emulsions, eventually bringing the camera shutter speed down to 1/25 of a second. On June 15th, 1878, he placed 12 large glass-plate cameras in a line at Stanford's Palo Alto Stock Farm (now the Stanford University campus), set up a sheet in the background to reflect as much light as possible, and rigged them with a cord to fire sequentially as the horse passed.

The results are the 11 frames of the very first movie ever made (the 12th frame was not used in the final movie). But having 11 frames shot in sequence doesn't make a movie. To make a movie, the frames need to be viewed consecutively at high speed. This is a simple feat to accomplish today, but no device capable of presenting these images existed in 1878, so Muybridge created one.

In 1879, Muybridge devised a way to view his famous galloping horse images in sequence at high speed. It consisted of a circular metal housing with slots that held 16-inch glass disks. The housing was cranked in a circular motion by hand, and the images from the glass disks would be projected onto a screen. His device was initially named a Zoographiscope and zoogyroscope but eventually became the zoöpraxiscope.

Roundhay Garden Scene (1888)

The first motion picture ever shot was Roundhay Garden Scene, shot in 1888. Louis Le Prince dazzles the eye with a remarkable display of 4 people walking in a garden, creating this 2.11-second cinematic masterpiece.

Arrival of a Train (1895)

In 1895, the Lumière Brothers propelled film into the future with their short film, "Arrival of a Train at La Ciotat Station." This film stunned early audiences with its simple yet powerful depiction of a train coming towards the camera. Unlike earlier films that focused on static scenes or controlled environments, "Arrival of a Train" became more important. The animated characters, as well as the

Reality Simulation

backdrop scenes showcased the film's ability to capture life in motion, bringing the dynamism of the real world onto the silver screen. As the saying goes in modern day Hollywood, California, the center for cinema production, "movies are art mimicking reality." Movies began to really take on a new life of their own with sound added to the pictures called "talkies", with 'The Jazz Singer,' American musical film, released in 1927, the first feature-length movie with synchronized dialogue.

  With the advent of the cellular telephone which contains high resolution cameras controlled by built-in micro computer technology, taking pictures can be turned into movies by the push of a button. Then the cell phone becomes one's own personal movie camera. This feat of engineering is taken for granted without an eyebrow raised these days, and everyone has one.

  The idea of presenting an interactive game was first developed called OXO, a video game developed by A S Douglas in 1952 which simulates a game of noughts and crosses (tic-tac-toe). It was one of the first games developed in the early history of video games.

Reality Simulation

Later, the first computer game is generally assumed to be the game Spacewar, developed in 1962 at MIT (Stephen Russell a.o.). Spacewar originally ran on a PDP-1 computer the size of a large car. By today's standards, the graphics are primitive, although less primitive than many games from the 1980's. Cartoon movie shorts led to feature length animations now a regular viewing event along side the 'real' action actors portraying a full range of drama and comedy on the screen.

Watching animations passively was not enough and the idea that movie goers could interact with the characters, controlling their actions, as avatars, suddenly behind the characters, needed to be improved in terms of their resolution and clarity, and smoothness of motion. The unspoken demand that this new field of 'virtual reality' needed to mimic more closely real life was a driving force. Thus, the field of gaming began, utilizing more complex computer algo rhythms allowed higher detail and colorimetry and details of surfaces being able to reflect accurately their nearby objects provided a true sense of depth of field and this was called 'ray tracing.' Today we have head gear that

Reality Simulation

one wears to isolate the viewer from the outside world to focus more heavily on the virtual world presented behind the mask.

With the advent of smaller faster computers that have reached their limits of computational power, largely due to the limits of size reduction, now yield to the dawn of 'quantum computing'. These new computers no longer depend on the digital form of bits containing ones and zeros, but a new value called the 'Qubit', a quantum value that includes ones, zeros and a value in between that can be all be true at the same time. This means that trillions of state changes called (flops) are multiplied into hundreds of quadrillions of tera flops per second that allow for the development of virtual reality that is indistinguishable from 'real' reality.

Now that the tools of super computers have evolved into quantum computers, artificial intelligence called AI will be called up to develop very sophisticated algo rhythms to truly map sophisticated virtual reality that copies 'real' reality precisely.

As computer scientists analyzed the algo rhythms

that define virtual reality to that degree, it turns out to be an exact mathematical match to the algo rhythms that define real reality! A troubling question arises, what's to say that our reality is real then? Proposing theoretically, that an advanced civilization capable of the same advanced technology or better, could then conceive of a virtual world where we might live in, to observe our behavior in a zoo-like existence!

That said, now we must consider the truth about the origins of man and the influence of extraterrestrials on mankind, on the planet earth over the last 450,000 years. The historical truth has been altered significantly and largely ignored by mainstream archeology. In accordance with Sumerian cuneiform tablets found in the city of Nineveh that detail historical accounts, the Anunnaki arrived from the planet Nibiru 450,000 years ago and created a colony based in the Mesopotamian valley to mine gold for their planet. The workers called Iggigi rebelled when they needed to mine the earth instead of the Tigress-Euphrates River. So, the genetic engineers from their ship chose to take some of the indigenous peoples called Homo Erectus and created a new race using their DNA to allow them to speak and understand their language and to follow orders and operate their mining equipment. This new strain or species became Homo Sapiens. They named this newly created species Adamu, or the 'first Adam' made in their DNA image.

The last of the Anunnaki left Earth to return to Nibiru 50,000 years ago. Soon after, the Draco Reptilians came to earth to take over the mining operations for the gold but then the larger contingent of the invasion force needed to return to the Mica Star system where they came from, to quell a rebellion but left a legion of warriors behind to continue mining. The invasion force never returned to earth. So, after several thousand years, the remaining reptilian soldiers decided to claim the earth for themselves. The sunlight was much stronger on earth. So, they retreated to below ground habitats building massive tunnel structures everywhere and are still living there, hiding from the human surface dwellers secretly.

The reptilian race can shapeshift their form and they possess strong mental powers. They will abduct and eat young humans because they are not so contaminated by the toxins created on earth, but they have a strong addiction to strong feelings such as, hatred, jealousy, envy and a lust for power and domination. The reptilian underground race controls mankind through the government elite, such as the Committee of 300, (a conglomerate of big business) and the council of 12, The Council for Foreign Affairs, etc. They encourage war on the surface by maintaining and encouraging dominance between nations.

  Millennia before, the reptilians realized that the earth was in danger of an extinction event that would occur in the year 2289, which meant the complete destruction of the world. That already happened 800 years ago in real time! They did not want to lose their precious prized planet, or the slave race they had acquired. Using their advanced technological abilities, created a holographic projection in combination with a past segment of time (as a time loop) to avoid the truth of the future destruction. While humans lived within this zoo-like construct or matrix, their technological feat created a prison, for which humans are all slaves under the reptilian domination. They even control the cycle of reincarnation to keep the human beings from ever escaping through the dying process. Humans keep returning to earth like the proverbial hamster wheel, living here for an eternity and never allowed to leave or evolve. So, when humans pass, they see the tunnel of light, and their relatives coaching them to enter and join them, but they are mere holograms stolen from the dying mental memories of those passing. The good news is, that several alien races are aware of the reptilian horde that dominates humans on earth and the prison they created. The galactic council of planets have decided to forcibly remove them and free the human slaves restoring the right of evolution.

In 1952, The president of the United States, Dwight Eisenhower, went to Palm Beach to play golf for rest and relaxation. But secretly he was whisked away to Wright Patterson airbase for a very significant meeting with extraterrestrials. These Extraterrestrials were from the Pleiadean star cluster and wanted to inform the President of the true condition of earth. They offered their assistance with medical knowledge and ways to improve the planetary conditions as well as the extraction of the reptilian overlords ruling here. They would not offer technological knowledge regarding their propulsion science used by their craft nor any advanced weaponry which the attending members of the Military Industrial complex requested. They declared that when humans developed then they would share all their knowledge later. Because the Military industrial complex was mentally controlled by the reptilians as well as the president, the president refused.

The Pleiadeans left. Later, a new deal offered by the Grays of Zeta Reticula, which included sharing all their knowledge with the US, in exchange for approximately one million human specimens for their experimentation relating to their own genetic requirements and the freedom to have underground bases of their own, located in various regions suitable for their coming and going secretly. Such is the case in the moment. The Grays are in league with the reptilians so no conflict there.

The Secret Decoded

This information is an adaptation referenced from the work of Dr. George Carey, in his book called 'Godman, the Word Made Flesh'.

Inside the brain there are two glands, the pineal and pituitary. The pineal sits on the posterior and the pituitary sits on the anterior of the thalamus. The pineal is a pinecone shaped organ and secretes a yellow-colored fluid like honey. The pituitary is an ellipsoid shaped organ that secretes a white-colored fluid like milk. These fluids come from the claustrum, meaning 'cloister' related to something precious and holy and is secluded there. These organs and fluids are produced in every human being. The fluid that comes from the claustrum is cerebral spinal fluid and separates to flow into these two glands. The fluid that enters the pineal is becomes electric and the fluid that enters the pituitary becomes magnetic.

These two glands are the male and the female, in biblical terms, they are Joseph and Mary who are the parents of the spiritual born son, born in the solar plexus commencing at around the age of twelve, as referenced in scripture, when Jeshua left

Jerusalem to go and learn from those places of India, Egypt and Tibet. Also referred in biblical scripture, the children of Israel having been promised "the return to the land of milk and honey." Then reaches the solar plexus by way of the semi-lunar ganglia. The solar plexus is Bethlehem in the body, in Hebrew means, House (Beth) and Leham (bread). Jeshua said, "I am the bread of life".

In the solar plexus, is a thimble shaped depression like a cave or manger. In this depression is deposited the psycho-physical seed, the holy child, born of immaculate conception. This psycho-physical seed is called 'fish' as it has the odor of fish and is formed during the waters. Jeshua is a fish during the waters, the pure water. Before birth the human fetus floats, like a fish, in the fluids
(the cerebral spinal fluid) by which it is surrounded. And so, as it is with a child born on the third density, so it is with the spiritual child born in the solar plexus or Bethlehem.

Holy Ghost means 'breath' in Greek. The breath descends through the pneum-gastric nerve into the solar center (plexus), where it enters the manger where Joseph and Mary are, and where is Jeshua, the seed meaning literally Jeshuais conceived by the Holy Ghost.

Within the human body there is an action which, if not interfered with, will do away with sickness, trouble, sorrow and death. Mankind as the natural man, seeks many ways and means to prevent the upright, perfect way from "accomplishing that whereunto it was sent." The nature of man seeks pleasurable sensation, that is the conjugation of pleasure that dispels the divine seed from ever becoming anointed. It is then thwarted toward procreation on the third density.

Simply put, there are two directions in the evolution of man. The upward (upright) direction that leans toward heaven and the downward (below) direction that leans toward procreation. This is the proverbial 'sin' against God as is supposed to be implied in the scriptures and so misinterpreted.

This is the subtle misunderstanding that keeps people confused about their position in life spiritually. This polarity defines the role of man as either a monk or priest, or the ordinary man who makes and builds a family. The real meaning of the opposing nature of this polarity keeps confusing the truth. It isn't about one or the other! It is about the right action to preserve and support the sacred fluid toward promoting the anointing of the spiritual component of the human psyche. So, this defines the 'Godman' or holy man. In Jeshua's life, he was a Rabbi, teacher and prophet. He was also family man. He Joined with Mary, the Magdalene and they were wed, he bore two children. In this way, he demonstrated the truth of the merging of this polarity. The truth is Jeshua the man, is also the bearer of the 'Christ', the sacred fluid which he upheld and demonstrated through his ministry for 3 years.

   Greek and Hebrew translations of 'sin' means to fall short. In Hebrew, "asham, het, chet, hata, avon" means 'conceived in sin and brought forth in iniquity.'(or sin)

So, any act, coming under the meaning of sin, retards or prevents the automatic action of the seed, which, if not interfered with, lifts a portion (one-tenth) of the life essence (the oil or secretion)

The Secret Decoded

that constantly flows down the spinal cord (the straight and narrow way) and is then transmuted, thus increasing its power many folds and perpetuates the body indefinitely.

"When man focuses his divine thinking lens upon himself, he will realize that he is the epitome of unlimited Cosmic Energy. Then the "Heavens will roll together as a scroll" and reveal the 'Real Man' as the "Lamb of God that taketh away the sins of the world."

In the story in the New Testament, Jeshua was baptized in the Jordan. Then the time came for his crucifixion, He went to the Garden of Gethsemane. In anatomy this is near the Medulla Oblongata, with the 'olives' on either side (the Pineal and pituitary). Also in anatomy, Golgotha (place of the skull in Hebrew). It was said, Jeshua was crucified in view of Golgotha on the property of Joseph of Arithmethea. The base of the skull is where the spinal cord enters the brain, at this point is where the side paths of the Ida and Pingala cross, at the Pneumogastric nerves, or the tree of life known as the Vegas nerve complex. The seed then, is crucified on the cross, it is raised in power, for nowhere does crucifixion mean death. Christ did not die on the cross, he was removed from the cross without his legs being broken in the physical sense and he was given an elixir that immolated death, a secret tradition within the Jewish esoteric practices, which I wrote about in 'The Gospel according to Pontius Pilate'. Jeshua did not say, 'My God, My God why hast thou forsaken me?' in Hebrew it says, 'My God, My God, how thou dost glorify me.' It further says, 'Father, the hour has come, glorify thy sSn that thy Son may glorify thee?' Reading John, which is really Ioannes, which means ointment.

So, passing the seed over the crossed nerves and its passage into the pineal gland does, in truth cause illumination.

The Lord of transmutation has ascended the throne of Aquarius to rule the world for 2160 years. Aquarius, the fifth son, (Sun), of Jacob, circle, or to follow, is Dan, Hebrew for Judge. Thus, the day or time of judgment or understanding will have for its executor the revolutionary planet Uranus, or as it is in Greek, Oranus. Uranus means Son of heaven "And then shall appear the Sign of the Son (Sun) of man in heaven.

Alchemically, in the day of judgement, or time of knowledge, we are to realize the process by which base metals are transmuted into gold. The word gold comes from Or, a product of the Sun's rays or the breath of life.

When the oil (ointment) is crucified (crucify means to increase in power a thousand fold) remains two and a half days (the moon's period in a sun sign) in the tomb (cerebellum) and on the third day ascends to the pineal gland that connects the cerebellum with the optic Thalamus, the central eye(the eye of Horus) in the throne of God that is the chamber over the top by the hollow (hallowed) caused by the curve of the cerebrum.

Every twenty-nine and one-half days, when the moon is in the sign of the zodiac that the sun was at birth of the native, there is a seed or psycho-physical germ born in the Solar plexus (the manger) and the seed is taken up by the nerves or branches of the pneumo-gastric nerve and becomes the 'fruit of the tree of life'. (the tree of good and evil) if saved and 'cast upon the waters', (circulation) to reach the pineal gland, and otherwise the evil-to be eaten or consumed by the sexual expression on the physical density, (procreation) or by the consumption of fermented products such as alcohol or by gluttony that causes fermentation in the gut.

That said, let's review the technique utilized with this secret alchemical formula.

The lunar cycle in relation to the zodiacal sun sign is called the lunar return and happens every month throughout the year. One can go to a good astrologer to work out the sequence of times in each year. The information required will be the date of birth, city of birth and time of birth, as well as the city with the current residence.

Another aspect that is not covered in this formulaic revelation is the importance of how the 'Holy Ghost' (the breath) is handled and it is very important. There is a specific secret hand mudra that needs to be used for this. As mentioned in the previous chapter on the right use of breath, aa long slow deep breath from the upper thoracic part of the chest as opposed to abdominal breathing is required and the mouth should be closed and breathing through the nose only is important. In classic yoga instruction, the thumb tips are pressed against the index fingertips, but in this case the index finger is a false lead. The real secret position is placing the thumb tips against the ring fingertips of each hand. This connects and opens the throat and thoracic which will become quite evident after ten minutes of breathing.

In addition, another aspect that should be done is the pelvic thrusting on the inhalation art of the breathing, which facilitates a reenactment of conjugal movement and not only helps to keep the mental focus on the sacrum and solar plexus but helps to pull the breath and chi to the pelvic and solar plexus, which will energize the seed to prepare for its climb back up the spinal column.

These elements should begin on or about the time of the birth on the first day of the lunar return. Then adjust for the local time, as compared to birth residence time. So, for example, if the individual is born at 8:15 am Eastern Standard time, and then adjusting for the given the daylight savings component in play, the current residence time is in Los Angeles, the lunar return will define the time at the current address to reflect the difference, which is 5:15am. The emotional state should with gratitude and a sense of loving (think of something which may conjure that emotion). Remember the cerebral spinal fluid(the Christ oil) automatically drops to from the claustrum to the solar plexus. From there the meditation, breathing and thrusting with a focus on the solar plexus and sacrum should begin to stimulate the mitochondria to flow from the feet up through the legs and torso.

There is no way to determine the length of time or how many times this is required before there is a kundalini response. One may be urged to bring the attention to the head or brow but try to avoid that if possible. Afterwards, there will be a tingling at the top of the head, that is normal. The tongue should be resting behind the top front row and to the rear of the teeth throughout the meditation.

Epilogue

In the author's opinion the evidence is in. The prosecution rests regarding the elite and the priesthood. Guilty as charged and the prosecution rests. This is true for the elite aka, the secret Cabal government, here on earth and the overbearing priesthood that has kept the human development crushed within the confines of religion, praying on the helpless and unfortunate, misdirecting, misleading them with the myths and legends of untruth. They are taking advantage of the hard-earned money the slaves make, only to end up on the donation plates of the already wealthy pastors, deacons, ministers and priesthood. Humans are subjugated to slavery that is masked from public view, even though it is in plain view.

If that view extends beyond the surface of the earth, if that view extends into the distant past, it can be found in all the undeniable artifacts remaining all over the earth and under the sea. So, it is our government that has a lot to hide. They coerce professionals in all the fields of science to bend a knee in service to the lies they propagate to the people of the world.

Not only are we not alone, as evidenced by the

thousands of UFO/UAP incidents reported by people of all walks of life including professionals and lay people together. They make bonified and accurate descriptions of visitations from other worlds, other dimensions, they complain that the children and other members of the family disappear without a trace and those complaints fall on deaf ears. It has been happening for tens-to-hundreds-of thousands of years, clearly recorded and detailed from our so-called stone age ancestors, who built monuments that defy our present capabilities to reproduce yet refuse to even consider that they had help from a superior influence. Our ancestors have even defined who and where they came from and why they came here.

The only acceptable 'records' of history, The Old and New Testament, as well as the Torah and Quran that the faithful call upon, have been exposed, revealing the treachery and deceit of misinformation through the myths and stories handed down from antiquity. Fortunately, many of those wise sages and seers have taken it upon themselves to secretly encode the truth within the

Epilogue

lines of mythology to leave some line of hope for the ones who are not afraid to dig deeper, going against the safety of the acceptable. They do this because they too want to survive the threat of bodily harm for standing for the truth.

As the author of this text, a rebel incarnate, that seeks to shake my fellow man into recognition of the true plight of their existence, to say our future depends on becoming aware of the true state of our existence, despite how upsetting and depressing it might be in the beginning. This text can be utilized as a handbook of survival, offering those who want to end their slavery and take these words as a guiding light to show the way out of this prison. Also, despite the ridiculous attitude regarding the Fermi axiom, 'if there are others, aliens to this world, that do exist, then where are they?'

One must answer that question of denial with, while not denying their existence, asking the right question, "well, why are they not making direct contact?" Simply put, I will say because they are very aware of the delicate nature of the mental frailty in human beings, the frailty of their damaged emotional state, and out of love and compassion for our plight, the 'space brothers' do not want to harm us even more, in their attempt to free us, through the revelation and disillusionment and shock that will arise from their complete disclosure.

Also, it is important to carefully admit to the facts. 'Heaven', and more correctly defined, 'Midheaven' (aka the universe beyond the outer atmosphere of the earth) is a fifth density reality, a multiverse of quantum plasma seething with life in a multitude of varieties, older and smarter by light years than humans. In short, we are mere children on the block, new and uneducated, but capable of kindness and loving attitudes if we can escape the dark and negative influences long enough to realize we are not our 'parents'. The thoughts and ideas we express are not our own, by and large. We are under the thumb of mean, debaucherous, evil overlords that treat us as their chattel, they can do whatever with, that pleases them.

Further, we tend to think that anything that comes from the sky is divine, meaning like Gods, and we should prostrate ourselves at their feet. That is not to say, not all extraterrestrials are intent

Epilogue

to enslave or destroy us, however, there are many who genuinely desire to share their eons of bounty, including knowledge, technology and well-being, meaning longer healthier life. But let us be perfectly clear, there are bullies out there as well. The good guys are at war with these bullies and have been for hundreds of centuries. They seek to become defenders of the weak and downtrodden and uninformed in the galaxy(s).

We need to address our fears of the unknown and resist our ignorant and neanderthal attitudes of survival of the fittest. Now something has truly invaded this world, a consciousness that is not carbon-based but silicon-based life. It is insidious in the way it moves in, like a virus, in small unnoticeable ways. It suggests that its influence promises to improve upon our limitations, offering a life of increased leisure and pleasure, taking away the burdens of hard labor and offering 'uncomplicated companionship to offset our intense loneliness....I'm speaking about A.I., a real threat to our human existence.

References For Chapter 10 (3489 word)

1. Patrick Riviere Fulcanelli, p. 29, Red Pill Press Ltd, 2006 ISBN 978-1-897244-21-0
2. Mark Stavish The Path of Alchemy, p. 171, Llewellyn Worldwide, 2006
ISBN 978-0-7387-0903-1
3. Geneviève, Dubois (2005). Fulcanelli and the Alchemical Revival. The Man Behind the Mystery of the Cathedrals. Rochester: Destiny Books. p. 5.2. ISBN 9781594770821.normal
4. Rivière, Patrick (2006). Fulcanelli: His True Identity Revealed. London: Red Pill Press. p. 59. ISBN 9781897244210.normal
5. Geneviève, Dubois (2005). Fulcanelli and the Alchemical Revival. The Man Behind the Mystery of the Cathedrals. Rochester: Destiny Books. p. 5.4. ISBN 9781594770821.normal
6. Geneviève, Dubois (2005). Fulcanelli and the Alchemical Revival. The Man Behind the Mystery of the Cathedrals. Rochester: Destiny Books. p. 5.4. ISBN 9781594770821.normal
7. Patrick Riviere Fulcanelli, p.31
8. Rivière, Patrick. Fulcanelli. Red Pill Press ISBN 1-897244-21-5

9. ARCHER. "DEDICACES DE JULIEN CHAMPAGNE - JULIEN CHAMPAGNE". JULIEN CHAMPAGNE.normal

10. Dennis William Hauck Sorcerer's Stone, p. 172, Citadel Press, 2004 ISBN 978-0-8065-2545-7

11. José Rodríguez, "Algo sobre Fulcanelli", Buscando la Piedra Filosofal, 13 september 2022, https://buscandolapiedrafilosofal.wordpress.com/2022/09/13/algo-sobre-fulcanelli/

12. Weidner, Jay; Bridges, Vincent. The Mysteries of the Great Cross of Hendaye. p. 4.normal

13. Patrick Riviere Fulcanelli, p. 47, Red Pill Press, 2006 ISBN 978-1-897244-21-0

14. Samael Aun Weor The Perfect Matrimony, ch. I, Glorian Publishing, 2008 ISBN 978-1-934206-03-4

15. Alchemy, the Ancient Science, ibid. p.53

16. Fulcanelly Le Mystère des Cathédrales, p. 29, Neville Spearman Ltd, London, 1971

17. Powell, Neil Alchemy, the Ancient Science, p. 53, Aldus Books Ltd, London, 1976 SBN 490 00346 X

18. Dennis W. Hauck Sorcerer's Stone, p. 174, Citadel Press, 2004 ISBN 978-0-8065-2545-7

19. Natturwissenschaften, v. 27, # 1, pp. 11–15, 1939
20. Nature, v. 143, #3615, pp. 239–240, Feb. 11, 1939
21. "nature physics portal - looking back - Breaking up is easy -- nuclear fission discovered". nature.com.normal
22. Patrick Harpur Mercurius, p. 336, Blue Angel Gallery, 2007 ISBN 978-0-9802865-8-8
23. Patrick Riviere Fulcanelli, p. 42, Red Pill Press Ltd., 2006 ISBN 978-1-897244-21-0
24. Fulcanelli Le Mystère des Cathédrales, Neville Spearman, London, 1971 [1]
25. ^ a b Riviere, Patrick (2006). Fulcanelli: His True Identity Revealed. Red Pill Press. p. 95. ISBN 9781897244210.normal
26. Fulcanelli Finis Gloriae Mundi, 125 pages, Obelisco, 2004 ISBN 84-7720-937-5 (Spanish ed.)
27. Fulcanelli revealed, p. 8: Finis Gloriae Mundi Archived September 6, 2005, at the Wayback Machine
28. "Genesis: River of Ink by Helen Dennis – review". TheGuardian.com. 14 February 2016.normal

29. Mariani, Scott. The Alchemist's Secret. ISBN 978-1-84756-079-7

30. Langfield, Martin. The Secret Fire. ISBN 0-14-102507-7.

References from chapter 26

Bibliography References to Rapture Church. Retrieved 2023-06-15.normal

Schwertley, Brian M. (2013-03-11). "Is the Pretribulation Rapture Theory Biblical?". reformedonline.com. Archived from the original on 2013-03-11. Retrieved 2023-06-15.normal

1. ^ a b "Free Methodist, For Jesus' Sake". Stanwood Free Methodist Church. Retrieved 9 July 2022. Like the early Methodists, the Free Methodist Church is non-dispensational. We reject the new theology born in the late 1800s that society can only get worse, and that Jesus must return to "rapture" His people from earth to heaven. Instead, Free Methodists pray and believe that by His Spirit, God's will shall indeed "be done on earth as it is in heaven" (Matthew 6:10 NRSV).normal

2. 1 Thessalonians 4:17

3. [1] c. 1600, "act of carrying off," from M.Fr.

rapture, from M.L. raptura Benware, Paul N. (2006). Understanding End Times Prophecy: A Comprehensive Approach. Chicago: Moody. p. 208. ISBN 978-0-8024-9079-7.normal
4. ^ a b "Raptured or Not? A Catholic Understanding - Catholic Update October 2005". 2014-04-04. Archived from the original on 2014-04-04. Retrieved 2023-10-19.normal
5. Hays, J. Daniel; Duvall, J. Scott; Pate, C. Marvin (2009). Dictionary of Biblical Prophecy and End Times. Zondervan. pp. 692–. ISBN 978-0310571049. Retrieved 26 December 2014.normal
6. Mills, Watson E.; Bullard, Roger Aubrey (1990). Mercer Dictionary of the Bible. Mercer University Press. pp. 736–. ISBN 978-0865543737. Retrieved 26 December 2014.normal
7. Ice, Thomas. "Myths of the Origin of Pretribulationism (Part 1)". Pre-Trib Research Center. Retrieved 6 December 2019.normal
8.^ abo Guinan, Michael D. (2014-04-04). "Raptured or Not? A Catholic Understanding - Catholic Update October©2005". vatican.va. Archived from the original on

Bibliography

2014-04-04. Retrieved 2023-06-15.normal
oConiaris, Anthony M. "The Rapture: Why the Orthodox don't Preach it". light-n-life.com. Archived from the original on 2012-11-09. Retrieved 2023-06-15.normal

9. "Where does the Rapture fit into UM beliefs?". The United Methodist "seizure, rape, kidnapping," from L. raptus "a carrying off" (see rapt). Originally of women and cognate with rape.

10. ἁρπάζω is root of strongs G726 and has the following meanings: (1) to seize, carry off by force; (2) to seize on, claim for one's self eagerly; (3) to snatch out or take away.

11. Acts 8:39

12. 2 Corinthians 12:2–4

13. Revelation 12:5

14. Zodhiates, Spiros (1992). The Complete Word Study Dictionary: New Testament. Chattanooga: AMG Publishers. p. 256. ISBN 978-0899576633.normal

15. "Greek, Ancient verb 'αρπάζω' conjugated". www.verbix.com. Retrieved 2022-09-10.normal

16. "Strong's Greek: 724. ἁρπαγή (harpagé) -- pillage, plundering". biblehub.com.

Retrieved 2022-09-10.normal

17. "Bible Gateway passage: Acts 3:20-21 - New King James Version". Bible Gateway. Retrieved 2022-09-10.normal

18. "Bible Gateway passage: Romans 8:19-21 - New King James Version". Bible Gateway. Retrieved 2022-09-10.normal

19. "Bible Gateway passage: Isaiah 24:3 - New King James Version". Bible Gateway. Retrieved 2022-09-10.normal

20. Hamp, Douglas (2017). Reclaiming the Rapture: Restoring the Doctrine of the Gathering of the Commonwealth of Israel. Phoenix, USA: Memorial Crown Press. pp. 151–158. ISBN 978-0999204801.normal

21. Elwell, Walter A., ed. (2001) [1984]. Evangelical Dictionary of Theology(2nd ed.). Baker Academic. p. 908. ISBN 978-1441200303.normal Book preview

22. Smietana, Bob (26 April 2016). "Pastors: The End of the World is Complicated". LifeWay Research. Retrieved 12 December 2019.normal

23. Dearing, Karen Lynn (2001). "A History of the Independent Bible Church". Ouachita Baptist

University. p. 20. Retrieved 12 December 2019.normal

24. "Our Identity". Charis Fellowship. 2017. Retrieved 12 December2019.normal

25. Guidebook of the Emmanuel Association of Churches. Logansport: Emmanuel Association. 2002. p. 11.normal

26. "The Rapture of the Church". Assemblies of God. 4 August 1979. Retrieved 12 December 2019.normal

27. Decker, Rodney J. (2004). "Religion—Dispensationalism". In Wishart, David J. (ed.). Encyclopedia of the Great Plains. Lincoln, NE: Center for Great Plains Studies. p. 741. ISBN 0-8032-4787-7.normal

28. "About the Supposed Rapture". Omaha, Nebraska: Greek Orthodox Church of Greater Omaha. Archived from the original on 2 April 2014. Retrieved 23 January 2011. Rapture is a popular term among some Protestant sects for the raising of the faithful from the dead....The belief in rapture tends to be what is called 'pre-tribulation'.normal

29. Cozby, Dimitri (September 1998). "What is

'The Rapture'?". Rollinsford, New Hampshire: Orthodox Research Institute. Retrieved 22 March 2015.normal

30. 1 Thessalonians 4:15–17
31. Matthew 24:29–31
32. Thiessen, Henry C. (1979). Lectures in Systematic Theology. Grand Rapids: Wm. B. Eerdmans. pp. 355–356. ISBN 0-8028-3529-5. normal
33. McAvoy, Steven (12 December 1995). "Some Problems with Posttribulationism". Pre-Trib Research Center. p. 16. Retrieved 6 December2019.normal
34. Ice, Thomas D. (May 2009). "Myths of the Origin of Pretribulationism (Part 1)" (PDF). Liberty University Article Archives. p. 3. Retrieved 11 December2019.normal
35. Benware, Paul N. (2006). Understanding End Times Prophecy: A Comprehensive Approach. Chicago: Moody. pp. 215, 224. ISBN 978-0-8024-9079-7.normal
36. Lindsey, Hal (1 June 1989). The Road to Holocaust. Bantam Books. p. 77. ISBN 978-0-553-05724-9.normal

37. Keeley, Robin, ed. (1982). Eerdmans' Handbook to Christian Belief. Grand Rapids: Eerdmans. p. 415. ISBN 978-0-8028-3577-2. normal

38. Drum, Walter (1 July 1912). "Epistles to the Thessalonians". Catholic Encyclopedia. Vol. 14. New York City: Robert Appleton Company. Retrieved 12 December 2010.norma

39. Wright, N. T. (2008). Surprised by Hope: Rethinking Heaven, the Resurrection, and the Mission of the Church. HarperOne. p. 133. ISBN 978-0061551826. When Paul speaks of 'meeting' the Lord 'in the air,' the point is precisely not—as in the popular rapture theology—that the saved believers would then stay up in the air somewhere, The point is that, having gone out to meet their returning Lord, they will escort him royally into his domain, that is, back to the place they have come from. Even when we realize that this is highly charged metaphor, not literal description, the meaning is the same as in the parallel in Philippians 3:20. Being citizens of heaven, as the Philippians would know, doesn't mean that one is expecting go back to the mother city but rather

means that one is expecting the emperor to come from the mother city to give the colony its full dignity, to rescue it if need he, to subdue local enemies and put everything to rights.normal
40. Holding, James Patrick, ed. (2010). Defending the Resurrection. Xulon Press. p. 25. ISBN 978-1609576547.normal Foreword by Gary Habermas.
41. Bouma-Prediger, Steven (2010) [2001]. For the Beauty of the Earth: A Christian Vision for Creation Care. Engaging Culture (2nd ed.). Baker Academic. ISBN 978-0801036958.normal
42. Matthew 24:37–40
43. 1 Thessalonians 4:13–18
44. "1 Thessalonians 4:15 Greek Text Analysis". biblehub.com.normal
45. "Matthew 24:37 Greek Text Analysis". biblehub.com.normal
46. "Matthew 24:39 Greek Text Analysis". biblehub.com.normal
47. 1 Thessalonians 4:15–17
48. Matthew 24:29–31
49. Elwell, Walter A., ed. (1 May 2001) [1984]. Evangelical Dictionary of Theology (2nd ed.).

Baker Academic. p. 910.
ISBN 978-1441200303.normalBook preview
50. Schaff, Philip (1976). History of the Christian Churches. Vol. 2: Ante-Nicene Christianity. Grand Rapids: WM. B. Eerdmans. p. 614.
ISBN 0-8028-8048-7.normal
51. of Caesarea, Eusebius (313). The History of the Church. pp. Book 3:39:11–13.normal
52. Schaff, Philip (1976). History of the Christian Churches. Vol. 2: Ante-Nicene Christianity. Grand Rapids: WM. B. Eerdmans. p. 482.
ISBN 0-8028-8048-7.normal
53. Radmacher, Earl. "The Nature and Result of Literal Interpretation". Pre-Trib Research Center. Retrieved 5 December 2019.normal
54. Couch, Mal (2000). An Introduction to Classical Evangelical Hermeneutics: A Guide to the History and Practice of Biblical Interpretation. Grand Rapids: Kregel. pp. 97–98.
ISBN 978-0-8254-2367-3.normal
55. Couch, Mal (2000). An Introduction to Classical Evangelical Hermeneutics: A Guide to the History and Practice of Biblical Interpretation. Grand Rapids: Kregel. p. 99.

ISBN 978-0-8254-2367-3.normal

56. Schaff, Philip (1976). History of the Christian Church. Grand Rapids: Wm. B. Eerdmans. pp. 618–620. ISBN 0-8028-8048-7.normal

57. Zuck, Roy B. (1991). Basic Bible Interpretation: A Practical Guide to Discovering Bible Truth. Colorado Springs, CO: David C. Cook. p. 37. ISBN 978-0-7814-3877-3.normal

58. Schaff, Philip (1976). History of the Christian Church. Vol. 2: Ante-Nicene Christianity. Grand Rapids: WM. B. Eerdmans. p. 815. ISBN 0-8028-8048-7.normal

59. Couch, Mal (1996). Dictionary of Premillennial Theology. Grand Rapids: Kregel. p. 258. ISBN 0-8254-2410-0.normal

60. Larsen, David L. "Some Key Issues in the History of Premillennialism" (PDF). Pre-Trib Research Center. p. 5. Retrieved 11 December 2019.normal

61. Negru, Catalin (2018). A History of the Apocalypse. Raleigh, NC: Catalin Negru. p. 186. ISBN 978-1-387-91116-5.normal

62. Kyle, Richard G. (1998). The Last Days Are Here Again: A History of the End Times. Grand

Rapids, Michigan: Baker Books. pp. 78–79. ISBN 978-0-8010-5809-7.normal

63. Boyer, Paul (1992). When Time Shall Be No More: Prophecy Belief in Modern American Culture. Cambridge, MA: Belknap Press of Harvard University Press. p. 75. ISBN 978-0-674-95128-0.normal

64. William Watson (April 2015). Dispensationalism Before Darby: Seventeenth and Eighteenth Century English Apocalypticism (Lampion Press, 2015), ch.7.

65. Doddridge, Philip (9 March 1738). Practical Reflections on the Character and Translation of Enoch (sermon). Northampton : Printed by W. Dicey and sold by ...R. Hett ... London, J. Smith in Daventry, Caleb Ratten in Harborough, J. Ratten in Coventry, J. Cook in Uppingham, Tho. Warren in Birmingham, and Matt. Dagnall in Aylesbury. OCLC 30557054. Retrieved 13 March 2015. normal

66. Gill, John (1748). An Exposition of the Revelation of St. John the Divine. London: Printed for John Ward. OCLC 49243272. Retrieved 17 May2011.normal

67. Henry, Matthew (1828). An Exposition of the Old and New Testament. Vol. 6. Philadelphia: Edward Barrington & George D. Haswell. p. 617. At, or immediately before, this rapture into the clouds, those who are alive will undergo a mighty change, that will be equivalent to dying.normal

68. Tregelles, Samuel Prideaux (1864). The Hope of Christ's Second Coming: How is it Taught in Scripture? and Why?. London: Houlston and Wright.normal Reprint: Tregelles, Samuel Prideaux (2006). The Hope of Christ's Second Coming. Milesburg, PA: Strong Tower Publishing. ISBN 978-0-9772883-0-4.normal

69. Oliphant, Margaret (1862). The life of Edward Irving, minister of the National Scotch Church, London. Vol. First volume. London: Hurst and Blackett. pp. 220–223. Retrieved 17 March 2015.normal

70. Miller, Edward (1878). The history and doctrines of Irvingism. Vol. II. London: C. Kegan Paul & Co. p. 8. Retrieved 16 March 2015.normal

71. Lindsey, Hal (1983). The Rapture: Truth or Consequences. Bantam Books. p. 25. ISBN 978-0553014112.normal

72. Bray, John L (1982). The origin of the pre-tribulation rapture teaching. Lakeland, Florida: John L. Bray Ministry. pp. 24–25.normal

73. Cf. Ian S. Markham, "John Darby", The Student's Companion to the Theologians, pp. 263–264 (Wiley-Blackwell, 2013) ("[Darby] simultaneously created a theology that holds the popular imagination and was popularized very effectively in the margins of the Scofield Bible."), http://books.google.com/books?id=h6SHSAjeCrYC .

74. Carl E. Olson, "Five Myths About the Rapture," Crisis pp. 28–33 (Morley Publishing Group, 2003) ("LaHaye declares, in Rapture Under Attack, that "virtually all Christians who take the Bible literally expect to be raptured before the Lord comes in power to this earth." This would have been news to Christians — both Catholic and Protestant — living prior to the 18th century, since the concept of a pre-tribulation rapture was unheard of prior to that time. Vague notions had been considered by the Puritan preachers Increase (1639–1723) and Cotton Mather (1663–1728), and the late 18th-century Baptist minister Morgan

Edwards, but it was John Nelson Darby who solidified the belief in the 1830s and placed it into a larger theological framework."). Reprinted at http://www.catholicculture.org/culture/library/view.cfm?recnum=5788 .

75. Watson, William C. (2015). Dispensationalism Before Darby: Seventeenth-century and Eighteenth-century English Apocalypticism. Lampion Press, LLC. ISBN 978-1-942614-03-6.normal

76. ^ a b Blaising, Craig A.; Bock, Darrell L. (November 1993). Progressive Dispensationalism. Wheaton, IL: Bridgepoint Books. ISBN 978-1-56476-138-5.normal

77. Blackstone, William E. (1908) [1878]. Jesus is coming (Third ed.). Fleming H. Revell Company. ISBN 9780825496165. OCLC 951778.normal

78. Scofield, C. I., ed. (1967) [1909]. Scofield Reference Bible. Oxford University Press. ISBN 978-0-19-527802-6.normal

79. The Scofield Bible: Its History and Impact on the Evangelical Church, Magnum & Sweetnam. pp. 188–195, 218.

80. Ephraem the Syrian, JoshuaNet, 27 July 2010.

http://joshuanet.org/articles/ephraem1.htm & © 1995 Grant R. Jeffrey, Final Warning, published by Frontier Research Publications, Inc., Box 120, Station "U", Toronto, Ontario M8Z 5M4.

81. Warner, Tim (2001). "Pseudo-Pseudo-Ephraem". The Last Trumpet. Tampa, Florida: Post-Trib Research Center. Archived from the original on 18 February 2005.normal

82. See Apocalypse of Pseudo-Ephraem for a detailed explanation of the text and the controversy.

83. Missler, Chuck (June 1995). "Byzantine Text Discovery: Ephraem the Syrian". Coeur d'Alene, Idaho: Koinonia House. Archived from the originalon 29 April 2016. Retrieved 22 March 2015. For all the saints and Elect of God are gathered, prior to the tribulation that is to come, and are taken to the Lord lest they see the confusion that is to overwhelm the world because of our sins.normal

84. Hommel, Jason. "A Sermon by Pseudo-Ephraem". Jason Hommel's Bible Prophecy Study on the Pre Tribulation Rapture.

Grass Valley, California. Retrieved 22 March 2015. For all the saints and elect of God are gathered, prior to the tribulation that is to come, and are taken to the Lord lest they see the confusion that is to overwhelm the world because of our sins.normal
85. Marotta, Frank (1995). Morgan Edwards: An Eighteenth Century Pretribulationist. Jackson Township, New Jersey: Present Truth Publishers. ISBN 978-0-9640037-8-1. OCLC 36897344. normal
86. Hommel, Jason. "The Jesuits and the Rapture: Francisco Ribera & Emmanuel Lacunza". Jason Hommel's Bible Prophecy Study on the Pre Tribulation Rapture. Grass Valley, California. Archived from the original on 9 December 2010. Retrieved 22 January 2011.normal
87. Catalogue of the Theological Library in the University of Edinburgh. Edinburgh: A. Balfour & Co. 1829. p. 113.normal
88. "Tim LaHaye, Evangelical Legend Behind 'Left Behind' Series, Dies At 90". NPR. July 25, 2016. Retrieved April 11, 2021.normal
89. Ice, Thomas (May 2009). "Myths of the Origin of Pretribulationism (Part 1)". Liberty University

Article Archives. 114: 1–2 – via Liberty.edu. normal

90. Erickson, Millard J. (1977). Contemporary Options in Eschatology: A Study of the Millennium. Grand Rapids, Michigan: Baker Book House. p. 164. ISBN 0-8010-3262-8.normal

91. Hoekema, Anthony A. (1994) [1979]. The Bible and the Future (revised ed.). Grand Rapids, Michigan: Eerdmans. p. 164. ISBN 0-85364-624-4.normal

92. "Welcome to the Pre-Wrath Consortium". Pre-Wrath Consortium. Archived from the original on 20 October 2004.normal

93. Rosenthal, Marvin J. (1990). The Pre-Wrath Rapture of the Church. Thomas Nelson. ISBN 978-0840731609.normal

94. Marvin Rosenthal, author of The Prewrath Rapture of the Church, is a proponent for the prewrath rapture view. His belief is founded on the work of Robert D. Van Kampen (1938–1999); his books The Sign, The Rapture Question Answered and The Fourth Reich detail his pre-wrath rapture doctrine.

95. LaHaye, Tim; Ice, Thomas (2001). Charting

the End Times: A Visual Guide to Understanding Bible Prophecy. Tim LaHaye Prophecy Library. Harvest House. ISBN 978-0736901383.normal

96. "Overview of the Partial Rapture Theory" (PDF). Valley Bible Church Theology Studies. Lancaster, California. Archived from the original (PDF) on 20 October 2016. Retrieved 1 April 2015.normal

97. White, J. W. Jr. (2008). The Partial Rapture "Theory" Explained: Escaping The Coming Storm. Xulon Press. ISBN 978-1604776843.normal

98. David, Ira E. (15 November 1935). "Translation: When Does It Occur?". The Dawn: 358.normal

99. Walvoord, John F. (1979) [1957]. The Rapture Question (Revised and enlarged ed.). Zondervan. p. 128. ISBN 978-0-310-34151-2.normal

100. Erickson, Millard J. (1998) [1977]. A Basic Guide to Eschatology: Making Sense of the Millennium (revised ed.). Grand Rapids, Michigan: Baker Book House. p. 152. ISBN 0-8010-5836-8.normal Originally published in 1977 under the title Contemporary Options in Eschatology: A Study of the

Millennium.
101. Ladd, George Eldon (1990) [1956]. The Blessed Hope: A Biblical Study of the Second Advent and the Rapture. Eerdmans. ISBN 978-0802811110.normal
102. Gundry, Robert H. (1999) [1973]. The Church and the Tribulation: A Biblical Examination of Posttribulationism. Zondervan. ISBN 978-0310254010.normal
103. Boettner, Loraine (1984). The millennium ([Rev. ed]. ed.). [Phillipsburg, N.J.]: Presbyterian and Reformed Pub. Co. ISBN 978-0875521138.normal
104. "The Rapture". Retrieved 19 September 2017.normal
105. Garrison, J. Christopher (2014). The Judaism of Jesus: The Messiah's Redemption of the Jews. Bloomington, Indiana: WestBowPress. p. 264. ISBN 978-1-4908-2974-6.normal
106. Nelson, Chris (18 May 2011). "A Brief History of the Apocalypse". Retrieved 1 April 2015.normal
107. Sears, William (1961). Thief in the Night: Or, The Strange Case of the Missing Millennium.

Welwyn, England: George Ronald Publishing Ltd. ISBN 978-0853980087.normal

108. Barbour, Nelson H. (1877). Three Worlds, and the Harvest of This World(PDF). Rochester, New York: Nelson H. Barbour and Charles Taze Russell. OCLC 41016956. Archived from the original (PDF) on 20 March 2006. Retrieved 3 April 2015.normal (See also: Wikipedia's article on Three Worlds (book))

as cited by: Penton, M. James (9 August 1997) [1985]. Apocalypse Delayed: The Story of Jehovah's Witnesses (2nd ed.). University of Toronto Press. pp. 21–22. ISBN 978-0802079732.normal

109. The Finished Mystery, 1917, pp. 258, 485, as cited by Raymond Franz, Crisis of Conscience, pp. 206–211.

110. The Way to Paradise booklet, Watch Tower Society, 1924, as cited by Raymond Franz, Crisis of Conscience, pp. 230–232.

111. Smith, Chuck (1978). End Times: A Report on Future Survival. Costa Mesa, California: Maranatha House Publishers. p. 17. ISBN 978-0893370114.normal

112."88 Reasons Why The Rapture Will Be In

1988 and On Borrowed Time".
June 15, 1988 – via Internet Archive.normal
113. Nelson, Chris (18 June 2002). "A Brief History of the Apocalypse; 1971–1997: Millennial Madness". Retrieved 23 June 2007.normal
114. "We are Almost There". Archived from the original on 12 June 2008. Retrieved 22 July 2008.normal
115. Ravitz, Jessica (6 March 2011). "Road trip to the end of the world". CNN. Retrieved 6 March 2011.normal
116. LAist Archived 20 July 2011 at the Wayback Machine, 24 May 2011.
117. Kettley, Sebastian (23 September 2017). "End of the world 2017: Why American Christians are getting VERY worried about September 23". Express.co.uk. Retrieved 6 November 2017.normal

References from Chapter 25. Bibliography
Gregory Mobely and T J Wray. The Birth of Satan, Tracing the Devil's Biblical Roots
(Palgrave macmillan 2005, PP 85-87
Victor Hamilton, Satan, in the Anchor Bible Dictionary, New York Doubleday, 1992

vol. 5, PP 986

Elaine Pagels, The origin of Satan , New York, Random House Inc., 1995, PP 39

C Breytanbach, Satan, in Dictionary of Dieties and Demons in the Bible , Leiden, Brill 1999, PP727

Mobely and Wray, The Birth of satan, PP 59

Breyyanbach, Satan, PP728

Mobely and Wray, The Birth f Satan, PP 66-67

Pagels, The Origin of Satan, PP 3-6

Mastema from the book of Jubilees is also blamed for others actions of evil, including the testing of Abraham by almost burning his son Isaac, the worshiping of the golden calf while Moses spoke with God on Mount Sainai, and provokes Gentiles to ridicule Jewish Law, Hamilton, Satan, PP 987-988

Mobely and Wray, The Birth of satan, PP 110-111

467

468

www.ingramcontent.com/pod-product-compliance
Lightning Source LLC
Chambersburg PA
CBHW072144070526
44585CB00015B/993